A VACATION GUIDE TO CANADA'S GREAT LAKES COASTS

ONTARIO

LAKE SUPERIOR

NORTH CHANNEL

GEORGIAN BAY

LAKE HURON

THE BOOKSTORE

ST. LAWRENCE RIVER

LAKE ONTARIO

LAKE ST. CLAIR

LAKE ERIE

The
LONG BLUE EDGE
OF
ONTARIO

DORIS SCHARFENBERG

WILLIAM B. EERDMANS PUBLISHING COMPANY

Library of Congress Cataloging in Publication Data

Scharfenberg, Doris, 1925-
The long blue edge of Ontario.
1. Ontario — Description and travel — Guide-books.
2. Great Lakes Region — Description and travel — Guide-books. I. Title.
F1057.S28   1984   917.13′044   84-10273
ISBN 0-8028-7046-5

ACKNOWLEDGMENTS

We wish to acknowledge the contributions of those who helped in the production of this book:

Doris Scharfenberg, for the photos in the book and on the cover;
Joel Beversluis, for the design and layout;
Randy Albosta, for the cover design;
Louise Bauer, for the maps;
Sandra Nowlin, for editorial supervision.

CONTENTS

CONTENTS

PREFACE

THE dearest influence of my growing years was a grandmother born in the 1870s on a scrub-poor farm just south of Meaford, Ontario, and Georgian Bay. During the trauma we called the Great Depression she had to share a room and bed with me, a wakeful child who would not sleep without a story.

Gran told of rides on a flatwagon pulled by the family's lone labor-saving device, a plowhorse, into Meaford and of a buggy trip to Toronto; of the one-room school and her two years of formal education . . . enough to turn her into an avid reader and life-long student. Sweets on the Queen's birthday; Sunday afternoon walks to a hill where she and her siblings could "see the blue," the long horizon of Georgian Bay.

My imagination grew close to Canadian life, albeit a life of another time. Seeking work, she and my grandfather became U.S. citizens but both remained Canadian at heart, and much of my early orientation was to the north and east of Detroit, to regions around Georgian Bay and towns close to home such as Amherstburg and Sarnia where we drove on family outings.

After finishing a book about Michigan's coast it was as natural as remembering childhood to think about the other side of the Great Lakes, the fabulous Ontario shoreline.

The writing, compiling, and exploring have been a labor of love and the best kind of education. Ontario, bigger than most of the nations of the world, is exciting and exceptional; past and present, wilderness and worldliness fit together like notched logs in a cabin. About 87% of the province's 1,068,582 sq. km. (412,582 sq. mi.) is back country, unnamed lakes and tundra. Wilderness: challenging, inviting, awesome, and *right there*. You can dine in a luxurious revolving restaurant high above Niagara Falls and at dawn on the next day be listening to a loon call across a mist-shrouded lake far beyond all roads. In restored forts, Victorian hotels, sleek glass towers, underground shopping malls, whitewater rivers, and a thousand museums, the door of time stands ajar.

The undulating pattern of the Ontario coast along the Great Lakes is 7,606 km. (4,726 mi.) long, offers sand as soft as any South Sea island, plus rock-bound stretches of chilling grandeur. Lighthouses, parks, cities, sanctuaries; a freshwater catalogue of every seaside scene.

This book has been directed to the budgeting general traveler (family, retiree, biker, boater) who is perhaps more interested in places to picnic than gourmet chic, and I have not gone into motel-hotel restaurant reviews except in the most casual manner (i.e., eateries in buildings of historic significance). There are many brochures on those matters; no one should have trouble finding fine food.

All prices quoted in this book are subject to change (alas!) but may help you know what to expect. Hours are also not written in stone and sometimes an attraction will close up altogether. If it is a serious matter I would advise calling ahead.

Please check with Chapter Ten for information about maps, travel associations, and more particulars.

The Ontario and Canadian Ministries of Tourism have been extremely helpful and generous with volumes of useful information and guidance. *Any* visitor will find enough material in the Ontario Information Centres to start a library.

My deepest thanks to John Bunt, Canadian Tourism Consul and Trade Commissioner, Detroit office, and his staff, especially his assistant, Robert Brown; to Sam McKelvey, Canadian Tourism and Trade Commissioner, New York office; to Shirley Teasdale of the Ontario Ministry of Tourism; to Suzanne Chicoine, Director of Public Relations, her assistant Mary Kenessey, and the rest of the Toronto Visitors and Convention Bureau staff; to the Eerdmans team; and to Mary Henry, who generously offered her typing skills. And a hug to you, Clara Kluge!

As we explore from Quebec's border to the edge of Minnesota, it is with a sense of gratitude that our incredible boundary is so easily shared; that all forts are relics and mutual friendship has far out-run the rivalries.

Like the lakes themselves, this too is a wonder of the world.

DORIS SCHARFENBERG

INTRODUCTION

THE GREAT LAKES drape with natural grace across the map of central-eastern North America, jewel seas of fresh water unmatched on earth.

It is hard to believe that the discovery of these lakes held any kind of disappointment, yet the rugged Frenchmen who first paddled and portaged through a primal wilderness weren't altogether pleased when they reached Georgian Bay, Huron, and Superior. They sought the tell-tale taste of salt water, but every drop was fresh. Priests seeking converts, traders and trappers, adventurers hoping to scoop up the nuggets of pure copper said to be waiting on the forest floor . . . all were alert for a clue to the Holy Grail of early continental exploration: a short-cut to the riches (or souls) of China. So strong was the belief in such a passage that Samuel de Champlain (founder of Quebec) gave his scout Jean Nicolet an elaborately embroidered robe to carry on the first trip across Lake Michigan. Surely the sweet seas would become salty, China would appear, and Nicolet would need proper attire for the emperor's court. Instead of Chinese, Nicolet was met by puzzled Indians, and China still half a world away.

In the 1600s, when the unknowns of the new world were as thick as clouds covering a November sun, such dreams died hard. It was over 150 years before the myth faded and the hard facts of geography were fully recognized. Those were the years of missionary explorers and hotly competitive fur traders, whose business was essentially antisettlement and prowilderness. The late 1700s, however, saw an incoming tide of 60,000 and more Loyalists escaping the American Revolution. Totally different from the solitary woodsmen who sought pelts, these were professional and educated people; community builders and farmers. The British government passed the Canada Act (first official recognition of "Canada" as a name) and divided the old province of Quebec into "Upper Canada" and "Lower Canada." Newcomer Loyalists were given land and the right to use UE after their names, referring to "United Empire."

Change accelerated like a revving motor, and the lands of the Great Lakes moved into new times. The French Revolution deeply affected northwoods commerce by killing off the upper-class fur customers in Europe, while the advance of the railroad, heavy immigration, etc. created a ravenous demand for lumber. Along the shores of Georgian Bay, Lake Superior, and Lake Huron nearly every community that wasn't a trading or military post began with a sawmill . . . more often a cluster of them. The discovery of valuable ores also produced a land rush, and commercial fishing brought in still another breed of entrepreneur.

To the Great Lakes, recorded history began yesterday as compared to regions of the Nile, and their geologic presence is a newborn feature of the planet. During the last of four ice ages, perhaps 18,000 years ago, moving glaciers dug trenches, piled up debris (morain) as they pushed ahead, then left pools of water as they melted back. Advance-retreat-advance; each time the pools had a different shape until the present outlines were left behind only 4,000 or 5,000 years ago.

Algonquins, Hurons, and Iroquois have their own versions of these beginnings, legends of the Manitou and His gifts of big-sea waters. For historians, geologists, and folklorists, the times and legends of the Great Lakes are a fascinating cache. Some tid-bits:

1679 • Robert Cavelier, Sieur de La Salle, built the first sailing vessel ever launched on the Great Lakes. The *Griffin,* loaded with furs, was also the first sailing vessel to sink—with only theories marking the spot.

1783 • The Treaty of Paris wound up the American Revolution and established the boundary between the U.S. and Canada, reaffirmed by the War of 1812 . . . a singularly senseless fray.

1816 • Canadians launched the first steamship, the *Frontenac,* on the Great Lakes. It burned in 1827 in the Niagara River.

1829 • The Welland Canal opened for traffic allowing vessels access to the midwest. By 1855 there were locks at Sault Ste. Marie.

1865 • Nearly 2,000 sailing ships listed as hauling freight on the Great Lakes.

1913 • Ten freighters lost, twenty wrecked during the worst storm ever known on the lakes.

1916 • Four freighters lost in one Lake Erie storm.

1959 • The St. Lawrence Seaway, a joint Canadian-American project, opens the Great Lakes to cargo ships of the world. . . .

Look, Monsieur Champlain, the Orient now comes to us!

The
LONG BLUE EDGE
OF
ONTARIO

RAIN DRAIN

Even though some of the rushing drainage through the St. Lawrence River has come a long way, the Great Lakes are not in a constant state of being flushed out. Studies of water at the deepest parts of the lakes reveal "pools" that have been there for centuries, whole areas moving at a glacial pace—if at all.

Ontario has 7,606 km. (4,726 mi.) of freshwater shoreline along the Great Lakes; 1,210 km. (752 mi.) of saltwater shore along Hudson and James bays. (Shorelines are measured to include sounds, and bays, and river mouths to a point where they narrow to the width of thirty minutes of latitude, and the distance at such point is included.)

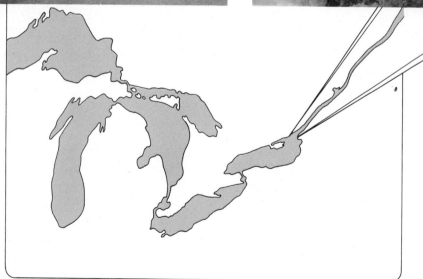

CHAPTER I
THE ST. LAWRENCE RIVER

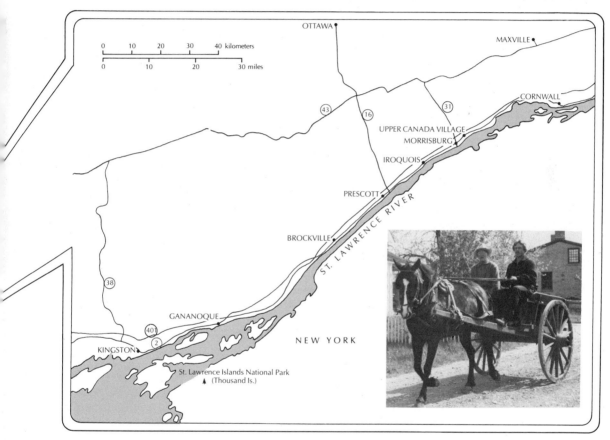

T HE WATERS POUR DOWNWARD, down through the Little Pic and Nippigon and Pukaskwa rivers into Lake Superior, from the French and Moon rivers into Georgian Bay, from the Manistique, Bayfield, Lynn, Pefferlaw, Pigeon, and a thousand other streams into lakes Michigan, Huron, Erie, and Ontario . . . into the greatest freshwater collection system on earth. By the time water reaches the eastern end of Lake Ontario it is barely halfway to the open sea. The St. Lawrence River, a long spout

3

arcing to the North Atlantic, is over 1,200 km. (800 mi.) long, a scenic, busy waterway that changes patterns as it goes: the Ontario end, strewn with rocky, forested islands; the International Rapids, a section for adventure and a barrier to past shipping. The torrent turns placid, widens into three lakes, pulls its banks together, then gradually broadens and deepens to the ocean.

Jacques Cartier was the first white man known to have visited the St. Lawrence River. It was 1534. In 1608 Samuel de Champlain established an initial settlement at Quebec. The river was a corridor toward the heart of North America, a lead followed by explorers, traders, immigrants. Its valley was a French possession until the end of the Seven Years' War when the British took control. U.S. claims to sections of the stream were not settled until the War of 1812.

When the St. Lawrence is spoken of, two visions form: One is of the Seaway, with great ships of the world entering and leaving our mid-continent. However, the 292-km. (183-mi.) portion of the Seaway on the St. Lawrence River is only *part* of the total project, which includes the Welland Canal and the locks at Sault Ste. Marie. Seven locks on the St. Lawrence lift vessels on a journey from Montreal to Toronto; most of the constructions are on the Canadian side.

The second "St. Lawrence vision" is of the river strewn with rocky, forested islands . . . *les Mille iles.* Years ago Arthur Godfrey made old radios buzz with a ditty about "finding love in the 1,000 islands." Love or a kingdom of your own, to judge by the number of mansions and cottages on these isolated dream worlds, and the number of tourists they've attracted for many years.

A third St. Lawrence picture coming more and more into focus these days is of an extensive parkway program that lets you skim along—or very close to—the river, from one carefully tended picnic area or campground to the next.

Loyalist country, settled by refugees from the American Revolution and still wearing the vestigial garments of the past, the St. Lawrence River shores are welcoming a new breed of escapee.

QUEBEC TO KINGSTON

Crossing the Quebec line into Ontario was once going from Lower Canada into Upper Canada, a region that saw 60,000 or more colonists loyal to the flag of England resettle after the American Revolution. The dominance of names like Laval, Trois-Rivieres, and Joliette gives way to Lancaster, Cornwall, and Kingston (i.e., the king's town), while the glistening river—at this point Lake St. Francis—beckons with universal language, unites with a flowing heritage.

Highway 401 and Co. Rd. 17 run along together and you pass the park and • GLENGARRY PARK campsite just east of the village of Lancaster. Take interchange 127 to south service road for picnic tables, a beach, refreshment stand, trailer dump, and 244 sites, 54 with electricity. Reservations, please: St. Lawrence Parks Commission, P.O. Box 740, Morrisburg, Ontario K0C 1X0. 613/543-2951.

Loyalists and United Empire Loyalists—not quite the same. Those colonists who joined the Royal Standard while still in America and then came across the border to stay under the British Crown are U.E.L. Those who simply decided that the British were a better bet than the inexperienced Americans, or stuck with the British flag for a host of other reasons, were Loyalists, the king's faithful.

Nor'westers and Loyalists have a museum housed in a gracious 1862 build- • MUSEUM ing, concentrating on the story of the North West Company, fur trading, and the Loyalist settlements. Located in Williamstown, just north on Co. Rd. 17, open Victoria Day—Labour Day daily afternoons, longer on Saturday. Small fee. Williamstown, Ontario K0C 2J0. 613/528-4292.

Now take Hwy. 2. Another campsite called **Charlottenburg Park;** more beach, boat ramp, 159 campsites with 54 electrified. (The **Raisin River Park** campground north of Hwy. 401 has a swimming pool, boat ramp, etc. All reservations taken through the Morrisburg address).

Cornwall

Ontario's easternmost city, named for the eldest son of George III, the Duke of Cornwall, and first town in the world with a factory lit by electricity. Far from the fields it grew in, cotton was turned into cloth in the Stormont Mill under pale bulbs installed by Thomas Alva Edison himself.

The city of 45,000 is the site of the **Robert H. Saunders Generating Station**, largest international spark-maker anywhere. Recent new developments include a shining **Civic Complex** next to the river, giving citizens a chance to see hockey games (the Cornwall Royals won the Memorial Cup in 1981), have conferences, dine, and be generally entertained. Try close-by Cornwall Square Mall (no rain in here) and Pitt Street Mall for shopping; Lamoureux Park for loafing, jogging, or pushups right in the same blocks.

CORNWALL ISLAND • With live-in authenticity, the **Indian Village and Museum** constructed by the North American Indian Traveling College shows the traditional buildings of the Cree, Ojibway, and Iroquoian people. The village is occupied during the summer by an Indian family who are glad to answer your questions. On Cornwall Island, after you cross the Seaway International Bridge, turn left just before Canadian Customs. Village open Victoria Day till Labour Day, Wednesday through Sunday 10:00 A.M. to 6:00 P.M. Museum open all year 9:00 A.M. till 4:00 P.M. Closed major holidays. Village: adults $2.50, children and seniors $1.50. Museum: donation accepted. North American Travelling College, R.R. #3, Cornwall, Ontario K6H 5R7. 613/932-9452.

HISTORIC HOMES • If you're "into" architecture and know a Georgian from Italianate, there's a house to enjoy on Hwy. 2 and Boundary Road (exit 125 from Hwy. 401). The **Inverarden Museum,** chosen as the finest example of Regency Cottage design in Ontario, is a fourteen-room dwelling open from April 1 to November 20, Monday–Saturday 11:00 A.M. to 5:00 P.M.; Sunday 2:00 P.M. to 5:00 P.M. Picnic area, washrooms, slide show on the building's restoration, special annual events (home brewing demos, for one). Box 773, Cornwall, Ontario K6H 5T5. 613/938-9585.

The **United Counties Museum** was the house of a United Empire Loyalist whose family occupied it for 113 years. Full of regional articles; a Broodwood grand piano is the collection's star player. On Second Street West, across from Domtar Paper Mills. Open May 1 to October 31 daily; Sunday, afternoons only. Practically free. P.O. Box 773, Cornwall, Ontario K6H 5T5. 613/932-2381.

Chamber of Commerce, 19 Second Street East, P.O. Box 338, Cornwall, Ontario K6H 5T1. 613/933-4004.

MAXVILLE • For children of the heather, thistle, tartans, pipes, and haggis, a true fling takes place every July in Maxville, only thirty-two km. (twenty mi.) north of Cornwall. Pipe band and Scottish dancers come to compete in the Glengarry Highland Games, North America's largest Highland gathering. Stirring moment (even for those w'nae Scot at all) is when the whole mixed mass of pipe bands comes together for a grand presentation. (Confession: Once I thought bagpipes were the worst sound this side of screeching tires. Now I love them. If you're of my ilk, listen and you may astonish yourself.)

The **Glengarry Pioneer Museum** is housed in an 1830 log inn, small cheese factory, log barn. A backward glance, open from Victoria Day weekend to Canadian Thanksgiving weekend; daily except Monday during July and August. $1.00. R.R. #1, Maxville, Ontario K0C 1T0. 613/527-5533.

Tiny Maxville (population 860) was thus named because so many arriving immigrants in the 1790s and early 1800s had surnames beginning with "Mac." More about Maxville and the Glengarry Games at the Cornwall Chamber of Commerce. Ask about *La Semaine Francaise,* a festival of arts, crafts, and Franco-Ontarian cultural traditions. French Week Pageant, parades, and *Fetes Populaire,* oui, oui!

Eleven islands appeared in the making of the St. Lawrence Seaway and • LONG SAULT PARKWAY Power Project, now linked like green jewels on a chain of roads and bridges for ten km. (six and one-half mi.) along the river section known as St. Lawrence Lake. Lawns aplenty, but three major developed areas for families to know about: **McLaren Campsite,** which has 211 campsites (50

with plug-ins), beach, boat ramp, trailer dump; **Woodlands Park** has 234 campsites, 48 with electricity, and a trailer dump; and **Miles Roches Park,** with 234 campsites (17 electrified), playground, beaches, refreshments, boat ramp . . . the works.

Standard fees: $2.00 a day for park use, up to $7.50 a day camping, depending on location and electricity. Reservations, Box 740, Morrisburg, Ontario K0C 1X0. 613/543-2951.

INGLESIDE • Home of Canadiana Pottery Limited, where you can watch the process from lump to lamp base. Bargain store, open all year. On Hwy. 2, just west of town.

FARRAN PARK • 115 campsites, 53 with electricity, and a playground area, refreshments, trailer dump, boat ramp. Off Hwy. 2, interchange 121 on Hwy. 401. For reservations, see Morrisburg, above.

MORRISON AND • Off Hwy. 2, it has 124 campsites, 20 with electricity. Nature trails, beach,
NAIRNE ISLANDS PARK trailer dump, playgrounds. For reservations, see Long Sault Parkway.

UPPER CANADA • **Crysler Farm Battlefield Park**—"The Americans are coming! The Ameri-
VILLAGE cans are coming!" So the Redcoats and the civilian sons of the soldiers-settlers who had served in such as the King's Royal Regiment of New York and Rogers' Royal Rangers stopped an invasion of Canada. In a bloody skirmish on the farm of citizen Crysler, the Americans lost 300 men, the British 181; Yankee plans to take Montreal were stifled forever. The date was November 11, 1813.

Today an obelisk commemorates the battle, a memorial building contains its remaining artifacts and a large mural of the scene, and a memorial garden pays tribute to those who fell. Meanwhile, another part of the Park property has been given new life as an alive-and-well piece of the past.

Upper Canada Village was never a place . . . never a real town. During the 1950s, when a deep sea canal and hydroelectric plant at Cornwall were constructed, eight villages in the low area near the old river banks were flooded, as were thousands of acres of farmland, including Crysler's farm. To save this part of its heritage, the Province of Ontario gathered buildings of special significance into a new site on higher ground under the name Upper Canada Village. (See Morrisburg.)

Nineteenth-century furnished houses, churches, work places, rail fences, and costumed staff hold a mirror to the way it was. There is talk of the

battle but the scene breathes deeply with peace; a church reflected in a mill pond, geese strolling on the street, the milkmaid tending her cow. "Peace" means being left alone to do your hard work.

Demonstrations of tasks as they were performed by those Loyalist settlers are part of the daily show at Upper Canada Village and special events focus in depth on home-farm skills (such as sheep shearing, working with wood, preservation of food, pig butchering, flailing of peas, etc.).

Thirty-four historic buildings, from bake house to boat shed, and restaurant, snack bars, gift shop. Open May 15 to October 15, 9:30 A.M. to 5:00 P.M. . . . slightly longer hours in mid-summer. Horse-drawn carryalls provide regular transportation between the far reaches of the Village and Cook's Tavern near the entrance. Adults $3.75, children 2-12 accompanied by adult $1.25. Family maximum charge $10.00. (Admission fees subject to change.) Contact St. Lawrence Parks Commission, Box 740, Morrisburg, Ontario K0C 1X0. 613/543-2951.

Will rev up old car buffs with its 1898 Locomobile Steamer, 1923 Durant, • AUTO WONDERLAND and at least fifty others. One and a half km. (one mi.) west of Upper Canada Village on Hwy. 2. Open May 15 to October 15, 10:00 A.M. to 6:00 P.M., slightly longer in mid-summer. Adults $2.50, seniors $2.00, students $1.50. Contact Auto Wonderland, 31 Pine Street, Morrisburg, Ontario K0C 1M0. 613/537-2105.

LAND OF THE NENIBUSH • Behind the stockaded walls, an authentic Indian village. The first Canadians' trials, battles, and life-style here to sharpen your appreciation of their role and contributions. On Hwy. 2, open daily 10:00 A.M. to 6:00 P.M. in June, till 8:00 P.M. in July and August; 5:00 P.M. until October 15. Adults $3.00, children $1.50. Land of the Nenibush, Box 856, Morrisburg, Ontario K0C 1X0. 613/537-8192.

RIVERSIDE CEDAR PARK • Pleasant, but camp city with room for 465 tents and trailers; 113 with electricity. Beach, playground, ramp, and dump, six km. (four mi.) east of Morrisburg on Hwy. 2. Reservations: same address.

MORRISBURG • Named for an early postmaster general of Canada. Morrisburg's citizens had to face a wet reality with the coming of the Seaway; either move or become adept at treading water. Their town was going to be flooded, so they pulled up to higher ground, but made a decision for which all future generations should be grateful. With brilliant feats of engineering and ingenuity, they hoisted, hauled, and secured selected antique buildings: rescuing them from the rising flood to create Upper Canada Village, eleven km. (seven mi.) down the road.

In spring and fall great numbers of migratory birds use the **Upper Canada Migratory Bird Sanctuary** as a fly-inn, but any summer visitor with an eye for spotting can see many wild birds remaining. From the last week in September until mid-November feeding time is at 2:30 P.M. daily. Free.

Morrisburg Chamber of Commerce, Box 288, Morrisburg, Ontario K0C 1X0. 613/543-3170.

Take Co. Rd. 4 for the backs of summer homes and glimpses of the river.

IROQUOIS • Western end of Lake St. Lawrence, "best little town by a dam site," as Iroquoians say, making reference to the Control Dam located here. Iroquois goes back to the 1700s, but not on the exact same spot; that's been flooded. The Iroquois Indians held pow-wows here, built their longhouses, and organized their ventures. The British built a fort and welcomed the United Empire Loyalists who fled the American colonies. Direct descendants are still in the vicinity.

The only Canadian deep sea lock in the St. Lawrence Seaway project is at Iroquois with a lot of grassy lawns about and a lookout to let you see the ships of the world as they exit the Great Lakes.

10

A VISITOR'S VOTE FOR OTTAWA

(Ottawa is definitely inland from *the long blue edge*, but well worth a visit.)

In 1858 there were heated debates about the choice of location for the capital of Canada. The selection would have to please both the French- and English-speaking citizens, should be a safe distance from the conniving Americans, and equidistant from Montreal and Toronto. Tales of how the final decision was made vary, but I like the one that has Queen Victoria—tired of the squabbling—pointing her royal finger at a spot on the Ottawa River called "Bytown" and saying "*We* have made a decision." Some of her loyal opposition were not amused, and one opponent consoled himself with ". . . any Americans who try to capture it will get lost in the woods." However, Bytown became Ottawa... and an excellent choice it turned out to be.

Small and beautifully situated on a high bluff, the newborn capital could start from scratch, planning streets, boulevards, and buildings suited to its role. They erected grandly traditional, gothic parliament buildings, government structures in chateau forms that today blend with modern box-glass walls to make a rich mix. Open-spaced downtown areas are the soul of graciousness and you can still see the country hills from mid-town, listen to debates of world importance, and start on a wilderness hike in the same hour. At the heart of the bi-lingual nation, Ottawa exudes a cosmopolitan élan. You are in North America . . . or maybe you are somewhere else.

Canada's Parliament Buildings are on Wellington Street, at the point called Parliament Hill. The House of Commons, the Senate Chamber, the Speaker's Chamber, and the Parliamentary Library (a beauty!) are quartered here. The block is crowned by the Peace Tower with a carillon of fifty-three bells, a memorial to World War I dead, where a light burning atop means Parliament is in session. Tours September to June, 9:00 A.M. to 5:00 P.M. Hours extended to 9:00 P.M. and weekends during July and August. Free.

OF COURSE, you must watch the **Changing of the Guard,** daily during July and August, an ancient military rite performed by the Governor General's Footguards and Grenadier Guards on the Parliament campus. They parade the "Colours," exchange compliments between old and new guards, walk in tin-soldier fashion to appreciative crowds of summer travelers. Band, Drum Corps; splendid show.

The National Arts Centre, opened in 1969, is a landmark structure in a different time frame. The building is in hexagonal units interconnected by landscaped terraces where fairs, exhibitions, and concerts are held in the summer. 2,300-seat opera house, 850-seat theater, 300-seat studio . . . and they can be all going at once, so check out the schedules in the newspaper. Located on Confederation Square, next to the Rideau Canal.

At the **National Gallery of Canada,** several thousand paintings, prints, sculptures . . . old masters and new talents. Elgin and Slater Streets, free. May through August, 10:00 A.M. to 5:00 P.M. daily. Shorter hours and closed Mondays the rest of the year. The **National Museum of Man and Natural Sciences** is just what it says, displayed with imagination. McLeod and Metcalfe streets, May to Labour Day, 10:00 A.M. to 5:00 P.M., closed Mondays other months. Free.

The **National Museum of Science and Technology** lets you in on their act. Push, pull, twist, and see what happens, or just look at the locomotives, old cars, airplanes, clocks, and what-have-you. Located on a grand spread of park, 1867 St. Laurent Avenue at Russell Road. 613/998-9520. For stamp collectors, especially, the **National Postal Museum** has a huge stock of stamps, mail boxes, models of mail-carrying ships, a replica of a Victorian post office. A sales counter, too. 180 Wellington, closed Mondays, but otherwise open daily 9:00 A.M. to 5:00 P.M. and Sunday afternoons. 613/995-9905.

The **National Aeronautical Collection,** ninety-five winged trophies from aviation history, with emphasis on the Canadian contributions, including the "Silver Dart," first powered heavier-than-air flight in the nation. 1345 Base Line Road, free, open weekdays, 9:00 A.M. to 4:00 P.M. **Canadian War Museum,** a showcase for weapons of all types and periods, even back to the days of French rule. Korean War, World Wars I and II. 330-350 Sussex Drive; free, but they like donations. Open Tuesday through Saturday, 11:00 A.M. to 5:00 P.M., slightly shorter hours from Labour Day till April 30.

Not exactly your average barnyard, the **Central Experimental Farm** has ornamental gardens, an arboretum, and a greenhouse as well as showcase herds of dairy and beef cattle, and crops. This is the Canadian Department of Agriculture's Research station, where you can visit the animal barns, take a wagon ride, have a picnic on the grounds. Guided tours during July and August. Sunrise to dusk, all year, free. On the Driveway at Maple Drive.

A pair of interesting houses: the *Laurier House,* home of two former prime ministers, Sir Wilfred Laurier and William Lyon Mackenzie King, and full of historic mementos. But wait until you see **Moorside,** sometimes called the "mystic temple of Canadian politics." There are relics from old Ottawa buildings on the grounds, part of occultist King's favorite retreat. He kept a crystal ball and fresh flowers before the portrait of his mother, held seances, etc. Less spiritual, more Canadian history there to peer into as well. Part of Gatineau Park, a wilderness park extending over 355 sq. km. (137 sq. mi.), only 13 km. (8 mi.) from Parliament Hill. Dining room, snack bar; free. 613/992-4231.

Ottawa's Byward Market has been going since the 1830s, a swirling mix of vegetable vendors, fruit farmers, fish, meat, eggs, specialties, and a great place to put together an as-you-go sandwich. Craft areas, outdoor cafe in summer. East of Chateau Laurier and one block north of Rideau Street between York and George. More to see: **Watson's Mill, Rideau Hall,** the **Royal Canadian Mint,** the **Royal Canadian Mounted Police Barracks, Ottawa City Hall,** etc. There are any number of tour boats and buses waiting to take you around; a splendid view of it all from Neplean Point Park, north off St. Patrick Street.

Come in spring when the gardens inspire a festival of coast-to-coast proportions. Hotel, restaurant, shopping, camping, and event information at the Visitors and Convention Bureau, 222 Queen Street, Ottawa, Ontario K1P 5V9. 613/137-5150.

Then cross over to Hull, Quebec and see how *that* town has bloomed in the last few years.

The 150-year-old Carman House Museum, parks, a beach, golf, tennis, and other reasons to pause in this village of 1,200 people.

More Iroquois information may be obtained from the Seaway Valley Tourist Council, Box 884, Cornwall, Ontario. 616/932-0299.

CARDINAL • Once known as Edwardsburg, another town with an early factory (this one made glucose) lighted by those new-fangled glowing glass bulbs in 1891. Thomas Edison himself did the installing.

GRENVILLE PARK • Just east of the Johnstown-Ogdensburg International Bridge. 115 campsites, 44 with electricity; trailer dump, beach, boat ramp, and all the fun things. Reservations at Morrisburg address.

International bridge to Ogdensburg, New York, a direct route from the • JOHNSTOWN
States to Ottawa. Sometimes called "Johnstown Corners" and listed under
Prescott in several guides.

Just east of Prescott, the fort was built during the War of 1812. It fell to • FORT WELLINGTON
ruins till the rebellion of 1837-38 when the present blockhouse and
officers' quarters were rebuilt. Now the National Historic Site is open from
May 16 to Labour Day, 9:30 A.M. to 6:00 P.M., shorter hours through October;
during the winter by appointment. Free. Box 479, Prescott, Ontario K0E
1T0. 613/925-2896 or 925-2897.

A shipping point for grain and industry and scene of the bright Prescott • PRESCOTT
Loyalist Days. Mock battle at **Fort Wellington,** antique show, coast guard
station open house—it all takes place in mid-July. Contact the Fort Wellington address and telephone.

Note the clock on Prescott's Main Street. Once in the old Town Hall, it is
now mounted so that you can see its works from sidewalk level.

I'm glad they didn't stick with their first name, Snarlington, because the • BROCKVILLE
connotation just doesn't fit. A busy home for 20,000 people and some
name-brand industries, Brockville is a ranking senior among Ontario communities. The houses have a British touch, the parks and gardens guietly
murmur "Hail Britannia," and it's not hard to find tea in the afternoon. A
walking tour in the heart of the early village with a map supplied by the
Historical Society is a pleasant way to change pace and get acquainted.

Go directly to jail, and the courthouse, an elegant neoclassical building
dating from 1842 and still functioning. Oldest remaining structure of its
type in Ontario.

Brockville is considered the eastern gateway to the **Thousand Islands,**
a gathering place for area boaters. Docking to transients at the Brockville
Yacht Club, 613/342-9083; Gilbert Marine Ltd., 613/342-3462, and St.
Lawrence Marina Sales, 613-342-0055. Gas, services, etc. Ask at the last two
places about boat rentals.

Brockville Chamber of Commerce, 51 East King Street, Brockville, Ontario K6V 1A8. 613/342-6553.

Past resorts and cottages on Hwy. 2, at Sherwood Springs you slip over to
the Thousand Island Parkway, a true river road in an area rife with motels,
places to eat, boat tours, and so forth. Ask and you'll certainly find.

CAMPSITES • Two places for campers between Brockville and Gananoque are **Brown's Bay Park and Campsite,** with spots for 108 RVs; 51 have electricity. Beaches for bathers, boat ramps for the water people. Eighteen km. (eleven mi.) west of Brockville; and **Ivy Lea Park** has 143 campsites, 34 electrified; trailer dump, beach, and playground facilities. Located at the entrance to Thousand Islands International Bridge, thirty-four km. (twenty mi.) west of Brockville, the big attraction here is **Skytown,** an entertainment complex with 122-m. (400-ft.) observation tower overlooking the St. Lawrence and the 1,000 Islands. Wax museum, aquarium, arctic display, the works.

ST. LAWRENCE ISLANDS NATIONAL PARK

Only a few of the Thousand Islands are part of the National Park System and even if those few were pulled together into one mass, this would still be Canada's smallest National Park . . . but also one of the prettiest.

The rocky isles, left smooth and barren by retreating glaciers, could support only the tiniest forms of lichen at first, but such is the determination of green and growing things that micro bits of decayed life and eroded rock eventually gave larger forms of soil to cling to; larger and larger until the stones support mini-forests of conifers and hardwoods plus abundant, less obvious plants and animals.

Having been a tourist magnate for many generations, the Thousand Island area has more resorts than Ford had cars. For those who would like to camp in the Park, fourteen of the islands have camping. The shore campground (sixty units, no electricity) is at **Mallorytown Landing,** Park headquarters. They'll supply you with a list of islands with docking and picnic facilities, others that are reserved for day-only nature hikes, etc. Write: St. Lawrence Islands National Park, Box 469, R.R.#3, Mallorytown Landing, Ontario, K0E 1R0 613/923-5241 or 923-5443.

Pronounced Gannon-ock-way. No two interpretations of the name are quite • GANANOQUE
the same, but it's an Iroquois word, a Loyalist settlement, and a Canadian-
American favorite stop. Although he wasn't the first settler on this site, a
fellow named Joel Stone, who fled from America with a price on his head, is
considered the town's founding father. Stone fought against George Wash-
ington and for this was given a grant of land where he built a lumber mill and
helped establish a number of other newcomers to the neighborhood.

Gananoque's docks not only launch a thousand Thousand Island tours
per season, but the town is a turning point for the Rideau Lake district, and
a shopper's feast of Irish linens, wool, and English china. Down by the
riverside, marinas, restaurants, and the world's largest aluminum passenger
vessels can be found.

This stop is on nearly every 1,000-Island tour schedule, something you • BOLDT CASTLE
don't want to miss. Plenty of people have constructed dream homes on
these rocky outcroppings, but George Boldt's dream was of King Ludwig
proportions. Boldt came to America poor but eager, wound up owning the
Waldorf-Astoria Hotel (among others), and decided that his beloved wife
needed an above-average retreat. Alas, dear Louise died before its completion; the whole sad story is told in this sixteenth-century-like landmark.

A Boldt Castle tour is included in some tour boat prices, or take a water
taxi from Alexandria Bay, New York. Adults $2.00, children 10-12 $1.25.
Contact: 1,000 Islands Bridge Authority, Collins Landing, Alexandria Bay,
New York 13607. 315/482-2501 or 658-2281.

Goulish foolishness and spooky stuff that kids love can be had in the
House of Haunts at the corner of Water and Main streets, mid-May to
mid-October daily. The fun might zap them into quietude when you pursue
the more elusive ghosts of the **Gananoque Historic Museum,** housed in
an 1840 Victoria Hotel. Large collection of military paraphernalia.

Newest Gananoque invitation is issued by the Siberian tigers of **1,000
Islands Wild Kingdom,** on Stone Street, Hwy. 32, just a growl from the
freeway. It's brand new and incomplete as of this writing, but has some big
cats, Ontario native beasts, and large plans for a petting zoo. "Cageless"
cages, the like. Prices and hours not yet available.

If you'd like to see the region by air, Clark's Marina—five km. (three mi.)
west of Gananoque on Hwy. 2—asks $25.00 minimum charge for a summer
flight for two people. Gananoque Air Services, Ltd., R.R. #3, Gananoque,
Ontario. 613/382-3951.

For more info: Gananoque Chamber of Commerce, 2 King Street East, Gananoque, Ontario K7G 1E6. 613/382-3708; summer 382-3250.

Kingston

The "king's town" didn't get the permanent assignment as Canada's capital, but its strategic location put Kingston in a vital role as guardian of the eastern extremity of Lake Ontario, the entrance to the St. Lawrence River and the Rideau water passage north. When the shooting broke out between British and Americans in 1812, **Fort Henry** was built to guard the Naval Dockyards serving the Royal Navy's Ontario fleet. In the following years defenses grew and the town that began as a fur trading post thrived under the fort's protective shadow.

Kingston is an impressive city today, home of Queen's University, St. Lawrence College, several federal prisons, a dignified city hall, museums, Canada's Royal Military College (equivalent of West Point or Sandhurst), and enough points of interest to keep you happily hiking around the shady streets for days. The midtown waterfront, for example, resembles a demure carnival. In a fairly compact area one can sit amid flowerbeds and strolling families next to the depot-turned-information office and watch a dancing fountain, children scrambling through a retired steam locomotive, tour and pleasure boats coming and going past the short, round tower of an old fortification . . . and the "something else" that is always going on.

Wearing walls of gray limestone, downtown Kingston has an Old World Victorian ambiance, buildings where the cornices and window caps are carved in scrolls from the past. (A delightful number of bookstores!) On three days of the week fresh produce and flowers are sold by individuals in the parking lot behind City Hall, a sight so common in Europe.

City Hall is a good place to start discovering Kingston. Look up; instead of a figure representing justice and truth or a lion-unicorn design, the dome on City Hall sports a weather vane, perhaps to show how political winds are blowing. Kingston was once the capital of Upper Canada and the classic building dominates the waterfront with authority. You can go through it from mid-June to September 1, Monday thru Saturday; upon request during the off season. Free.

Across the street (in front of a former train station where the **Bureau of Tourism** hands out Kingston information) is a tractor train that will take you on a one-hour, nonstop ride past the best of old and new Kingston. Eight tours a day, last weekend in June thru Labour Day. Adults $3.00, children 5-12 $1.00, small children free. Family maximum $6.00.

By 1812 Kingston was the largest town in Upper Canada, and all supplies • FORT HENRY coming from the east passed or paused at its docks to get to points beyond. Because of the importance of Kingston and the Royal Naval Dockyards, an earth and wood fort was built. Later additions of stone blockhouses, stone ramparts, barracks, storerooms, arsenals, and more made Fort Henry a formidable stronghold. The high command decided to play it even safer, however, and four fortress-towers (called **Martello Towers**) were built at half-mile intervals to protect the city's waterfront and provide cross fire if the Americans decided to invade. A needless bit of defense spending; the nations were becoming friends.

When you go through the sentry tunnel the year flips back to 1867. One hundred twenty-five university and high school students take over as the **Fort Henry Guard,** a hand-picked group given historically accurate training in infantry drills, artillery salutes with muzzle-loading cannon, etc. You get to watch these exercises daily, and during July and August on Wednesday and Saturday at 7:30 P.M. (weather permitting) a colorful Ceremonial Retreat is a Fort Henry highlight. Visitors are advised to check ahead for this event, as occasionally the Guard goes on tour. Adults $2.75, children 6-15, $1.00. May 15-October 15, 9:00 A.M. to 5:00 P.M., slightly longer in mid-summer. Gift shop (open all year), snack bar, and David, the mascot goat, who will pose for you. Contact St. Lawrence Parks Commission, Box 740, Morrisburg, Ontario K0C 1X0. 613/543-2951.

Does this town collect things! A peek at the museum list:

One of the largest specialized military museums in the country traces the • CANADIAN FORCES history and development of message apparatus. Open daily 1:00 P.M. to COMMUNICATIONS AND 4:00 P.M., closed weekends in off-season. Admission. Vimy Barracks, Hwy. ELECTRONICS MUSEUM 2 East, 613/545-5395.

ROYAL MILITARY COLLEGE OF CANADA MUSEUM • Housed in the Fort Fredrick Martello Tower, it tells the history of Canada's military education and the achievements of its graduates. Extensive weapon collection, relics of the old Royal Dockyard, etc. Open daily late June until Labour Day, other times by arrangement. Admission charged. Royal Military College Grounds. 613/545-7369.

MARINE MUSEUM OF THE GREAT LAKES • A waterfront collection of models, helms, flags, hulls, a freighter, etc. Parts and pieces of the whole Great Lakes naval scene, displayed in a recently renovated, enlarged show. Library and archives, store, shipbuilders gallery, engine room. Open mid-April to mid-December, 9:00 A.M. to 5:00 P.M. Admission $2.25 adult, $1.25 students and seniors. 55 Ontario Street, Kingston, Ontario. 613/542-2261.

PUMP HOUSE STEAM MUSEUM • Only one like it in the world; everything is operated by steam. Built in 1849, completely restored, it will enchant all those who love old equipment that does the job. At 23 Ontario Street near the Marine Museum. Open mid-June to Labour Day, 10:00 A.M. to 5:00 P.M. daily except Fridays. Adults $1.50, students and seniors $1.00. 613/546-4696.

MURNEY TOWER MUSEUM • Built in 1846, one of the finest martello towers in North America; full of military and pioneer information. Open late May to September 30, daily. Adults 50¢. Kingston Historical Society, Box 54, Kingston, Ontario. 613/542-4687.

KINGSTON FIRE DEPARTMENT MUSEUM • In a firehall at Brock Street and Clergy, fire-fighting equipment and documents from 1856 to the present. Open daily 9:00 A.M. to 3:00 P.M. and 7:00 to 9:00 P.M. Free. 613/548-4001.

BELLEVUE HOUSE NATIONAL HISTORIC PARK • Home for a while to Sir John Alexander Macdonald, Canada's first Prime Minister and an architect of Canadian Confederation. A jewel of a house, the Victorian idea of an Italian villa set in its own private park. Guides in period costumes tell you more about Macdonald and what the elite lived like in his times. May through Labour Day 9:00 A.M. to 5:00 P.M., a little longer in mid-summer. Closed holidays. Free. 35 Centre Street.

AGNES ETHERINGTON ART CENTRE • A major and very attractive Eastern Ontario gallery, showcasing important touring exhibitions and events. Permanent collection of fine Canadian and European paintings, prints, etc. Open Tuesday to Saturday 10:00 A.M. to 5:00 P.M.; Sunday 1:00 to 5:00 P.M. Free admission. Queen's University, University Avenue at Queen's Crescent. 613/547-6551.

"To be ignorant of what occurred before you were born is to remain a child. For what is the worth of human life unless it is woven into the life of our ancestors by the records of history?"
Cicero, 46 B.C.

Ask at the **Bureau of Tourism** about schedules for the Kingston Symphony, the Kingston Choral Society, and the Kingston Summer Theatre. The latter holds forth in the century-old Grand Theatre on Princess Street, and is one of a surprising number of Kingston theater groups.

KINGSTON MILLS • Once a guardian of the Rideau Canal, now a place to observe the life-style
BLOCKHOUSE   of an 1839 soldier. Muskets are fired occasionally to remind you of its long-gone purposes. May 20 to Labour Day, 9:00 A.M. to 4:00 P.M. (closed 12:00-1:00). Free. Kingston Mills Road a little bit north of Hwy. 401. 613/359-5377.

The waters around Kingston are so superb for sailing that they've been the scene of Olympic competitions and hosts to an annual Canadian Olympic Training Regatta, late August-early September. Contact 198 King Street East, Kingston, Ontario K7L 3A4. 613/544-2508.

MILLER MUSEUM • Shows Ontario's mining development, geology of the Kingston area, forma-
OF GEOLOGY   tion of the ancient limestone reefs, metals of the earth. A free display, open
AND MINERALOGY   9:00 A.M. to 4:30 P.M., Monday to Friday. Miller Hall, Queen's University, Union and Division Streets. (An undecided crossroad?) 613/547-2798.

INTERNATIONAL • They say it was the winter of 1886 when schoolboys shot some pieces of
HOCKEY   wood across the harbor ice and the game of hockey was born. Even though
HALL OF FAME   Kingston lacks a big national team, they claim the right to tell the world it all started here. Pictures, equipment, mementos. Open mid-June to mid-September, Alfred and York streets. Adults $1.00, students 50¢. Box 82, Kingston, Ontario K7L 4V6. 613/544-2355.

MACLACHAN • Back toward Gananoque a bit, but usually listed among Kingston's muse-
WOODWORKING   ums, this white cedar log house built in 1853 has a theme: "Wood in the
MUSEUM   service of man." Carpentry tools, augers, bow saws, adzes, chisels; equipment for making all kinds of wood products. Handyman haven. Located in Grass Creek Park. Adults $1.00, children 50¢. P.O. Box 966, Kingston, Ontario K7L 4X8. 613/542-0543.

From Gananoque and Kingston, etc., there are a dozen tour boat companies offering trips through the islands, up the Rideau to Ottawa, and around the eastern reaches of Lake Ontario.

For further info, Kingston Bureau of Tourism, 209 Ontario Street, Box 486, Kingston, Ontario K7L 2Z1. 613/548-4415 or 548-4416.

The trillium, official floral emblem of Ontario since 1937, is also called wake-robin or white lily. Very pretty, but don't take one home . . . it's illegal to pick them.

THE RIDEAU CANAL

Glance at an area map and note the curious pattern of lakes and rivers stretching to the northeast almost as though their beds were raked by a massive tool. (The "tool" was a glacier.) The military strategists of the 1820s saw that these waters could be connected, with locks to handle differences in water level, and boats would then be able to travel to Canada's northern interior via the Ottawa River. Another war with the Americans was surely coming, they argued, and the St. Lawrence River was an enemy target; a canal system would bypass such a hazard.

At that time it was a monumental project, begun in 1826, finished in 1832. The war, happily, never came, but the twentieth century and vacationers, pleasure boaters, and new life-styles did.

Today the Canal is a top Ontario attraction. 198 km. (124 mi.) long. Starting in Ottawa, the Canal follows the course of the Rideau River to Upper Rideau Lake, goes through a man-made canal to Newboro Lake, through the Cataraqui River to Kingston. Throughout are forty-five locks, including those on the connecting route to Perth.

At Ottawa eight locks lift boats into the system; fun to watch, but stand back—the currents and undertows can be dangerous. The Kingston Mills Blockhouse, the Lockmaster Anglin Visitor's Centre, marshes and parks, walking trails, and canalside villages . . . take a ride on the Rideau! Contact Superintendent, Rideau Canal Office, 12 Maple Avenue North, Smith Falls, Ontario K7A-1Z5. 613/383-5170.

CHAPTER II
LAKE ONTARIO

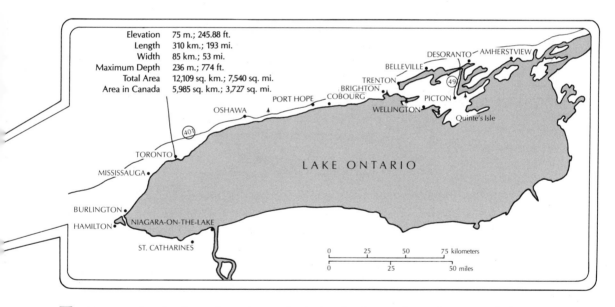

Elevation	75 m.; 245.88 ft.
Length	310 km.; 193 mi.
Width	85 km.; 53 mi.
Maximum Depth	236 m.; 774 ft.
Total Area	12,109 sq. km.; 7,540 sq. mi.
Area in Canada	5,985 sq. km.; 3,727 sq. mi.

I N CHICAGO there's a fountain-sculpture depicting the Great Lakes as five sisters holding basins, and the water pours from the standing "Superior" sister to Michigan, Huron, and Erie to the kneeling Ontario, smallest member of the allegorical quintet. Ontario is looking aside, as if toward the great ocean where the contents of her bowl will flow. Or is she watching the human stream of explorers, priests, traders, and immigrants—the incoming tides of history—entering, changing, using, and often abusing their gift of fresh water?

23

In the early days Samuel de Champlain found this to be a tough Indian neighborhood, made worse when his men killed two Iroquois chiefs. For *many* moons the lake was prudently by-passed by paddling up the Ottawa River and going north via Lake Nippissing and the French River to Georgian Bay. Maps were drawn of the north before the regions of Lakes Ontario and Erie were fully known. Eventually this territory was called Upper Canada and became a Loyalist refuge.

Today the biggest percentage of the provincial population lives near Lake Ontario's shores.

Some interesting marine archeology is going on in the western sector of the lake, where two fighting ships of the War of 1812 have been located almost intact. Eventually it is hoped that they will be on display—masts, cannons, and even a maiden figurehead—in a special waterfront park being readied by the city of Hamilton.

AMHERSTVIEW TO OSHAWA

AMHERSTVIEW • Two chapters in this guide begin with communities named for Lord Amherst; this one and the chapter taking us up the Detroit River. Both have strong Loyalist backgrounds, both are pretty spots to be in. Stop at the Fairfield White House on Hwy. 33 at Fairfield Park for a tour through a prized example of an affluent Loyalist's mansion, built around 1793.

MILLHAVEN • The ferry to Amherst Island leaves every half hour for the seventeen-minute crossing. Passengers over 14, 25¢; autos and driver, $1.25. What will you see? A relaxed, rural island where time has never left a slow trot.

ADOLPHUSTOWN • Crossroads home of the United Empire Loyalist Museum. Worldly goods of the immigrant Loyalists, the story of their struggles, settlements, and contributions. Open late May to Labour Day, daily.

At the end of the road, a free ferry to Glenora and Prince Edward County, better known as **Quinte's Isle.**

Prince Edward County

The county, named to honor Prince Edward, Duke of Kent and father of Queen Victoria, has a shape that defies description. That's part of the

delight, however, because the constantly twisting roads and scores of inlets, beaches, bays, and points guarantee against that feeling of having seen it all before. Not "born" an island, Quinte won a right to the title when the Murray Canal was dug, severing Prince Edward from the mainland.

The Loyalists who first settled here were a determined and righteous lot. They built churches before schools or roads, were sticklers for law and order. A high of prosperity came in the late eighties when the bays had schooners coming and going with loads of grain and the sawmills were buzzing. Remnants of times long gone are everywhere and you can just guess that some of the houses you pass are well into their second century.

There is no best way to drive around; you drive and backtrack, circle and detour past the farms and resorts that brace the local economy.

Day use only, no fee, and a grand place to eat lunch and watch the ferry • LAKE come and go from Glenora. A high cliff with a lovely view on one side of ON THE MOUNTAIN the road, a mountaintop lake on the other. Camera fodder. Legend claims PROVINCIAL PARK the lake, 61 m. (200 ft.) *above* nearby Lake Ontario, is fed underground directly from Niagara Falls(!)

A town from the 1780s, once called Hallowell till re-named after a major- • PICTON general in the Napoleonic Wars, Sir Thomas Picton. Largest community on Quinte's Isle and now growing in fame as a gathering place for artists and craftsmen. That handsome Greek revival building on the hill is the district courthouse, dating from 1832 and still in use. John A. Macdonald, first prime minister of Canada, had to defend himself against charges here, an accusation of assault that turned out to be a practical joke. 44 Union Street, open weekdays all year. No charge to go in and look around.

There are six area museums dwelling on Quinte's history, which means a lot of overlap is inevitable, yet all have something different. Mary Magdalene Church, built in 1823, has been converted to the **Prince Edward County Museum** along with the fully furnished rectory. Union and Church streets.

Picton's Bay, wide and placid, brings in the boaters. Launching, gas, pump-out facilities at the town dock or the Prince Edward Yacht Club.

With Picton as base, a list of Quinte points of interest:

THE AMELIASBURGH • Comprised of an 1868 church, furnished log cabin, two early barns, black-
MUSEUM smith shop, grist mill, and other structures. Special displays and demonstrations, down Co. Rd. 19, six km. (four mi.) west of Hwy. 14 in the village of
Ameliasburgh. Open weekends in spring and fall; daily except Monday
from July to Labour Day. Adults 50¢, children 25¢. Contact the township
office, Ameliasburgh, Ontario K0K 1A0. 613/962-2782.

BIRD HOUSE CITY • A tweeting metropolis located in the Macaulay Mountain Conservation
area. Birdhouse-sized reproductions of historical buildings in Prince Edward
County built and donated by members of the community. Take Union
Street out of Picton to Co. Rd. 8, just past town limits.

MARINER'S PARK • On Co. Rds. 9 and 13, about sixteen km. (twelve mi.) south of Picton. You
MUSEUM will be looking at the second oldest lighthouse on Lake Ontario in a park
with large anchors and engines salvaged from the lake. About 3,000 items
relating to the sailing-fishing history of the area. Very appealing picnic area,
too. Donations accepted. Open June through Thanksgiving; July-August
daily 10:00 A.M. to 5:00 P.M., weekends in June and from Labour Day to
Thanksgiving. Box 399, Picton, Ontario K0K 2T0. 613/476-4572.

SCOTT'S MILLS • In Milford, thirteen km. (eight mi.) south of Picton, open for viewing on
weekends during July and August. A reconstructed grist mill from 1810,
Scott's sits at the west end of Milford Mill Pond and offers picnic tables
along with grinding information. Especially photogenic in early morning.

NORTH MARYSBURG • (**Rose House**) Waupoos, an early settler's home furnished—along with its
MUSEUM loft and shed—as would befit Marysburg's early comers. East of Picton,
twenty-one km. (thirteen mi.) down Co. Rd. 8. Open daily, 1:00-6:00 P.M.
There are also museums in Wellington (former Quaker meetinghouse,
399-3041) and Bloomfield (the **Quinte Educational Museum and
Archives,** a school-theme display; 393-3153).
The **Glenora Fisheries Research Station** would be a choice place to
ask about your fishing prospects. Open Tuesday to Sunday, 1:00-5:00 P.M.
Quinte has six (no camping) conservation areas, at least seven places to
play tennis, three golf courses, and seven public boat-launching sites and
docks plus *many* privately operated marinas. Public tie-ups at Wellington,
Point Traverse, Northport, green point, South Marysburg (head of bay).
For exact locations, resort names, fish reports, moon risings, and bug

counts, stop at the Quinte's Isle Tourist Association, 116 Main Street, Picton (Box 50), Ontario, K0K 2T0. 616/476-2421.

Second largest community in the county, where a neat park adorns the • WELLINGTON waterfront and the talk is boats, fishing, and mushrooms. Get your fill at the **Wellington Mushroom Farm,** east of the village on Hwy. 8. For fanciers of "olde" architecture, the senior house in the region is a 1786 Wellington home of stone: an original Quaker meetinghouse survives as the **Wellington Community Museum;** and **Tara Hall,** built in 1839, is an historic manor house open for tours and the sale of antiques. Daily, July-Labour Day; after that, it's open by chance or appointment. Quinte's Isle is into antiques like Hershey is into chocolates.

Fishing addicts will note that Wellington is situated on both West Lake and Lake Ontario. For sailors coming in from the big lake, a government dock at the liquor store provides gas, pump-out, and facilities.

In two sections (merged with Outlet Beach Provincial Park), with excellent • SANDBANKS swimming, sunset-watching, beach hiking, camping. 412 sites, none with PROVINCIAL PARK electricity; self-guided trails, interpretive program and building, boat rentals, and store within a short distance. Sandbanks, R.R. #1, Picton, Ontario K0K 2T0. 807/934-2995.

Meanwhile, back on the mainland. . . .

We cross the Bay of Quinte Bridge to Belleville, but first must say a word or two about the immediate east.

The town got its start when the Loyalist settlers needed a mill and the • NAPANEE government built one on this site. An ambitious Scot, Alan McPherson, rented the project and prospered tidily. His home, now restored as a museum, testifies to success. On the river, north of Hwy. 2, open daily late May to mid-October.

When water-power meant industrial expansion, Napanee did well with tanneries, carding mills, paper mills, and foundries, along with the profitable grist. The oldest furniture factory in Ontario has operated here since 1835.

At 97 Thomas Street East, the old county jail puts limestone walls around more pieces of the past. If you have ancestors from the area to look up, here's the place to come: **Lennox and Addington County Museum.** Open afternoons all year.

DESERONTO • Good place to come for a swim in the Bay of Quinte or to find a campsite. Top fishing and marina facilities, another gateway to Prince Edward County. On the Sunday closest to May 22, the Mohawk Indians celebrate the landing of their tribe at Deseronto in 1784; a reenactment to which all visitors are welcome. In 1710 four Indian "Kings" traveled to England, were driven through the streets of London with great ceremony, and were presented at the Court of Queen Anne. She gave the guests of honor medals, a Bible, a communion table, and a fine set of communion ware, some of which is used in the service at Christ Church on the day of the "landing." The "Mohawk Silver" is the oldest and most valuable silver in Canada today. In splendid tribal costumes the members of the Tyendinaga Indian Reserve also remember the great peacemaker, Deganawida, a Huron by birth, Mohawk by adoption. Monuments to renowned Mohawks can be seen in the ancient graveyard.

BELLEVILLE • This writer is usually a little put off by towns that shout "We're the Friendly City!" with smiling daisy signs, etc. At Belleville, it's true, however. In walking around and asking questions, there was much sweetness and some light. Even a "parking ticket" (I was in violation) was just a gentle no-no; no fine.

Among 35,000 there *will* be grouches, but not at the Sunday afternoon band concert at the bandshell at **Zwick's Park.** (Near the bridge to Quinte's Isle.) Numerous aging stone and clapboard buildings, a picturesque old City Hall, and tree-filled neighborhoods make bustling Belleville appealing. Excellent marina facilities, sports of all kinds, a dozen fine parks.

On Tuesdays, Thursdays, and Saturdays a **Farmers' Market** with fifty to seventy-five vendors selling maple syrup, flowers, and produce flourishes behind City Hall on Pinnacle Street. Flea Markets are once a month at the Quinte Sports Centre or Ben Bleecker Auditorium; bargains abound in factory outlets around town.

HASTINGS COUNTY • Started life as a Victorian mansion called "Glanmore." Elegant. Period furni-
MUSEUM ture, Canadiana collection, extensive European and Oriental objects d'art, and a gathering of lighting devices dating back to the Stone Age. 257 Bridge Street East. Open all year: June-August, Tuesday to Friday 10:00 A.M. to 5:00 P.M. and Sunday afternoons, but closed Saturday. From September to

May, open Tuesday to Sunday afternoons, closed Monday. Adults $1.00. Hastings County Museum, Belleville, Ontario K8N 1P4. 613/962-2329.

Another area sawmill, early schoolhouse, some agricultural machinery that • O'HARA MILL MUSEUM shouts of hard work. Directly north of town, five km. (three mi.) northwest of Madoc on Hwy. 7. Open Victoria Day weekend thru Labour Day, 9:00 A.M. to 4:00 P.M., pending sufficient staff. Have a picnic; grill, shelter provided. Moira River Conservation Authority, 217 North Front Street, Belleville, Ontario K8P 3C3. 613/968-3434.

If you'd like to take a two-hour tour through the **Corby Distilleries Ltd.,** gather seven or more of your friends together and make an appointment. J. P. Wiser Distillery, R.R. #1, Corbyville, Ontario K0K 1V0. 613/962-4536.

Ask about cheese, too, when you go to the log cabin information office at 183 Pinnacle Street next to the bridge. P.O. Box 726, Belleville, Ontario K8N 5B3. 613/962-4597.

Water-oriented city at the southern entrance to the **Trent-Severn Water- • TRENTON way** (six of the system's forty-four locks are nearby); also western gate keeper for Quinte's Isle. Boat-conscious Trenton has over ninety docks available on a seasonal or daily basis for pumping out, getting gas, repairs, and the rest.

The largest air station of the **Canadian Armed Forces** spreads its wings on the edge of town. You can explore the hangars and planes on "Armed Forces Day," usually the second Saturday in September. Military bands and an air show, demonstrations of the latest equipment. Quite a contrast to Fort Henry.

Trenton's early industry was lumber, but that dwindled as textiles, ship-building, and other manufacturing grew. In 1918 the whole place was nearly blown to Ottawa when a munitions plant exploded, and exploded, and exploded . . . all night long. Miraculously, no one was even injured, but the town hurt financially for a time.

Today Trenton has top shopping (ask about the factory outlets), is known as the "Pickerel Capital," and sends some 1,600 or so boats up the Trent-Severn system in a season.

The Chamber of Commerce, 97 Front Street, P.O. Box 536, will give you maps, motel and campgrounds lists, suggest places to eat. Trenton, Ontario K8V 5R7. 613/392-7635.

29

BRIGHTON • Named for the sunshine city on the south coast of England, Brighton's population of 3,000 doubles with summer resort and cottage people. Lots of apple orchards are nearby, as well as pick-your-own farms. Big event is the **London-Brighton Antique Car Rally** in May, but antique anythings are year-round attractions; good browsing country. Stop at the **Proctor House Museum,** a grand mansion overlooking Lake Ontario. Open daily, late June to early September.

PRESQU'ILE PROVINCIAL PARK • A long splint of land curling like a green hook back toward the coast, it is—as the name states—almost an island. A lovely park with trails and bikeways, fishing, swimming, lighthouse (closed), and 393 campsites, 24 with electricity. Excellent interpretive program and museum; a favorite haunt of bird watchers during the spring and fall migrations. Reservations: Presqu'ile, R.R. #4, Brighton, Ontario 613/475-2204.

Pretty, pleasant road. You'll probably start singing in the car.

COLBORNE • Small (population 1,760) but ready to fill your car, serve you supper, give you information.

GRAFTON • Home of the **Barnum House Museum,** an outstanding Georgian structure well-stocked with chinaware, furnishings, and tools of early settlers. May–October, Sunday afternoons; daily during July and August. P.O. Box 38, Grafton, Ontario K0K 2G0. 416/349-2724.

THE TRENT-SEVERN WATERWAY

Like switchbacks on a road coming down the mountain, the route from Georgian Bay to Lake Ontario zig-zags and turns, widens and narrows 384 km. (240 mi.). If boats could fly, that would be a little over 160 km. (100 mi.).

Fortunately, they can't, as there's hardly any voyage more enjoyable than going down (or up) the Trent-Severn, lifted and lowered from one lake to the next on watery elevators, and passing the scenic green heartland of the lower province.

Houseboats, canoes, rowboats, and rafts follow the trail of the early traders, thankful for not hav-ing to get out and shoulder their craft as they go to the next lake. Used today almost exclusively for recreation, there are stores, marinas, historic sites, and fish (walleye, pike, bass) just over the rail as you go through locks with names like Glenn Miller, Lovesick, and Swift Rapids. The hydraulic lift locks at **Peterborough** are rare and interesting; the big chute marine railway near **Port Severn** the only one of its kind.

Drifting and dreaming, Trent-Severn style, is tranquility as a happening.

Once called Amherst, then Hamilton; when Princess Charlotte married • COBOURG
Prince Leopold of Saxe-Coburg the name was changed again (with a mild
misspelling) to honor the pair.

Much of its Victorian architecture survives handsomely, and you will
hear a lot of United Empire Loyalist tales in their historic accounts. Go first
to **Victoria Hall,** an 1860 municipal building of generous size and decora-
tion housing the Cobourg Art Gallery. Canadian, European, American,
Eskimo art, and imaginative shows such as jukebox art, etc. The small but
choice display is free, open Tuesday to Friday 10:00 A.M. to 5:00 P.M., for two
hours on Friday evenings, Saturday and Sunday afternoons. 416/372-0333.

Don't leave without exploring the rest of the building, mostly open to
the public and in regular use. Victoria Hall's Provincial Courtroom was
patterned after London's Old Bailey with rich, dark woodwork. Hall and
Gallery at 55 King Street West.

Marie Dressler, Wallace Beery's constant rolling-pin-wielding costar, was
born in a 100-year-old house that's now a popular restaurant. 212 King
Street West.

The Scots go to it again in the annual **Highland Games** in Donegan Park, very early in July. The authentic kilt-swirling pipe-blowing works. Adults $3.00, students $1.00, children under 12 free with an adult. 416/342-5667.

Chamber of Commerce, 55 King Street West, Cobourg, Ontario K9A 2M2. 416/372-5831.

PORT HOPE • I have no wish to conduct a beauty contest among lakeside towns, but if such a competition came up, Port Hope would be a finalist. An Indian settlement, a French mission, a trading post—it's been them all. First it was named Smith's Creek, then Toronto, and finally Port Hope, a reflection of the feelings of Loyalists fleeing from the States.

Of interest is **St. Mark's Church,** oldest surviving church in the Anglican Diocese of Toronto, built in 1822. The Chamber of Commerce offers a guided "Heritage Tour" of P. H. homes, churches, and public buildings.

The **Thomas Gallery** at 26 Ontario Street is open daily, all year, with exhibits of contemporary Canadian artists. 416/885-6973.

One of Canada's most famous trout streams, the **Ganaraska River,** running through town, is said to have a spectacular trout run in April. For more information, 27 Queen Street, Port Hope, Ontario L1A 2Y8. 416/885-5519.

BOWMANVILLE • Now fused with Clark and Newcastle, was once a milling town. Of the several flour mills originally there, only one, **Vanstone's Mill,** has survived. The **Bowmanville Museum,** a home of the 1860s, has the details on local history among its remnant artifacts: an old-time store, toys, crafts, furniture, and bric-a-brac. Nice setting and you're welcome to picnic on the grounds.

BOWMANVILLE ZOO • The largest private animal collection in Ontario, this zoo has earned a reputation as a kind of fertility clinic for rare and shy mammals and birds. Starting with a bear and a few raccoons, Keith Connell began this family operation that has expanded to herds of deer and llamas, zebras, emus, and parrots . . . plus a long list of relatives. Though thousands of visitors come each year and petting or feeding is encouraged, a camel giving birth has a privacy priority and sometimes sections are roped off. Open daily 10:00 A.M. till dusk, April 15 to November 15. Adults $3.00, children and seniors $1.50. Family $9.00. 340 King Street East, Hwy. 2, Box 154, Bowmanville, Ontario L1C 3K9. 416/623-5655.

Close to the big cities, here's a spot favored by duck hunters and fall • DARLINGTON
migration watchers. 359 campsites (a city of its own), 102 with electricity.   PROVINCIAL PARK
Swimming, boating, trails, interpretive program, and building. R.R. #2,
Bowmanville, Ontario L1C 3K3. 416/723-4341.

Oshawa

"Crossing of a stream" is what the name meant to the Indians, but the
stream is hard to find in this city, small only because neighboring Toronto is
so large. Oshawa is home of General Motors of Canada, and the auto
industry plays a major role in civic life.

This museum has motorized marvels and classic standards in glistening • CANADIAN
jewel-shape, more than fifty vehicles dating from 1900 to 1964. Canada's   AUTOMOTIVE MUSEUM
contribution to transport development is at 99 Simcoe Street South, just
north of Hwy. 401 (turn off at interchange 70). Open all year, Monday to
Friday 9:00 A.M. to 5:00 P.M.; Saturday 10:00 to 6:00; Sunday afternoons.
$2.50 adults, $1.50 seniors. Less for students and young children. Osawa,
Ontario L1H 4G7. 416/576-1222.

A stone from every battlefield where Canadians served in World War I has • OSHAWA'S MEMORIAL
been used to construct a monument. Weekly band concerts are part of the   PARK
summer program in the downtown park, popular with brown-bagging
office workers and strolling families.

R. S. McLaughlin was a hard-working Scotsman who made good by building • PARKWOOD
(with his father) Canada's first automobile in 1907. Parkwood, his home, is
one of three heritage houses luring Oshawa visitors. If-you-have-it-spend-it
is not the usual Scot attitude, but McLaughlin went lavish in home-building
with dark carved paneling, fifty-five rooms, antique furniture, barber chairs,
bowling lanes, eight-jet showers, and all the kingly fixtures. The gardens are
measured in acres, with ribbons of flowers, stripes of lawn, fountains, and
ornamental trees. June through Labour Day, daily, 10:30 A.M. to 4:30 P.M.,
shorter hours the rest of the year. Adults $3.00, seniors $1.50, students
$1.00. No pets on the premises, please. Special times are the Lilac Gardens
in spring, Rose Garden in June, and Chrysanthemum Show in fall. 270
Simcoe Street North, Oshawa, Ontario L1G 4T5. 416/579-1311.

HENRY HOUSE AND • Two restored homes have a variety of displays from an old bar to an early
ROBINSON HOUSE tourist cabin. Both houses are in the Lakeview Park area: Henry House on the
northwest corner of Henry Street and Lakeview Park Boulevard; Robinson
House on Simcoe Street South at Lakefront. 50¢ admission, both houses.
416/728-6331. 416/723-3818 off-season.

ROBERT MCLAUGHLIN • This contemporary showplace for the Painters Eleven (founded in Toronto
GALLERY in 1953) changes exhibitions monthly, featuring Canadian art. Civic Centre,
open all year, daily 10:00 A.M. to 6:00 P.M., Saturday 12:00 noon to 5:00 P.M.,
Sunday 2:00 to 5:00. Robert McLaughlin Gallery, Civic Centre, Oshawa,
Ontario L1H 323. 416/576-3000.

SCUGOG SHORES • Seven buildings are north of Oshawa on an island in Lake Scugog. The
HISTORICAL MUSEUM name lacks poetry, but it's a pretty spot with a pioneer cabin, re-created
general store, church, period house, and items of settler-Indian significance.
Co. Rd. #7 off Hwy. 7A. April–November, mornings and afternoons (closes
for lunch). Adults $1.00.

WHITBY • A garden with a difference in this city of 33,000, said to be home of the
marigold. The Cullen Gardens and Miniature Village has reproductions of
over 100 historic southern Ontario buildings placed in a garden setting.
Makes you want to shrink and move in. Dining facilities, plant and gift shop,
too. North on Taunton Road, open daily all year.

TORONTO—ONTARIO VERVE CENTER

Toronto clearly did things right. When it was considered foresighted for
cities to replace aging neighborhoods with more expressways, Toronto
citizens said, "Maybe we shouldn't. . . ." When other large cities' satellite
communities were declaring independence forever, Toronto's civic sisters
said "Let's make it a family," and Etobicoke, Scarborough, East York, North
York, and York took communal vows. Instead, they went ahead with underground rapid transit and buses but didn't rip up the old streetcar tracks.
Toronto built a radically new city hall without throwing the wrecking ball
at the old one.

Seldom has a city been so smart. Today Toronto has as much pizzazz,
high-rise splendor, antique architecture, and boulevard grace as any city

on the continent. Its reputation as a cosmopolitan giant and hot spot for the good life has shot real estate prices into the ozone, but it has lured a whole generation of newcomers—with more new ideas.

Success, some say, has made Toronto citizens irrationally smug. Understandable. After going along for years as a "mature" lady in tweeds (or worse—at times the nickname was "Hogtown"), today Toronto's the belle of the ball and her dress keeps getting fancier. What new tower, hotel, mall is next? True, the city is not utopia and the most casual reading of the *Toronto Star* reveals a share of human woes, wasted funds, charitable intentions gone wrong. However, with sixty ethnic minorities and a population creeping toward three million, Torontoans have a right to be proud. Visitors feel safe, you can get around easily, and the variety is stimulating.

If you have only one day to spend in Toronto or would like a high-impact-super-screen-special-effects initiation to help you line up your priorities on what *not* to miss, take yourself to **"The Great Toronto Adventure"** currently at 131 Bloor Street West. More than a movie (sixty projectors), T.G.T.A. is an exciting one-hour presentation of all the sights, sounds, history, neighborhoods, and general Toronto clamor or glamour. Adults $3.50, children $1.75. Every hour on the hour, 11:00 A.M. to 7:00 P.M., seven days a week.

For this guidebook tour we begin with times past. . . .

OLD TORONTO

It started as a fur-trading site, grew to a colonial settlement, and became Capital of the old "Upper Canada." In spite of periodic set-backs (two fires, a cholera epidemic, the American invasion), assets of geography and energy pushed growth. Amid the warmest, most fertile, and most populated sections of the province (even the "far north" is easily reached), the city's position as financial and merchandising hub was assured early on. Waves of immigrants, bringing skills and an eagerness to work, turned out to be a prime resource. In historic homes and halls, bits and pieces of the past tell their own role in the drama:

Toronto's first military post. Although the original establishment dates • FORT YORK from the year 1793, it's 1812 when you enter the gates. Bedrooms, game rooms, sitting rooms for the officers; barracks for the boys. The Battle of York is given a rerun on film, while out in the yard the Fort York Guard puts on periodic artillery drills and musket firings. Year-round; May 1 to Labour Day open 9:30 A.M. to 5:00 P.M. Adults $2.50, children and seniors $1.25. Toronto Historical Board, Stanley Barracks, Exhibition Place, Toronto, Ontario M6K 3C3. 416/366-6127.

MACKENZIE HOUSE • Home of Toronto's first mayor and leader of the Rebellion of 1837. William Lyon Mackenzie was a printer whose business has been reestablished in the back room of this charming house, using equipment from way back then. 82 Bond Street, two blocks east of Yonge Street at Dundas. Open all year, Monday thru Saturday 9:30 A.M. to 5:00 P.M., Sunday and holidays, noon to 5:00 P.M. Adults $1.25. Tea served from 2:00 to 4:00, $2.00. Reservations required on weekends. Contact same address and phone as Colborne Lodge.

SCADDING HOUSE • Owned by an historian of Toronto, Henry Scadding, and closely tied to Trinity Church, this nineteenth-century dwelling was in the way when the big glassy Eaton Centre was about to be built, and so it's now 45 meters from its original site. A community center for children, where Canadian artifacts are sold as part of fund-raising efforts. West of Yonge Street, south of Dundas. Or step out Eaton's Trinity Square exit. To see the very oldest

ITEM
FROM THE MACKENZIE
PRINT SHOP

Recipe for Preserving Children

1 large grass field
1 dozen children
2 or 3 small dogs
a pinch of brook & some pebbles

Mix the children and dogs well together. Put them in the field, stirring constantly. Pour brook over the pebbles and sprinkle the field with flowers. Bake in hot sunshine and when browned remove to the bathtub.

house in town, go to the **Canadian National Exhibition** grounds where a little log cabin with the same name, the **Scadding Cabin,** is under the protective eye of the Toronto Historical Board.

In the oldest part of town . . . York, Toronto of the 1800s. . . . **St. James Cathedral**—the mellow gothic cathedral on King Street East was built in 1853 without a steeple. Twenty years later the inspiring spire was added, visible to mariners far out on the lake and marking the location of the city. It is the tallest steeple in Canada . . . on one of the loveliest churches.

In the mid-1800s the Victorians were high on the Renaissance tradition, and here is one of the best examples. Jenny Lind and Tom Thumb, the celebrated midget, were part of the parade across the stage of the Great Hall where the list of luminaries is its own history book. The building faded into hard times but was restored to original splendor as a Centennial project in 1967. Jarvis and King Street East. 367-7986. • ST. LAWRENCE HALL

Directly south, past the New St. Lawrence Market (where the action gets heavy on Saturdays) and across Front Street is the **St. Lawrence Market** . . . senior, and decidedly more alive. It was built in 1844 as Toronto's first municipal hall, lost that job when the Bay Street Hall was built, and now is given over to the sale of steaks and sausages, salmons, sardines, zucchini, strudels, and all things edible. Upstairs you'll find a Market Gallery, operated by the city, with exhibits often taken from the town archives. The Market is open from 7:00 A.M. to 5:00 P.M., a little later on Friday; closed Sunday and Monday.

Walk west from here on Front Street to a couple of Toronto "monuments"; the **Gooderham (flatiron) Building,** a photogenic contrast with the slick glassy towers behind it, and the **Royal York Hotel.** Don't walk too fast to miss seeing the back of the three-sided antique; it's decorated with a four-and-a-half story mural that looks like the side of a house painted on fluttering canvas. Some of the windows are real, some are painted, and when a real person looks out of a real window he or she becomes part of the graphic. Toronto is full of fun new tricks on old surfaces.

The Royal York, once billed as the largest hotel in the British Empire, has recently been redone, but they still call the various stations at the main desk "wickets." Very British. Cross the street to **Union Station** (if it's rainy there's a tunnel from the lower level of the York). Not too old (opened in 1927, replacing an earlier grand station) but very impressive in an age when such proportions are hard to find. The twenty-two massive pillars across the front are over twelve m. (forty ft.) tall. Go in and wander around a while.

OLD CITY HALL • Across from Nathan Phillips Square, keeping watch on its successor, is the second of three city halls, constructed in 1899. Today it houses the Provincial Courts. The clock in the tower was deliberately constructed to be seen down Bay Street and has a nice authoritative gong to it, but is apt to go on the fritz when you need it most, according to the home folks. Note the gargoyles under the ledges—said to be portraits of city councilmen who perhaps were too tight with the stonemason's pay. Or maybe they're there because the council had a disagreement with the architect, E. J. Lennox. Bay and Queen streets.

The building with the Corinthian portico across the Square is **Osgoode Hall,** headquarters of the Law Society of Upper Canada since the 1830s. Not generally open for tours, you might get special permission to peek in at the classical central hall and library. Meanwhile, note the narrow iron gates, devised to keep the cows out when this was a more bucolic scene.

CAMPBELL HOUSE • This gracious Georgian colonial in the heart of the city belonged to Sir William Campbell, Chief Justice of Upper Canada from 1825 to 1829, and reflects the prosperity of that time. Upstairs is a model of early Toronto and a diorama of the Toronto fire. 160 Queen Street West at University Avenue. Open all year, 9:30 A.M. to noon, 2:30 P.M. to 5:00 weekdays; weekends and holidays May 15-October 10, afternoons only, noon to 5:00 P.M. Adults 75¢, seniors 50¢, children 25¢. Toronto, Ontario M5H 3H3. 416/597-0227. (Don't miss the pretty little back yard.)

CANADIANA BUILDING • **The Royal Ontario Museum**—Where history buffs are like kids at the park, eying early Canadian room settings, silver and glass, and an enormous collection of prints, drawings, and maps. Ceramics, a Quebec panelled room, coins, medals, and all the artifacts of Canada-growing-up. Open Monday to Saturday, 10:00 A.M. to 5:00 P.M., Sunday 1:00 P.M. to 5:00 P.M. Free. 14 Queen's Park Crescent West, just opposite the Ontario Parliament Buildings, about five minutes of walking south of the Royal Ontario Museum.

Contact Royal Ontario Museum, 100 Queen's Park, Toronto, Ontario M5S 2C6. 416/978-3640.

In 1892, when architect Richard Waite was put in charge of a committee to • PROVINCIAL
select someone to design a new legislative building, he looked over the PARLIAMENT BUILDING
hopefuls and selected himself. The results were grandiose and expensive,
but the interior is worthy of the office. Sixteen years after completion, the
West Wing, housing offices and a library, burned down. The replacement
was meant to be fireproof and used a lot of white Italian marble, so the two
ends of the building do not look alike. There is a simplicity about the white
walls and dark woodwork that is striking, and the red-carpeted Legislative
Chamber is most impressive. Open to the public July, August, September,
January, tours every half hour beginning at 9:00 A.M. till 3:30 P.M. weekdays.
Free. Contact Suite 150, Legislative Building, Queen's Park, Toronto, Ontario
M7A 1A2. 965-4028.

Here's that gem residence with a mentality older than anything called • CASA LOMA
Canadian. Sir Henry Pellatt, soldier, financier, and industrialist, liked castles
and, since there was a shortage of same in Toronto, built a full-scale one,
Casa Loma, with medieval-to-Georgian touches plus some Gothic on the
side. Marble and glass, paneling and mantlepieces imported from Europe,
and Scottish stonemasons who built the castle wall around the six-acre
site (cost estimated at a dollar per stone) . . . things like that. No expense
was spared. The Great Hall has a sixty-foot ceiling, priceless bronze doors
open to the Conservatory from a hallway copied from Windsor Castle, and
an 800-foot tunnel leads to the mahogany-stalled stables. When Sir Henry
needed to get away from all this he went down secret staircases to the
wine cellar.

   Times changed and Pellatt, faced with new realities, vacated Casa Loma
in 1923—sixteen years before his death. The castle was taken over by the
City of Toronto for taxes. For years it was a fantastic white elephant, until
the Kiwanis Club entered an agreement with the city and Casa Loma
became a tourist attraction.

   Open daily, 10:00 A.M. to 5:00 P.M. Hours subject to change. Adults $2.00,
students $1.00, seniors 50¢. Casa Loma, 1 Austin Terrace, Toronto, Ontario
M5R 1X8. 416/923-1171.

   More of the past is present at **Todmorden Mills Park,** 67 Pottery Road,
just east of Don Valley Parkway (accessible from either Bayview or Broad-
view avenues). Two pioneer homes, paper mill, train station, and a non-
producing brewery make up the "village." The **Gibson House,** which put

walls around a family of nine, is furnished as it would have been in 1851. 5172 Yonge Street (behind the post office) up in Willowdale. 225-0146. **The Grange,** Dundas Street West at Beverly (downtown), is part of the Art Gallery of Ontario, an elegant Georgian house restored as a living showcase for the 1830s. 977-0414.

The **Thomson Park Museum** is housed in three buildings dating back to 1850, with furnishings of even earlier years showing rural domestic life. Brimely Road, Lawrence Avenue East, from Victoria Day to Thanksgiving. **Enoch Turner Schoolhouse** was donated by a civic-minded citizen when the town council voted against funds for a public school as an unnecessary expense. 106 Trinity Street all year. 863-0010. **Montgomery's Inn,** a ten-minute walk north from the Islington subway station, is a choice example

of Loyalist or late Georgian design. Mr. Montgomery was an Irish immigrant, and his tidy establishment has been restored to the time when the inn was hub of local festivities. 4709 Dundas. 236-1046. The **Redpath Sugar Museum** serves afternoon tea, a sweet touch. Artifacts and pictures tell how the Redpath family and their sugar industry got started in Canada. Free. Weekdays 10:00 A.M. to 3:30 P.M., closed noon hour. 95 Queen's Quay East. 366-3561.

You can smell the cooking, candlewax, forge fires (and, well, sometimes • BLACK CREEK
the horses), and hear the sounds of the early 1800s. A harness shop, general   PIONEER VILLAGE
store, inn, farm house, etc. are among the thirty restored structures. Jane Street and Steeles Avenue West, 1000 Murray Ross Parkway. Adults $4.00, seniors $2.00, children $1.75. Family $8.00. Open from late March to December 31. Mid-summer hours 10:00 A.M. to 6:00 P.M., till 4:30 P.M. on weekends and holidays.

Ask about their calendar of events, from sheep-shearing days to shingle-making demos. Black Creek Pioneer Village, 5 Shoreham Drive, Downsview, Ontario M3N 1S4. 416/661-6600.

Sits in beautiful High Park, donated by the builder, John Howard, to the • COLBORNE LODGE
City of Toronto. Howard came to York (Toronto's earlier name) from England, became a prominent architect, and named his house in the country after one of his benefactors. Built in 1836 with round chimneys and low verandas and filled with his watercolor drawings. Open all year, 9:00 A.M. to 5:00 P.M., half-days on weekends and holidays. Adults $1.25. Contact Toronto Historical Board, Stanley Barracks, Exhibition Place, Toronto, Ontario M6K 3C3. 416/595-1567.

New Toronto

"New" Toronto is the last 100 years with futuristic features. A trolley car reflected in the glassy walls of a big bank; a Victorian hotel window staring at a space needle. Antique sellers do a big Sunday business on a spiffy *new* waterfront locale. Start there, on the edge of Canada's largest inland port.

Built on landfill, this is an imaginative complex with too much going on for • ONTARIO PLACE
any single visit. The Forum, a handsome indoor-outdoor amphitheater, is

41

home for bluegrass, symphonies, ballet, pop singers, and circus acts. A geodesic dome called the Cinesphere shows those wide-wide films that you fly or swim into, leaving only a body in your seat. There are sales pitches and explanations of Ontario's wonders, picnic-grounds, award-winning buidings, a dozen restaurants, an amusement park with special kids' attractions (like the forest of massed punching bags), pedal boats, and an Oriental temple gong if you want to sound off. The naval destroyer HMCS *Haida* is tied up at one end, open to visitors; a showboat is tied to a dissecting waterway with Dixieland bands, et al., and you can tie your own boat to the Ontario Place Marina if there's docking space that day. 955 Lakeshore Boulevard West, mid-May to mid-September. Adults $4.00, children under 12 unaccompanied $2.50, accompanied $1.00. Toronto, Ontario M6K 3B9. 416/965-7711.

HARBOURFRONT • Much completed, much in progress, this 92-acre lakefront development is the site of 3,500 yearly events and an ambitious list of daily pleasures. Music, art, sailing courses, ethnic festivals, literary readings, drama, films . . . all are part of the Harbourfront project. A schedule of events is published every week in the newspapers, or you can call 364-5665 to find what half-hundred things are going on. One summer favorite: the Sunday antique sale.

At 553.33 m. (1,815 ft.) and 130,000 tons (about the weight of 22,214 • THE CN TOWER *large* elephants), the CN has become to Toronto what the great leaner is to Pisa. You can zip 1,100 feet up this new trademark to the restaurant, lounge, nightclub, outdoor (but well screened) or indoor viewing levels in glass-faced elevators, and, if that's not enough, "inside" elevators will take you to a Space Deck at the 1,500-foot level. On a clear day you can see to the ground.

The Tower is the tallest free-standing structure in the world; taller ones are braced with cables. On ground zero are shops, eateries, a reflecting pool, electronic games, pedal boats, and other amusements. CN (for Canadian National . . . they also run trains and hotels) Tower, 301 Front Street West, Toronto, Ontario M5V 2T6. 416/360-8500.

A place and an event, a century-old institution that is to the big slick show • CANADIAN NATIONAL places what country music is to Broadway. Down home displays of jams, EXHIBITION jellies, and quilts, cows, chickens, and everything that has ever gone into any country fair . . . except that this is the *whole* country: Canada, second largest in the world. Band concerts, Ferris wheel, cotton candy, and obviously a good time to be had by all. The Exhibition grounds house other events and some permanent displays, are easily found off West Lake Shore Drive, across from Ontario Place.

Won the architectural sweepstakes for imaginative design when it was • CITY HALL erected in 1965. A Finnish genius, Viljo Revell, designed it—through much controversy—and the citizens are rightfully pleased. Between the two curved buildings and the domed Council Chamber, the setting (Nathan Phillips Square) is complete with walkways, a grouping of play equipment for youngsters, a Henry Moore sculpture, and a reflecting pool that becomes a skating rink in winter.

There are free guided tours daily all year, at frequent intervals. Tourist Centre and cafeteria in the basement are open during the week. Public Information Division, 100 Queen Street West, Toronto, Ontario M5H 2N2. 416/947-7341.

This one's up for grabs: grab the lever, see what happens; pull the rope, • ONTARIO push the button, twist the dial, and watch the results. A thousand exhibits, SCIENCE CENTRE most of them designed to let you see the "whys" as well as the "whats" of sound, light, computers, physics, mathematics, wheels, and robotics . . . and why we can't believe our eyes. A stunning set of connected buildings that follows the contours of a hill in a ravine area. A busy day with thirty busloads of school children going through can be a little hectic, but O. S. C. is 100 percent for grown-ups, too. (I love it, I love it!) Refreshments, gift shop, et al. 770 Don Mills Road, Don Mills, Ontario M3C 1T3. 416/429-4100.

ECOLOGY HOUSE • Grow supper in a tank, put the sun to work. Energy efficiency, solar heating systems, soil-less gardening, better insulating, etc. demonstrated in a mid-town house, 12 Madison Avenue, east of Spadina and just north of Bloor. Open all year from Wednesday through Sunday, noon to 5:00 P.M.. Free. 416/978-6477.

METROPOLITAN • Where are the West Beskids and how do you build a floodgate? Don't even
TORONTO LIBRARY   think up a question; just go to this most unlibrarish library and stare about. Four tiers of galleries look down on main floor fountains, greenery, elegance. The elevators have glass walls but there are seats you can vanish into. Reference only, no carry-outs; was research ever so pleasant? 789 Yonge Street. 416/928-5211.

METRO TORONTO ZOO • The 700 acres are home for 3,500 beasts and birds; cream of the creature crop. With native trees and landscape care, the animals are placed in next-to-natural habitat without distracting bars, etc. They watch you as you travel through their various domains (areas designed to represent different climatic regions of the world) on a monorail system and/or trackless train, but *they* don't seem too interested in humans. It's a well-done show with some very handsome buildings and special events such as Meet the Zoo-keeper days during the summer months. Hwy. 401 at Meadowvale Rd., just east of Don Valley Parkway. Adults $4.00, seniors and youth $1.50, children under 4 free. Metro Toronto Zoo, P.O. Box 280, West Hill, Ontario M1E 4R5. 416/284-8181.

HIGH PARK MENAGERIE • More animals. Birds, bison, buffalo, deer, yaks, llamas, and swans. (See
OR PADDOCKS   **Colborne House** location.) Visit barnyard friends at **Riverdale Farm,** overlooking the Don River in the middle of East Toronto. Go back to a nineteenth-century farm with horses, cows, pigs, chickens, goats, and those stars of our picture-book days. Open all year, 9:00 A.M. till dusk. Free.

Canada's largest public showcase ranges from art and archeology to zoos of • THE ROYAL
a different sort . . . the microscopic, extinct, or exotic as seen through the ONTARIO MUSEUM
life sciences. Invertebrates, reptiles, arthropods; dinosaurs revisited. Vast
Oriental and Egyptian collections, and visiting exhibits such as "Alexander,"
"Treasures from the Tower of London." A new series of galleries depicts life
around the Mediterranean in far-gone days as you walk through a centuries-
old Islam market, and are given glimpses of Imperial Rome. Topnotch.
Open daily 10:00 A.M. to 8:00 P.M., Monday to Saturday, Sunday 10:00 to
6:00. $2.50 adults, family $5.00. Children, students, seniors $1.25. 416/
978-3704.

Part of the ROM complex. Lie back in reclining chairs and watch the stars • MCLAUGHLIN
come out. Constellations, planets, black holes, and galaxies; four times a PLANETARIUM
day the universe comes closer. Adults $2.25, students-children-seniors $1.25.
(Senior citizens free on Tuesdays.) 416/978-8550.

    Both museums are at 100 Queen's Park, Avenue Road at Bloor. University
subway at Museum Station.

Well, the kids *will* love it, but I have trouble warming up to fake brown • CANADA'S
mountains. Think juvenile and enjoy a Salt Water Circus with performing WONDERLAND
sea lions and dolphins, browse in the shops and bazaars on "International
Street." *Five* rollercoasters ought to rearrrange your brain cells: clinging to
a youngster as you go through these gyrations is a new form of family
togetherness. All kinds of rides and musical events at six-million-dollar
Kingswood Theatre; Happyland of Hanna Barbera. General admission
includes all free attractions, starts at $10.95. A whole set of ticket prices,
including season passes, is offered. Take Hwy. 400 North, exit at Rutherford
Road (about twenty mi.). Open late May to late September, longer hours in
mid-summer. Canada's Wonderland, 7725 Jane Street, Concord, Ontario
L4K 1B6. 416/669-5620.

Art-Full Toronto

Henry Moore in front of City Hall; Gerald Gladstone's "Universal Man"
beside the CN Tower; Toronto's artistic flair even shows up in subway
stations, such as the mosaic mural called "Spadina Summer Under All
Seasons" . . . flowers in tile. For more conventional settings, see the
following:

ART GALLERY • More than 8,000 works from the Old Masters to tomorrow-modern, in-
OF ONTARIO cluding the largest public collection of Henry Moore works in the world.
Frans Hals, Augustus John, Alex Colville, Oldenburg, Tom Thomson, Renoir,
and Rothko . . . any big name you can pull out of the art-world hat.
Canadian art from the eighteenth century, traveling shows, and loan exhibits
from other major galleries—it's all here. **The Grange** (mentioned earlier)
is also part of the big, beautiful A.G.O.O. Open Tuesday to Sunday, 11:00
A.M. to 5:30 P.M., Wednesday and Thursday till 9:00 P.M. The Gallery Shops
and the Restaurant are open seven days a week. Adults $2.00, students and
seniors with cards 75¢ . . . as of this writing. 317 Dundas Street West (walk
west from St. Patrick subway station or transfer to Dundas Street Streetcar),
Toronto, Ontario M5T 1G4. 416/977-0414.

THE MCMICHAEL • It means a little drive to the country but it's too much a part of the
CANADIAN COLLECTION Canadian art scene to miss. In a newly remodeled and most appropriate of
buildings, 1,000 works of the "Group of Seven" Canadian artists and their
contemporaries are shown to full impact. The gallery has thirty long rooms,
uses enormous old timbers and fieldstone on a hilly, pine-filled setting,
fairly singing "Oh Canada!" Also works of West Coast, Inuit, and Woodland
Indians. McMichael Canadian Collection, Kleinbergh, Ontario L0J 1C0.
416/893-1121.

Ask what's going on at **Prime Canadian Crafts,** 229 Queen Street West
(593-5750); the **Isaacs Gallery,** 832 Yonge Street (923-7301); **Canadian
Centre of Photography and Film,** 596 Markham Street (536-5400);
The Wildlife Gallery, 18 Birch Avenue (922-5153); **Albert White Gal-
lery,** 25 Prince Arthur Avenue (923-8804); **David Jean Gallery of Fine
Art,** 2158 Queen Street East (690-6404).

. . . and of course, Harbourfront's let-the-pipes-show **Contemporary Art
Gallery,** a great popular success. At the foot of York Street; call 364-5665.

THE MARKET GALLERY • This public show operated by the City of Toronto is located in the renovated
section of the South St. Lawrence Market, and locale of the first City Hall.
95 Front Street at Jarvis. Open all year, Wednesday-Friday 10:00 A.M. to 4:00
P.M., Saturday open at 9:00 A.M., Sunday 1:00 to 4:00. Free; refreshments
available in the Market. 416/947-7604.

Of Cameras and Stanley Cups

Just as the food being served to the next table looks like the item you should have ordered, the special museum or tour of your companion's interest can be where you wanted to go. Try:

Home of the Stanley Cup. There is a continuous film show of great hockey moments, as well as trophies, sweaters, sticks, personal stories, and memorabilia of the game. **Exhibition Place** (between Stadium and Food Building), Lakeshore Boulevard West, across from **Ontario Place.** Open all year. Mid-May to mid-August 10:00 A.M. to 8:00 P.M., till 5:00 P.M. Monday, till 10:00 P.M. during Canadian National Expo. Shorter hours after Labour Day, closed Monday. Adults $2.00, seniors, students $1.00. Contact 63 Purdom Drive, Downsview, Ontario M3H 4X2. 416/595-1345.

• HOCKEY HALL OF FAME

A two-hour tour that focuses on a top hobby-profession, shows how film is made, how cameras are put together. Free, but you must make an appointment. 416/766-8233, Ext. 6686.

• KODAK CANADA, INC.

Located in the former Officer's Quarters of Stanley Barracks, it shows the Great Lakes freshwater heritage from the days of fur trading to the present: How inland routes spurred development; sail and steam advances, etc. At Exhibition Place overlooking Lake Ontario near Princes' Gate, Lakeshore Boulevard West. Open all year, 9:30 A.M. to 5:00 P.M., Sunday and holidays afternoons only. Write to Toronto Historical Board, Colborne Lodge address and telephone.

• MARINE MUSEUM

Seventy-two vintage vehicles from 1901 to 1933, and a couple dozen miniature cars showing the evolution of our number one transport. Call first; the collection may be on tour. 416/789-3432. 760 Lawrence Avenue West, one block east of Dufferin.

• THE CRAVEN FOUNDATION AUTOMOBILE MUSEUM

Toronto—A Park Place

Walk all you want to; a park bench is never too far ahead. High Park, the Zoo, and the picnic areas of other attractions have already been mentioned so I'll stay here with the waterfront grasslands.

TORONTO ISLANDS • Catch the ferry at the foot of Bay Street (behind the Toronto Hilton Harbour
PARK Castle) for a ten-minute joy ride to the islands of Centre, Ward, and Olympic. Where else can you get so much for so little? Sailboats, the city panorama, glowing sunsets . . . besides the chance to relax in picnic-goers' heaven. There are bikes and fishing equipment (a trout pond at Harlan's Point) to rent, a small amusement park, tennis courts, swimming, refreshments, and a restaurant where you can sit sipping something cool as you stare about. Completely delightful and inexpensive; *don't* miss it.

During busy summer hours the ferries run every twenty minutes, more usually every half hour till 11:30 P.M. Round trip $1.00, less for kids and seniors. Any questions, call 367-8193 and 367-8194. P.S. No camping.

THE BEACHES • For visitors the designation **"Ashbridges Bay Park"** may seem confusing: this *long* stretch of grass and boardwalk near **Greenwood Race Track** and **Kew Gardens** is called The Beaches. On the edge of a homey old neighborhood, this was once a separate resort community, but the city's growth

enclosed it years ago. A little short on picnic tables, but lots of benches to sit on while the joggers or boats go by. Marina, swimming, food concession at one end, a feeling of space all along. Drive east on Lakeshore or take the Queen Street Trolley and get off near the end of the line.

The land rises along the Scarbough lakefront into strange, peaked sandstone • BLUFFERS PARK formations; bluffs with a surrealistic look to them. Best for photos in the morning. There are walks and places to sit out on small peninsulas, a marina, washrooms, no concessions. Take Brimely south from Kingston Road.

Bluffers is close to the water but a whole series of parks can be found atop the cliffs. **Rosetta McLain Park** (gardens) down Glen Everst Road; **Cathedral Bluffs Park** on Cathedral Bluffs Drive; **Cudia Park,** on Pine Ridge to Meadowcliffe Drive; **Sylvan Park,** Bethune to Sylvan Avenue; and **Guildwood Park** surrounding the impressive **Guild Inn** where a collection of historic architectural souvenirs sits in beautifully landscaped settings. Parts (fireplaces, facades, entries) from former Toronto-area buildings. Privately owned but open to the public, off Guildwood Parkway; and **East Point Park** where the bluffs look toward Highland Creek. Take Lawrence Avenue south to Beechwood Grove Drive.

These scenic spots on the heights are not recommended for rambunctious family outings, but are quiet retreats where you could bring a sandwich and a good book. All south off Kingston Road.

ROUGE BEACH PARK • An excellent sandy beach, good fishing, and a view of the **Rouge Marshes.** The **West Rouge Canoe Club** at the east end of the park will give you lessons in canoeing, kayak racing, and water safety . . . if you're more than ten years old. Take Island Road, east off Port Untion Road, south to Rouge Hills Drive.

ALLAN GARDENS • Bounded by Carlton and Gerrard, Jarvis and Sherbourne, masses of color outdoors and in, plus tropical plants given all-season protection in a classic Victorian greenhouse. Open daily, 10:00 A.M. to 5:00 P.M.

West side:

MARIE CURTIS PARK • Lake Shore Boulevard at 42nd Street. A family-oriented playground with wading pool, beach, boat launching ramp.

HUMBER BAY PARK • (West)—From Lake Shore Boulevard west of Park Lawn Road is a new spread of lawns and waterside fun. Great view of Toronto skyline; lots of boats to watch.

HUMBER BAY PARK • (East)—South from Lake Shore, opposite Park Lawn Road and separated from the other park by Mimico Creek. Good fishing, model boat ponds.

More pleasant spots are along Lake Shore, at Ontario Place, Harbourfront, etc. Ask at Tourist Information for Metropolitan Toronto Parks folder.

I Bought It in Toronto

EATON CENTRE • The biggie place for buying, with connections to **Simpsons,** et al. The Centre has 300 stores under a high glass arch where a flock of sixty realistic fiber glass geese seem about to land. You wouldn't be surprised; the place is big enough. Take note of the soft-sculpture (among other media) store ads, other imaginative commercial art. Access to the subway and other shopping areas is readily available, too.

There's good browsing for discount clothing bargains on Spadina near Queen Street; for high chic try the **Yorkville** area (North Bloor between Avenue Road and Yonge Street). The **Hudson's Bay Company,** the third merchandising giant, is there, too.

MIRVISH VILLAGE • Lined with art galleries, antique shops, and bookstores, and some classy little places for dinner.

Of a different stripe is **Honest Ed's Department Store** on Bloor Street

West where signs proclaim Ed's insanity for such low prices. ("Honest Ed's childish . . . his prices never grow up"). Ed Mirvish, the name behind the Village, is also behind the discount circus.

In addition, every ethnic neighborhood has its own shops (we'll get to that) and the great North-American-ethnic malls are easily found. Look in the paper for notices of flea markets, antique bargains, used books, whatever interests you.

There are blocks of underground shops where I suspect credit card addicts have gotten lost and are never seen again. (The natives are friendly; they'll tell you where you are). If you go down the steps on the corner of Bay and Queen streets, for example (next to old City Hall), you enter **The Lanes**, which runs under the enormous Sheraton Centre Hotel or under the new City Hall, where you can find jewelers, barber shops, restaurants, the works. These places go on and on under the big banking buildings for mysterious—to the stranger—distances.

The Tourist Bureau people will be tickled to give you shopping info. Keep all your receipts and apply for a tax refund if you've spent more than $100—be sure to pick up a brochure and application at the border.

The World in Mini-Tour

Unless you stay in your hotel room with your head buried in a pillow, you'll see that Toronto is a mirror to the world. Wars and famine and the lure of opportunity have brought countless waves of immigrants from time to time, but since World War II newcomers from Europe as well as Asia, Latin America, and the East and West Indies have come in record numbers. Name your ancestor; your relatives are here. So venture out and experiment with taste, try some new food, buy a sari, kobe, or carved room divider.

The corner of Gerrard Street and Coxwell Avenue on the east side of the **Yonge Street** artery marks the heart of the **East Indian community,** with its pulsing bazaar selling carpets, Indian silks, brass, and incense. The twang of Indian music seems to add extra flavor to the curry, tandori, and bar-becued chicken served in the local restaurants.

Toronto's **Greektown** is also eastside along Danforth Avenue where a good percentage of the city's 80,000 Greeks live. You can see a hundred Zorbas toasting each other with retsina (a dry Greek wine); bring on the moussaka, baklava, feta cheese, and olives—but be warned about the coffee! Grecian urns, postcards of the Acropolis, Greek language records, and grocery stores should be explored, too.

West of Yonge Street: Outside of Rome, Toronto is said to have one of the largest Italian-speaking populations in the world. Over 450,000 Eee-tal-yan-ee make the area so **Italian** that the local library carries predominantly Italian literature. Lots of good food—pasta, gelati (ice cream)—music, of course, and high-quality bargain-priced tailors. Dufferin Street and St. Clair Avenue, west side, will put you al centro. (Did you know that Toronto is farther south than Venice?)

Reggae and calypso fans will follow a beat to St. Clair Avenue and Bathurst Street, **West Indian territory.** (Be thankful the West Indians settled of the *west* side and the East Indians on the *east* side because it's so much easier to give directions!) Shops selling carpets, records, and clothes from behind the same counter are fun to poke through. BIG local event is a **Caribana,** a festival with parade, razzle-dazzle floats, super-sequined costumes.

If grandpa was **Portuguese** you'll feel at home in and around College and Grace streets; a likeable area even if you're Incan. They are fond of bright yellows and pinks on their houses, a lure for out-of-town photographers. Portuguese bakeries and fish markets are part of the **Kensington Market** to which the neighborhood extends. In summer the market is a scramble of loud voices, haggling in every language around. The best bargains in Portuguese lace can be found here, too.

Toronto's **Chinese** population is generations old, substantial, and by no means confined to traditional restaurants or stores. After catering so long to the western palate, they cook for their own tastes now—you should go and try the real thing. Of course you'll find paper parasols, embroidered blouses, paper kites, cameras, and magazines of Chinese movie stars. **China Court,** at 210 Spadina, is North America's first and only indoor shopping mall of traditional Chinese design. More than two dozen shops carry Oriental apparel, food, candies, and souvenirs.

There is no way to include every group in this brief space, such as the Hungarians (40,000), the Ukrainians (80,000), the Germans (170,000), or Filipinos, Arabs, Koreans, Malaysians, Mexicans, etc. The Tourist Bureau people have lists and lists and *lists,* with all the "wheres."

Toronto on Stage

Think of being able to go to a different *live* performance every evening for a month and never repeat, thanks to the rare enthusiasm shown for the lively arts in this cultural greenhouse.

At this world-class hall you sit beneath lights that resemble a mega-bulb • ROY THOMSON HALL aurora borealis and listen to the superb Toronto Symphony, the Mendelssohn Choir, or touring performers. The Symphony's home is at King Street West, between Wellington and Simcoe streets.

One of the giants (3,200 seats), this is home base for the Canadian Opera • O'KEEFE CENTRE Company and the National Ballet of Canada. A restaurant in the Centre handles before or after dining. Front Street at Yonge.

Close to its hundredth birthday, this grande dame is still an acoustical • MASSEY HALL wonder. Caruso was here, but so was Gordon Lightfoot; i.e., it's an everybody place. 178 Victoria Street (at Shuter). 363-7301.

A Toronto Centennial Project in 1967, this beautiful, up-to-date structure • ST. LAWRENCE CENTRE features a 483-seat Town Hall for concerts or lectures and group discussions, plus an 863-seat theater with a resident Repertory Company. 336-1656.

With gold brocade and gilded trimmings, it's "royal" all the way. London and • ROYAL ALEXANDRA New York plays, local productions once in a while. 260 King Street West.   THEATRE Going all summer. 593-4211.

During hockey season, standing room only, no matter how the team is • MAPLE LEAF GARDENS doing. In the summer, rock concerts, conventions, revivals, etc.
The Forum at Ontario Place, the Kingswood at Canada's Wonderland, Hart House Theatre, Bayview Playhouse Theatre . . . and we haven't begun to mention the little revues for audiences of under 200 such as those at Second City, a dinner-theatre in The Old Firehall, 110 Lombard. 863-1111. Check the paper for titles, talents, and times. You can buy half-price tickets on the day of performance and full-price tickets to small nonprofit performing arts companies under the Five Star Tickets program. Opera, ballet, top shows. Includes Shaw fest and Stratford, too. Cash only, sales final, first-come, first-served. Ask at Toronto Visitors Information.

This book will not get into restaurant critiquing, especially not in Toronto where there are more than 4,000 establishments selling meals on a plate. Again I refer you to the Tourist Guides, or ask some people who live here where they go out to eat.

A few general tips for getting around town:

Toronto's streets are laid out in a grid pattern running north-south, east-west, with Yonge Street as the dividing line. Bloor Street, going across east-to-west, is considered "mid-town" when it crosses Yonge. Some street names change after crossing Yonge.

TORONTO TRANSIT SYSTEM • An efficient bus, trolley, streetcar, and subway service with interconnecting routes throughout the city. The subway consists of three lines:

> Bloor-Danforth—running east-west
> Yonge Line—running north-south
> Spadina Line—also running north-south

Cash fare is 85¢ for adults, six tickets or tokens for $4.00. Please note that surface vehicle operators do not carry change or sell tickets. Tickets/tokens must be purchased at subway booths or specially designated variety stores. For Transit information call 484-4544 and ask about the **Trolley Tour** of Toronto.

METRO TORONTO CONVENTION & VISITORS ASSOCIATION • Offers a special Infoline: 979-3143; with Information Officers ready to give assistance on attractions, dining, shopping, entertainment, etc. Infoline is available during normal business hours. During summer months the service is extended until 6:00 P.M.

As an additional service, during summer months, the Association also operates Toronto Information kiosks located at strategic points throughout the city. These kiosks, which operate seven days a week, are easily identifiable by their red and white signs and colorful photo panels featuring Metro events and attractions.

Guided Tours

TORONTO HARBOUR AND ISLANDS BOAT TOURS • Ride in glass-topped boats for one-hour excursions around the harbour, waterfront, island lagoons. Foot of Yonge and Queen's Quay, beside the Harbour Castle Hilton and Captain John's Floating Restaurant. Or, at Ontario Place on East Island. Hourly departures. Mid-summer from 10:00 A.M. to

8:00 P.M., shorter hours in spring and fall. Adults $6.00, children $3.00. Boat Tours International, 5 Queen's Quay West, Toronto, Ontario M5J 2H1. 416/364-2412.

A red sail for the sun set; tour the Harbour on a forty-foot trimaran, the "Tapo Wingo" (the hull is white, sails red), eight times a day . . . on into the evening. Adults $9.95, youth $7.95. Call "Trolley" number below.

• TORONTO BY TROLLEY

Rock as you roll along learning about the city from a restored jewel of the street railway department. The deep red carriers stop at **Fort York** for a visit, are good vantage points for photographs. Forty-minute tours, departing from the Royal York or the Sheraton Centre, twice a day, each place. Adults $9.95, children $4.95. Toronto by Trolley, Inc. Suite 2304, 44 King Street West, Toronto, Ontario M5H 1E2. 416/869-1372.

• GREY LINE TOURS

More than a dozen city and area bus tours, can last from one hour to whole day. 416/469-5136.

Special Events

Or, is there life after the Canadian National Exhibition? (See under "new" Toronto.)

• CARIBANA

A Caribbean caper, sending up warmth like a Gulf stream, and catering to all things calypso. Steel bands, fruit and straw markets, limber limbo-tics, art show amid splashy costumes, parades, pageantry. Lasts a whole week. On **Olympic Island** (part of Toronto Islands Park), end of July, beginning of August. Contact Caribbean Cultural Committee, 632B Yonge Street #1, Toronto, Ontario M4Y 1Z8. 416/925-5435.

• METRO INTERNATIONAL CARAVAN

A time when the international communities set up special pavilions, "passports" are sold, and you can take special Caravan buses to entertainments, souvenir-hunting, jazz, opera, a mini-world of exotic foods, and all that good stuff. Usually the third week in June. Contact Metro International Caravan, 263 Adelaide Street West, Fifth Floor, Toronto, Ontario M5W 1Y2. 416/977-0466.

• QUEEN'S PLATE

The oldest continuously run stakes race in North America; entries are Canadian-foaled three-year-olds at one and one-quarter mile. Woodbine (where Secretariat made his last start). Call 675-6110 for details.

THE LAKE SIMCOE ESCAPE

A favorite weekend destination for Metro Toronto motorists or those sailing through the Trent Severn Waterway, Lake Simcoe is lined with small towns, resorts, cottages, etc.; Barrie and Orilla act as senior hosts.

BARRIE One hundred six km. (sixty-six mi.) north of Lake Ontario on Hwy. 400, Barrie makes a good central point from which to explore. A harness racing track, the Elmvale Jungle Zoo, the Robert Phillip Museum of Time are all on the list of attractions. The **Simcoe County Museum & Archives** tells the story of man in Simcoe County from cave days to the twentieth century. Ten pioneer buildings and some traveling displays, Canadian crafts gift shop. About eight km. (five mi.) north of town on Hwy. 26, open all year, daily 9:00 A.M. to 5:00 P.M., Sunday afternoons.

ORILLA Something you might not have seen lately; a **Buffalo Ranch.** Described as a herd of "wild buffalo," they pose like regular cows on the rangeland, along with elk and deer. Take Horseshoe Valley exit from Hwy. 400. Guided tours daily during the summer, weekends spring and fall. 705/835-2000.

The home of **Stephen Leacock,** a much-loved, funny, witty, and shrewd Canadian author is nothing to laugh at. A white nineteen-room colonial mansion of great charm, it was designed by Leacock and built in 1908. Located on Atherley Road at Old Brewery Bay, off Hwy. 12B, east edge of town. Open mid-June to Labour Day daily, 10:00 A.M. to 5:00 P.M., other times by appointment. Call Museum 705/326-9357 or 326-2107.

Three Provincial Parks: Mara, McRae Point, Sibbald. Bass Lake P.P. is nearby. Full facilities.

Boating facilities, golf, wind surfing, water skiing, resorts, cottages to rent . . . contact the Georgian Lakelands Travel Association, Simcoe County Complex, Midhurst, L0L 1X0. 705/726-9300.

TORONTO FLOATING • At Ontario Place, about the third weekend in September, **Mariposa Folk**
BOAT SHOW **Festival** series, Harbourfront.

Toronto has two race tracks and four professional sports clubs: the Argonauts (Canadian Football League), the Blizzard (soccer), and the Blue Jays (baseball, American League) have their home games at **Exhibition Stadium,** Exhibition Place; the Maple Leafs (National Hockey League) play at Maple Leaf Gardens. For info contact: 416/595-1131 or 595-1149 (football); 416/977-4625 (soccer); 416/595-0077 (baseball); 416/977-1641 (hockey).

MISSISSAUGA TO NIAGARA-ON-THE-LAKE

MISSISSAUGA • In 1974 a pair of towns with the pedestrian names of Streetsville and Port Credit joined the communities of Mississauga and—landwise—turned themselves into one of the largest cities in North America. The name came from the Mississauga Indians who sold the land to the crown in 1805. Half a dozen early villages emerged in the area; stage coach and train stops on the way to Toronto. However, Toronto came to be the big rail center and the villages grew into towns with some sizable businesses but mostly giving living space to its burgeoning neighbor. Today's Mississauga has more than 1,500 industries, a mushrooming skyline of condos and apartments, over 148 parks, and 270,000 people. Canada's busiest airport sprawls on its northern edges; the blue horizons of Lake Ontario gleam against its southern shores.

Preserves a saltbox-style farmhouse and reconstructed barn to show home life as it was for an 1830 Loyalist pioneer from Georgia. On Orr and Meadowbrook Road, from Q.E.W. exit on Southdown, east to museum. Open Saturday to Wednesday daily. 416/822-4884. • THE BRADLEY HOUSE MUSEUM

Heritage Highway #2 continues through the downtown thick of things; at Oakville we are halfway between Toronto and Hamilton. Stop at the Old Post Office in **Lakefront Park** (pigeonholing mail from 1835 to 1857) for a little local history, pioneer equipment and maps, the story of the harbor. Oakville's founder was one Col. Chisholm and its first mayor was Chisholm's son. • OAKVILLE

From the mostly sacred to the sometimes profane; Glen Abbey, monastery, became **Glen Abbey,** golf club, with champion Jack Nicklaus designing the layout. Each year the Canadian Open held here draws top international professionals. Also home of the **Canadian Golf Hall of Fame,** Museum, and Library. Open all year, Monday–Friday 9:00 A.M. to 4:30 P.M., other times by appointment. No charge to browse around. Dorval Drive, exit off Q.E.W. North to North Service Rd., west to golf club.

The Ford Motor Company offers public tours of their large assembly plant. Three-week (or more) notice is often required, so plan ahead. Call 416/845-2511, ext. 1276.

A day-use only park with an 1890s farm among its assets. Fully operational agri-biz as Grandpa knew it, plus a miniature farm where the kids can see and touch lambs, calves, etc. Walking trails, biking, or swimming in Canada's largest man-made "lake." Eight flood-lit tennis courts. Interpretive Building and program. • BRONTE CREEK PROVINCIAL PARK

BURLINGTON • A stop at Burlington's breezy waterside Travel Information Office will make old-house buffs delirious with anticipation. In the racks are brochures for four Burlington self-guided tours for drivers and walkers; leading them past more than seventy vintage homes with gossipy bits and pieces of their history: ". . . this house has the Gothic gable . . . bought by . . . who owned the drug store next to the bank"; ". . . the lumber was purchased in exchange for two pigs. . . ."

What you see as you walk and drive around is a highly livable city of 111,000 with plenty of places to eat, shop, and be merry. You might try doing some of each in the **Village Square**, a block in the older downtown area, rebuilt into boutiques and restaurants.

At the **Burlington Cultural Centre** visitors watch local artists at work, purchase samples at the Arts and Crafts Shop. Open daily except Mondays, 425 Brock Avenue (across from Spencer Smith Park). 416/632-7796.

JOSEPH BRANT MUSEUM • Housed in a Georgian-style reproduction of the Mohawk chief's house . . . believe it or not. Brant was known to his relatives as Thayendanegea, leader of the Six Nations Indians during the American Revolution, fighting for the British. After the war both Indians and Loyalists crossed into Canada and Brant, who was given a medal by George III, built an untraditional house perhaps to inspire a trend away from the smoke-filled longhouses of his brothers. Exhibits include masks of the Iroquois False Face Society (a religious group of healers), nineteenth-century tools, dolls, etc. An excellent costume collection. Open all year, Monday–Saturday 10:00 A.M. to 5:00 P.M., Sunday afternoons only. Adults 75¢, students 50¢.

ROYAL BOTANICAL GARDENS • Between Burlington and the region known as Hamilton-Wentworth (usually listed under the latter) is a gardener's Valhalla, a photographer's Elysian field. Two thousand acres of bee-yu-tiful flower beds, natural parkland, wildlife sanctuary, paths, wooded ravines, and cactus under glass domes. Fifty km. (thirty mi.) of trails indicate something of the size of this blooming wonder-world. Lilac dell, rose garden, children's garden, demonstration garden, rock garden; and a big visitor's orientation center to explain, teach, and do research. Anyone who has ever stuck a seed in a flowerpot will love it. Art shop, tea room; open all year 9:00 A.M. to dusk. Plains Road at Highways 2 and 6. Royal Botanical Gardens Centre, 680 Plains Road West, Burlington, Ontario; R.B.G., P.O. Box 399, Hamilton, Ontario L8N 3H8. 416/527-1158.

Inland a mite, but worth a detour for antique buyers. • WATERDOWN

Wonders never cease. Here in the land of the pine and trillium, where rain • DUNDAS
is bountiful and rattlesnakes are in zoos, is the **Cactus Capital** of Canada.
The firm of Ben Veldhuis Limited has a one-hectare (two-acre) greenhouse
with thousands of cacti, succulents, and plants that prick. There's even a
"Cactus Festival" in August.

A modern, yellow brick building on the corner of Park and Albert, has a • DUNDAS HISTORICAL
large collection of dolls and stories about the past. Diverse exhibit, open all   MUSEUM
year, May-October Monday-Friday, 10:00 A.M. to 4:00 P.M. Sunday afternoons.
Free. 139 Park Street West, Dundas, Ontario L9H 5G1. 416/627-7412.

Hamilton

This city of 312,000, where the Canadian steel industry flexes its biggest
muscles, has a certain stainless beauty. Hamilton-Wentworth is the name of
the county, penetrated by the long Hamilton Harbour and backed by the
Niagara escarpment.

   Downtown, park your car as close as you can to Main Street and MacNab
and walk around awhile. The Bay-Main-McNab-Hunter block contains four
widely divergent points of interest:

A handsome structure of Georgian marble, Italian mosaics, and some inter- • CITY HALL
esting murals that highlight the Council Chamber.

The way it was . . . in civic building styles. Romanesque, Italian marble • OLD PUBLIC LIBRARY
pillars, et al.

There're computerized information systems, push-button exhibits, films, • CANADIAN FOOTBALL
and tributes to Canadian football greats. Open all year, daily except Sunday.   HALL OF FAME
Late May to Thanksgiving, 10:00 A.M. to 4:00 P.M. Late November to May,
afternoons only. Adults $1.25, seniors and students 75¢. 58 Jackson Street,
Hamilton, Ontario L8P 1L4. 416/528-7566.

Home of a *prosperous* nineteenth-century family, it has all its original • WHITEHERN
interiors, family antiques, silver, paintings, books, etc. intact. Open all year,
11:00 A.M. to 4:00 P.M. mid-summer, afternoons only during other seasons.
Adults $1.25, less for students and seniors. 41 Jackson Street West, Hamilton,
Ontario L8P 1L3. 416/522-5664.

South, across from the Old Library, is **Hamilton Place,** modern stages for the performing arts where there is almost always something going on. If not, try the adjacent **Hamilton Convention Centre.** Up on the fifteenth floor, all the Hamilton-Wentworth tourism information you can possibly use.

THE ART GALLERY • Next to the Centre is the third largest gallery in Ontario, home of a major
OF HAMILTON   collection of Canadian art. Over 4,000 paintings, graphics, and sculptures by Canadian, British, American, and European artists, plus several dozen regional or national shows a year. Open all year, Tuesday through Saturday 10:00 A.M. to 5:00 P.M., Thursday evening 7:00 to 9:00 P.M. Sunday, afternoon only.

Don't leave without looking at the eighteen-ton poured concrete mural on the Education Centre next door, donated by Hamilton's Dutch community.

Keep wandering south, this time to Lloyd D. Jackson Square, across King Street. The new **Hamilton Public Library** is also the unlikely site of a Farmers' Market on the lower floors. Growers from all over southern Ontario come on Tuesday, Thursday, Friday, and Saturday to vend their veggies, flowers, cheese, and fruit.

Two blocks east, the **Hamilton History Museum** illustrates the city's history through photographs and attic treasures.

DUNDURN CASTLE • Hamilton's house of houses, which you may pass on your way in; off York
Boulevard. Sir Alan Napier MacNab was a soldier-statesman of swashbuckling character; as they say, a lot of swash and little buckling. Historians are fairly kind as they recount MacNab's bravery in battles at Fort Erie, Lundy's Lane, and Saranac Bridge, as well as his forays to quell the Mackenzie Rebellion, his career in Parliament as Prime Minister of Provinces of Canada, etc. They call him generous (he once paid bail for all the men in the Hamilton prison so they could flee ahead of a cholera epidemic) and forceful, but one who made enemies and was too stuck on having his own way. Whatever; MacNab's castle shows the bright extravagant nature of a rare Victorian. On a grand lawn that sweeps down to the Hamilton Harbour, thirty-six-room Dundurn Castle was the first Tuscan-style villa in North America and is resplendently refurnished in the brocades and damasks of its time. Demonstrations of the domestic arts are in the

basement kitchen and summer months are enlivened with a kilted piper playing beneath the trees. (Tour buses are "piped" in.)

The floodlit castle makes a stunning backdrop for warm weather musicals on the front lawn, but that's not the end of its attractions. The **MacNab Arms Restaurant, Cockpit Theatre,** museum store, aviary with tropical birds, historical playground, and the **Hamilton Military Museum** are all on the grounds. MacNab went in for cock fighting and built a fancy little arena which is now used for *much* better purposes; a charming children's threatre with puppet shows, summer concerts, festivals, etc.

In the Military Museum are uniforms, equipment, and weapons dating back 200 years, plus displays on loan from other Canadian museums. Open seven days a week, year-round except Christmas and New Year's Day. From 1:00 P.M. to 4:00, from 11:00 A.M. during summer. Adults $1.00. 523-5681.

Hours are the same for the Castle. Adults $2.00, seniors $1.50, students $1.00. 416/522-5313.

The Old Dundurn Castle Restaurant, licensed for beer and wine; call 527-3303 for reservations.

Dundurn Park, York Boulevard, Hamilton, Ontario L8R 3H1.

P.S. Like Sir Henry Pellett of Toronto's Casa Loma, MacNab played the regal role with too much gusto and died broke, his home in the hands of the tax collector.

CHILDREN'S MUSEUM • On Main Street East, houses a series of children's programs, each covering a subject and involving the audience in the show. 1072 Main near Gage Park. Call 549-9285 to find out what's happening next.

CANADIAN WARPLANE • Missions accomplished, veteran planes wait for the next signal, at Civic
HERITAGE MUSEUM   Airport. A Mitchell B-25, three Harvard Trainers, Corsair, Tiger Moth, etc., plus more under construction. During the third weekend in June the CWH sponsors one of Canada's largest airshows, featuring a flying demonstration of thirty or forty World War II aircraft. Museum hours from April 1 till the end of October, daily 10:00 A.M. to 5:00 P.M. November through March, weekends only. $2.00 adults, $1.00 youth, seniors.

To enlist (or just ask questions): Canadian Warplane Heritage Inc., Hamilton Airport, P.O. Box 35, Mt. Hope, Ontario L0R 1W0. 416/679-6567.

MOHAWK TRAIL • Same neighborhood, at 360 Mohawk Rd. west of Hwy. 6; a century old and
SCHOOL MUSEUM   restored with desks, slates, books, and bell. The one-room school lives again. Free, open 1:00 to 4:00 P.M. during July and August. 527-5092.

For a panoramic vista, go to **Sam Lawrence Park,** via Wellington Street up the hill, east on Arkledon. Of course the Grey Line sightseeing people are full of tour ideas. Call 527-4444 if you're tired of driving yourself.

A healthy segment of the Niagara-Bruce Hiking Trail angles around Hamilton on the edge of the Niagara Escarpment, a cliff formation going from these regions off-and-on all the way to Wisconsin. Scenic overlooks as close as beads on a string.

WENTWORTH HERITAGE • Unless you're pushing 100 you're not likely to remember a community as
VILLAGE   portrayed in this collection of thirty-plus historic buildings. The sweet side of life before painless dentistry, penicillin, and hot water flowing from the faucet . . . i.e., log cabins, a blacksmith shop, tea room, rockers on the front porch of the general store, and yummies cooking on the open hearth.

Beautifully shaded picnic areas, gift shop, buggy rides. Open from April to the New Year, 10:00 A.M. to 4:00 P.M., closed Mondays. Adults $4.00, children $1.00, a family $10.00. Wentworth Heritage Village, Rockton, Ontario L0R 1X0. (Take Hwy. 8.) 519/647-2874.

Although it is in Wentworth-Hamilton County, this farmhouse is operated • BATTLEFIELD HOUSE by the Niagara Parks Commission as one of their historic museums, a chink in the story of the American-Canadian struggles. Interpreted by guides and audiovisual aids, the Battle of Stoney Creek and pioneer life in the Niagara Peninsula emerges. The interesting two-story frame house is open 11:00 A.M. to 5:00 P.M. during the summer season, shorter hours in spring and fall, Sunday afternoon only in winter. Take Q.E.W. to Centennial Parkway. Anyone over 12, $1.00. Niagara Parks Commission, P.O. Box 150, Niagara Falls, Ontario 416/356-2241 or in Stoney Creek, 662-8458.

For more Hamilton area data: Hamilton-Wentworth Visitors and Convention Bureau, City Hall Plaza, Hamilton, Ontario L8P 1L4. 416/525-7011.

As Q.E.W. zips along near the shore there are motels, food, gas, and places to swim near every exit.

It's a smaller world than you thought at Tivoli's miniature wonderland • VINELAND where the architectural giants of the world have been reduced to 1/50th of their real size. Want a picture of the Eiffel Tower, St. Peter's, the Kremlin, etc. for your album? On the shore of Lake Ontario, take Victoria exit, cross over Q.E.W., turn right on Prudhomme. Open May through September most of the day but longer hours in mid-summer. Adults $4.50, seniors $3.00. Box 90, Vineland, Ontario L0R 2E0. 416/562-7455. Motel, water slide, go-karts nearby, too.

On R.R. #24 at Vineland, 5.6 km. south of the Q.E.W., has seventy campsites, • BALL'S FALLS walking trails, plus historic interest. Scenic spot for a picnic.   CONSERVATION AREA

110 km. (69 mi.) from Toronto: 19 km. (12 mi.) from **Niagara Falls;** even • ST. CATHARINES if St. Catharines didn't have location going for it, the town would still be one of the better—and prettiest—places to visit. They live up to their "Garden City" image, put on fourteen festivals per year, and would probably do so even if the fermented juice of the grape were not high on the list of local products. Around town:

The Art Centre and Gallery shows Canadian, American, and European art, • RODMAN HALL sculpture, drawings, and tapestries. The Hall also offers schedules of lectures and concerts, children's program. Open all year, closed Mondays.

LAKE ONTARIO

9:00 A.M. to 5:00 P.M., Saturday and Sunday afternoons, Wednesday evenings. Free. 684-2925.

An entrenched St. Catharines institution is the **Farmers' Market** held at the corner of James and Church streets next to City Hall. This is fantastic fruit country and more than seventy stands can be counted during the peak of the season. Tuesday, Thursday, and Saturday, 6:00 A.M. to 5:00 P.M. When the Market Day falls on a holiday, vending is done the day ahead.

ONTARIO'S TOASTLINE: THE WINE-TASTING LIST

In the early 1800s an immigrant from Germany came to Canada, settled in a little river valley west of Toronto, and decided what the country needed most was a good native wine . . . just like his Rhineland. Johann Schiller knew his territory; he is now recognized as the first commercial wine-maker in Ontario. Today there are about ten wine-producing companies and the St. Catharines' area is a good place to explore the harvest, see how it's made, and have a sip.

JORDAN & STE. MICHELLE About one quarter of all grapes grown locally are bought by this firm, winner of more than 100 medals in world competitions. Monday to Friday, tours at 10:00 A.M., 1:00 P.M., and 3:00 P.M. 120 Ridley Road, St. Catharines, Ontario L2R 7E4. 416/688-2140.

ANDRES WINES LTD. Canada's largest vintner with six operations in the country. Tours between 10:00 A.M. and 4:00 P.M., Monday to Friday, Saturday tours by appointment. Kelson Avenue and Q.E.W. P.O. Box 550, Winona, Ontario L0R 2L0. Access Casablanca Boulevard from St. Catharines, Fifty Road from Hamilton. 416/643-4131 or toll free 1-800-263-2170.

BARNES WINES, LTD. The senior member of the winemaker's group, Barnes started producing in 1873. Tour the old-new place of business from April through November, between 9:30 A.M. and 3:00 P.M. Located on Martindale Road at the Q.E.W., St. Catharines. 416/682-6631. P.O. Box 248, St. Catharines, Ontario L2R 6S4.

BRIGHTS WINES LTD. One of the older establishments, the original building and cellars are still part of the plant. Tour center where two massive wooden tanks once stood. Tours available year round, Monday through Friday at scheduled times between 10:00 A.M. and 4:00 P.M. 4887 Dorchester Road, Niagara Falls, Ontario L2E 6V4. 416/357-2400.

Niagara-on-the-Lake Wineries:
INNISKILLIN WINE INC. A lot of displays showing the wine-making process, housed in an antique barn. No tours, however, as of this writing. Wine boutique. South on Niagara Parkway, on Line 3, Service Road 66. 416/468-2187.

CHATEAU DES CHARMES WINERY A small cottage industry where only a dozen folks can fit in the wine-tasting room at once, so in summer everything is outside. Creek Road and Line 7. 416/262-5202.

NEWARK WINES Offers tours and tastes, just west of Virgil on Hwy. 55. 416/468-7123.

COLIO WINES LTD. In Harrow, Essex County, forty-seven km. (twenty-nine mi.) south of Windsor on Queens Road. One of the area's most popular vintners invites you in any time of year except September and October. Tours on Wednesdays 5:00–9:00 P.M., but you must arrange in advance. Box 372, Windsor, Ontario N0R 1G0. 519/726-5317 or 738-2241.

For other names and more information, write to the Wine Council of Ontario, One Yonge Street, Suite 2104, Toronto, Ontario M5E 1E5. 416/366-7763.

No one should miss the chance to stand next to a giant canal lock and watch a freighter go down (or up) like a fortress in a slot. Do so at the **Lock Three Observation Platform** on the Welland Canal; take the Glendale Avenue exit from Q.E.W., then follow the signs. An information booth to tell what's happening is open from mid-May till early October. • WELLAND CANAL

The Welland is star of the show at the **St. Catharines Historical Museum** where several exhibits focus on its early stages. Military, industrial, pioneer history; plus a fire-fighting gallery featuring an old steam pumper. 343 Merritt Street, open all year. 9:00 A.M. to 7:00 P.M. from Victoria Day to Labour Day, afternoons after that. Adults 50¢. St. Catharines, Ontario L2T 1K7. 416/227-2962.

No camping here unless you have wings, but you can have a waterside picnic (no swimming, either) and see what hops along. On Lakeshore Road. • HAPPY ROLPH BIRD SANCTUARY CONSERVATION AREA

THE WELLAND CANAL

For a magnificent reason known as Niagara Falls, no freighter is going to get very far traveling up *that* river; the Welland Canal with lift locks was built to connect Lake Ontario and Lake Erie, enabling lakers and ocean ships to continue into mid-continent. Although the Falls' height is 54 meters (176 feet), there is a 114-meter (332-feet) difference between the levels of the two Great Lakes, and eight giant locks take care of the raising and lowering. The toughest challenge is getting past the Niagara escarpment, so it follows that most of the lock activity is at the north end of the canal.

Even though a lock is a basically simple device whereby water from the high side fills a compartment, then is drained (lowering the boat) till level with the low side—easy on paper—the Welland Canal is a world-class feat of engineering begun on St. Andrews Day in 1824. The first canal opened for small boats in 1829, carrying vessels to the Niagara River above the Falls. Due to the swift current of the Niagara River, however, the last part of this canal was abandoned and rerouted to Gravelly Bay (now Port Colborne) on Lake Erie. At one time it took more than forty locks to do the job of the present system, and canal depth has increased from three meters (nine feet) to more than ten meters (thirty feet).

Today's lock system in brief:

Lock 1; at St. Catharines on Canal Rd. north of Lakeshore.

Lock 2; farther south on Canal Rd. north of Carleton St. The banks of the canal provide nice places for a picnic.

Lock 3; with an observation platform, Canal Rd. north of Glendale Ave. Excellent view of lock operations, picnic area, snack bar, rest rooms, tourist information.

Locks 4, 5, and 6; The twin flight locks of Thorold allowing simultaneous locking of ships in both directions.

Lock 7; Thorold, the last lift over the Niagara Escarpment.

Lock 8; and viewing stand; Port Colborne, south of Hwy. 3. One of the world's longest locks.

Three most eventful events:

THE ROYAL CANADIAN • *The* rowing match of North America, attracting heavy competition and
HENLEY REGATTA   huge crowds. The 100th anniversary of the regatta was in 1982; it takes
place in the Henley Course, usually early in August. $2.00. Less classy fun is
the annual Raft Race around a mile course set on Lake Ontario. Mid-July.

NIAGARA GRAPE AND • When the leaves are turning and the air getting crisp, a harvest celebration
WINE FESTIVAL   with open air concerts, dances, sports events, art shows, gourmet dinners . . .
with just the right wines, of course. A parade, too, plus a lot of marching
around in the region's 27,000 acres of vineyards.

FOLK ARTS FESTIVAL • For two full weeks, featuring concerts, open houses by various ethnic
clubs, true ancestral costumes, beer garden, parade, etc. (which stands for
Ethnics Take Charge). From late May through the first week of June (of
course there's a queen).

For more about these and other St. Catharines' parks, marinas (there are
twenty-nine docking facilities), nearby camping possibilities, and all other
travel details, stop at their visitor information booth or call 416/684-2361.
Ask about that merry-go-round (a *real* one) in the park.

NIAGARA-ON-THE-LAKE • The Q.E.W. curves toward Niagara Falls, dipping past the upper eastern
corner of the peninsula, and that's the way it's generally been. Time and the
mainstream of commerce took a short-cut, and Niagara-on-the-Lake was
left to live quietly in its own world; one that hasn't caught up with the
calendar.

The only trouble with picture-book Niagara-on-the-Lake is that it's been
"discovered" . . . something bound to happen when they started up the
Shaw Festival. You just can't keep these jewels hidden forever.

In 1678 LaSalle's party of explorers were said to have paused here where
remains of an old Indian settlement were found. One hundred years later
some families who did not sympathize with the American Revolution relo-
cated on the far banks of Lake Ontario to establish the town of Newark,
soon to become capital of the colony of Upper Canada. Newark, however,
was just too close for comfort to the scheming Americans for a capital to
feel safe, so that assignment was turned over to York (Toronto). However,
when hostilities broke out in the War of 1812, both cities suffered. With
strange illogic, the Americans burned Newark (*and* York) but left the
next-door Fort George alone. Burning a village and ignoring a fort was
pretty cowardly, and roused British ire to victorious levels.

The name changed, the tempers of the times cooled, and Niagara-on-the-Lake rose again to a new era. Now you *must* park your car and walk around this museum of a town with its "fish-scale" shingles on mansard roofs, gingerbreaded Victorian wonders, antique shops, bake shops, and fudge shops, picket fences and trees that turn each street into a gothic hall. Step into the Niagara Apothecary Museum, and imagine you have a toothache. How about the pink stuff in the big bell jars? The "drug store" has its original walnut and butternut fixtures, crystal gasoliers, and rare bottles. (No hair spray or sand pails.) 5 Queen Street at King Street. Open noon till 6:00 P.M., mid-May through Labour Day. Free.

Half a block away is the Niagara Fire Museum with a collection of fire equipment used from 18*16* to 1926. On King Street, open late May through the summer, hours depending on public interest.

Opened in 1907, making it the oldest local history museum in Ontario. **• NIAGARA HISTORICAL** Twenty thousand treasures from basement, hay lofts, and back rooms; mili- **SOCIETY MUSEUM** tary displays, old gowns, church items, bric-a-brac. 43 Castlereagh, two and a half blocks from the main intersection. Open May 1 through October 31 10:00 A.M. to 6:00 P.M.; November 1 to April 30, afternoons only. Adults $1.00. Niagara-on-the-Lake, Ontario L0S 1J0. 416/468-3912.

The citizens are now working on their courthouse, a handsome three-story structure built to serve as the seat of a united county government. The courthouse held the town's first library, was also the original home of the renowned Shaw Festival. Municipal offices occupied the premises till 1970. Plans are to restore the library facilities, provide a reception room and Lord Mayor's office, and refurbish the Grand Hall on the third floor. Look it over as you stroll . . . then see if you can't have lunch in the Greenhouse Room of the marvelous old Prince of Wales Hotel.

If you don't like it here, I suggest taking your next vacation on an ice floe.

The BIG event is the colossally successful Shaw Festival, now starring a new 830-seat playhouse and the only professional troupe in the world devoted exlusively to Shaw and his contemporaries. The Shaw Festival is not just plays, but lectures, discussions, and reviews. Three locations for all this. Contact Shaw Festival, Box 774, Niagara-on-the-Lake, Ontario L0S 1J0. Box Office, 416/468-3201.

It will seem to some people that **Niagara-on-the-Lake** should include a bit about Fort George. Reasonable, since Fort George and the town are a matched couple, and the town's limits include the Fort. However, the book needed Fort George where it is because it faces the Niagara River and is much a part of that coastal segment.

Coming next, the Niagara River and Fort George.

ONTARIO FACTS AND FIGURES

From the Iroquois language the word *Ontario* means "rocks standing near the water." This might have been a reference to the cliffs of Niagara Falls.

Ontario is bigger than Spain and France combined. It is one and a half times bigger than the state of Texas.

Believe it or not . . . Toronto is on a line just *south* of Venice, Italy.

Highest point in Ontario is the 665-m. (2,183-ft.) Ogidaki Mountain.

Ontario's north-south distance is 1,730 km. (1,075 mi.); its east-west distance is 1,690 km. (1,050 mi.). Ontario has 177,388 sq. km. (68,490 sq. mi.) of inland water.

Ontario is Canada's most populous province with 8,676,000 as of the 1982 estimate.

Toronto is Canada's largest city, metropolitan population estimated at 3,000,000 in 1982.

European origins: British Isles 67%, France 10%, Germany 5%, Italy 4%, Netherlands, Poland, and Ukraine 2% each.

Ontario is home to three major Indian groups: the Chippewa, Huron, and Iroquois. In the early 1600s the most densely populated area in what is now Canada stretched between Georgian Bay and Lake Simcoe where 30,000 Hurons lived in about twenty villages. These people acted as middlemen to French fur buyers, trading with more distant tribes and then carrying furs to white posts on the St. Lawrence River.

CHAPTER 3
THE NIAGARA RIVER

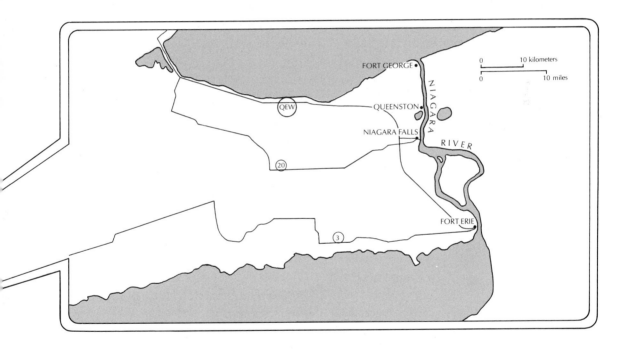

F ROM FORT GEORGE TO FORT ERIE along the spectacular **Niagara Gorge,** past the thundering
wonder of **Niagara Falls,** runs one of the best-kept parkway systems in the country, serving
one of the top tourist areas of the world. It's a short trip as traveling miles or kilometers go, but a
long haul if you want to see *everything* . . . which you can't and maybe wouldn't want to do.

While the river churns its way from south to north we explore from north to south, stopping to peer into the gorge now and then and wonder at the engineering powers of water. This is the tip end of the Niagara Escarpment, an enormous coral reef (limestone) formed eons ago when the region was beneath a warm sea. The remains of the ancient formation are seen as a cliff running up through Ontario, along the eastern side of the Bruce Peninsula, on Manitoulin Island, into Michigan along the Garden Peninsula (at Fayette), and finally ending on the Door Peninsula in Wisconsin. There are breaks and dips, yet the ridge is unmistakable and the Niagara River tumbles over a section of it. Twelve thousand years ago the Falls was eleven km. (seven mi.) downstream from its present position, a point more nearly in line with the sharp hill-cliff you see driving to or from Hamilton.

Until the early 1950s the rate of erosion was about one m. (three ft.) a year, but international water diversion controls have slowed the rate to a third of that per ten years.

The first *known* European to have approached the river and falls was Jesuit priest Father Luis Hennepin in 1678, more than half a century after Champlain, Brule, and Company traveled up the Ottawa River finding their way to the upper Great Lakes. Lake Ontario was largely the domain of the fierce Iroquois, and to avoid them meant leaving the lower lake regions unexplored until later dates.

Since Hennepin wrote of his sightings, their fame has spread, and through the years pilgrimages to Niagara have brought artists, poets, presidents, kings, honeymooners, and home folks. Twelve million a year is the present pace.

The region's military history gets a thorough review at the two forts, Brock's Monument, and other museums. However, the history of any area has seldom had as many colorful side stories to tell as this one . . . tales of daring and desperation, money schemes and fame dreams. Among your souvenirs should be a good book on the subject.

FORTIFYING TERMS

A SHORT GLOSSARY OF MILITARY TERMS USED IN FORTIFICATIONS

Banquette: A step running inside the parapet for the troops to stand on, while firing over it.

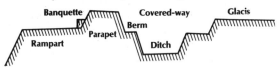

Barbette: A platform on which guns are placed to fire over the parapet. Barbettes can have various shapes, according to requirements.

Bastion: A projecting part of the fortification, usually pentagon-shaped and made of earthworks.

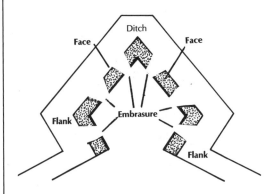

Battery: A number of guns placed regularly for combined action; also a platform where guns are placed within the fortification.

Berm: A narrow level space between the foot of the parapet and the scarp of the ditch, designed to prevent the moss of the earth in the parapet from sliding into the ditch.

Blockhouse: (1) Detached small fort for controlling strategic points. (2) An edifice constructed chiefly of timber, normally two-storied and loopholed for firing.

Breastwork: A fieldwork of earth thrown up breast-high, a sort of makeshift parapet.

Casemate: A vaulted bomb-proof chamber (like a cellar) built into the rampart and provided with embrasure, gunports, or loopholes for defensive purposes.

Covered-way: A secure road of communication all around a fortress outside the ditch, having a banquette from which fire may be brought into the glacis.

Curtain: The part of the fortification that connects the bastions.

Ditch: A large, deep trench made around the whole body of works, generally 15–18 feet deep and 50–100 feet wide. The earth excavated from this trench serves to raise the ramparts and the parapets. When it contains water, we describe it as a wet ditch. Practically all engineers prefer dry ditches, because of the maintenance problems of wet ditches (stagnant water, frost action, etc.). Ideal solution is where the ditch can be inundated temporarily during siege. Ditches are called "lined" when the slopes are supported by stone or brickwork.

Embrasure: An opening made in the parapet for guns. They have widening angles from within for sweeping effect.

Escarp or Scarp: A steep bank or wall immediately below the rampart.

Face (of work): Generally those parts which project toward the attackers and away from the main body of works.

Flank: Any part of the fortification designed to defend another part by fire.

Fortification: The art of constructing military works, the object being to increase the power of the users by their use.

Garrison: A body of soldiers stationed in one place for the purpose of defense.

Glacis: A gentle, sloping earthwork, commencing from the covered way and stretching toward the country. Every part of it should be covered by fire. Walls conceal the escarp revetment.

Gorge: Any part of the works, where no rampart or parapet exists; usually the lowest part.

Loophole: A narrow vertical opening, normally wider on the inside, for shooting through. (Hence, "find the loophole." . . .)

Magazine: A heavily and well-constructed building normally of stone or brick, in which to store gunpowder, ammunition, armament, and provisions. Powder magazines required extra-heavy construction.

Martello Tower: Self-contained fortress towers with fighting areas, quarters, etc. to defend harbor entrances.

Palisade: Strong, pointed wooden stake. A number of them fixed deep in the ground and in close proximity create a defensive work. They are often placed parallel to the covered way on the glacis and also in the ditch and ramparts.

Parapet: A defense of earth or stone to cover the troops and armament from the enemy's fire and observation. It is the exterior side of the rampart.

Postern (Sally-Port): A vaulted passage under the rampart to allow communication from the interior to the ditch.

Ramp: An inclined place in a rampart to facilitate ascent.

Rampart: A mound of earth for the defense of a place and capable of resisting artillery fire. It should be wide enough on the top to allow the passage of troops and guns, and it is surmounted by the parapet.

Redoubt: A small, self-defensive, heavily constructed works without flanking protection (e.g., for battery), and located at strategic points.

FORT GEORGE TO FORT ERIE

FORT GEORGE • The British Army Headquarters, Fort Niagara, was on the wrong side of the river after the American Revolution; another border decision of the Jay Treaty that rubbed salt in English wounds. They had to rebuild a stronghold and chose a spot overlooking the river mouth and the budding village of Newark (Niagara-on-the-Lake). The new post was destroyed in the War of 1812, captured by the U.S. Army, partly rebuilt, and finally reoccupied by the British.

The two countries, however, outgrew any need for staring at each other

via cannon sights, and the fort rotted into oblivion until a history-conscious generation came along to reconstruct and refurbish. Fort George became a **National Historic Park** in 1969. Visitors are greeted by a guard in period uniform, given a booklet for their self-guided tour, and turned loose to inspect the guardhouse, bastions, quarters, kitchens, blockhouses, magazine, and anything else that could made the establishment secure and independent.

Military life was harsh and discipline showed little mercy, but the green grasses of summer across the parade grounds soften history's grim side while sharpening its lessons.

Open all year. Mid-May to June 20, 9:00 A.M. to 5:00 P.M. July 1 to Labour Day, 10:00 A.M. to 6:00 P.M. Labour Day to October 31, 10:00 A.M. to 5:00 P.M. November 1 to May by appointment only, weekdays 8:00 A.M. to 4:00 P.M. Adults $1.00, children 50¢, subject to change. Write: Superintendent, Niagara National Historic Parks, Box 787, Niagara-on-the-Lake, Ontario L0S 1J0. 416/468-2741.

Just about one and a half km. (one mi.) south of Niagara-on-the-Lake, a • MCFARLAND HOUSE Georgian brick house built in 1800 by James McFarland and used as a hospital by both the British and American forces during the War of 1812. Picnic tables and refreshments on the grounds. Open May 19 to June 30, weekends, July 1 to September 13, Saturday through Wednesday. Adults 75¢, children under 12 free with adult. Niagara Parkway. 416/356-2241.

A tall, impressive monument to Sir Isaac Brock, British hero and general • QUEENSTON HEIGHTS killed during the War of 1812. Climb the stairs inside for your daily workout to the panoramic view of river and tree-filled landscape. Free, mid-May to Labour Day. Beautiful gardens *every*where, thanks to the Niagara Parks Commission and School of Horticulture. You can hardly miss the grand twelve-m. (forty-ft.) **Parkway's Floral Clock,** world's largest, that blooms with a different design in flowers every year, using at least 25,000 plants.

The Queenston-Lewiston Bridge will short-cut you to New York. Don't even think it.

Laura Secord walked a tough thirty-two km. (nineteen mi.) through brush • QUEENSTON and swamp to tell the British garrison that Americans were planning to attack. This was 1813, and her warning helped turn a defeat into a victory.

The house where Mrs. Secord raised seven children (and overheard the plot) has been restored, contains a fine collection of Upper Canada furniture, and is enhanced by a rose garden with flowers *she* planted. Partition Street, Box 1812, Queenston, Ontario L0S 1L0. 416/751-0500.

THE SCHOOL • One-hundred-acre campus welcomes visitors to its continuous (until the
OF HORTICULTURE snow falls) show. Rose garden, floral fountain; the school grounds are enough to make anyone want to enroll. 416/356-8554.

You're getting *close* to the Falls now. . . .

NIAGARA GLEN • If it weren't for the overwhelming presence of the Falls, here's a spot that would get more press coverage. A former channel of the river, you enter down a steep flight of wooden steps to a ledge, then down paths to the riverbank. Sheltered by the high walls, the glen supports plant life not too common in Ontario, is full of small fossils and traces of long-gone life forms. About four km. (two and a half mi.) of winding trails in this nearly remote nook. Guided nature walks are conducted free of charge from late June to Labour Day, 10:00 A.M., noon, 2:00 and 4:00 P.M., Friday through Tuesday.

SPANISH AERO CAR • Go over a whirlpool in *that?* Yes; *that* contraption is safe. A Spanish engineer, Leonardo Torres-Quevedo, designed the car for a group of Spanish businessmen who thought a ride across the gorge over the whirlpool would be a money-maker. For long years it wasn't, but patronage has increased steadily since World War II, and the car has carried as many as 2,600 passengers in one day. Niagara Parkway, four km. (two and a half mi.) north of Horseshoe Falls. 416/356-2241. Adults $2.00, students $1.00.

GREAT GORGE TRIP • Down to the river via elevator, then a short hike to the edge of the Whirl-
AND NIAGARA pool Rapids, a whitewater challenge with rare takers. The barrels and
DAREDEVIL GALLERY assorted padded tanks used by those who *did* try to boat through (now forbidden by law) are on display. 4330 River Road, P.O. Box 186, Niagara Falls, Ontario L2E 6T3. 416/356-0904.

NIAGARA FALLS • *"All of the pictures you may see, all of the descriptions you may read of these mighty falls can only produce in your mind the faint glimmer of the glowworm compared with the overpowering glory of the meridian sun"* (John J. Audubon).

Purple prose indeed, but how can you overstate the sight of a wide river flowing straight down for 54 m. (176 ft.) with a roar, sending up an eternal tower of mist, gleaming, churning, and foaming its way toward the sea? There is a hypnotic power in just watching the flow, watching the river race faster as it nears the edge, the awesome force of its plunge.

The most visited scenic attraction in North America, perhaps in the world, easily reached by car or train, N.F. has attracted people by the millions and *attractions* by the score. Every conceivable entertainment, fast food, oddity collection, fun-o-ride, animal act, and souvenir that has made a nickel anywhere has come to the Falls. One good revolving tower seemed to inspire another; one wax museum molded the next.

That's the bad news if you're touchy about crowds. The miracle and good news is—except on hot summer weekends when the throng swells to tens of thousands—the scene remains quite lovely. As soon as you move

a kilometer or two up or downstream from the brink (*any* day) there are places in the long Niagara Parkway to stretch out beneath trees with ample space to spare.

In the mid-1880s the cliff edge (called "The Front") was a genuine mess. Freak shows, gambling halls, hawkers; an ersatz Chinese pagoda, menagerie, tea rooms, and more with barkers at their doors competing with the cries of buggy drivers and snake oil salesmen. The only exception was the **Niagara Falls Museum,** and all reformers made note of that fact.

The excesses aroused concern, and after much struggling, legislation was passed to restore the river edge to scenic beauty via a Parks Commission. It took many years but they did a superb job. The clutter of slap-dash buildings was swept away, monuments and historic points restored, flowers planted to add blankets of color. Money earned from souvenir sales in the remaining buildings takes care of the costs and makes the whole parkway completely self-sustaining.

Be aware that Niagara Falls, Ontario, is not just a big water drop with amusements up and down every street. It is a friendly little burg with a *real* downtown east of the tourist area, good shopping, a VIA station, and the **Niagara Falls Visitors Centre.**

Niagara Falls special events include a Blossom Festival in May, the Harvest Festival in late October, and a Winter Festival in January . . . when the waterfall's spray has festooned the shrubs and trees with icicles and the river is more like a glistening white shelf. Quiet, frosty winter is a good time to come.

Niagara Promotion Association, P.O. Box 111, Niagara Falls, Ontario L2E 6S8. 416/356-2521.

Things to do and see:

MAID OF THE MIST • Take one of these sight-seeing boats for a view that will rinse out your brain cells. The name has been applied to a long series of boats, beginning with a

---

There's one born every minute . . .

The Falls' souvenir business got started when an enterprising wag picked up pieces of calcite called "Surf Stone" (white rocks) and found he could sell them as "petrified spray." When the supply ran out he imported more from elsewhere, made some into jewelry.

FALLS FACTS

The two cataracts are separated at the brink by Goat Island, and illuminated with alternating white and color lights one and a half to three and a half hours every evening, length of time depending on the time of year.

—The Canadian Horseshoe Falls is 54 meters or 176 feet high and the American Falls is 56 meters or 184 feet high.

—An estimated 34.5 million Imperial gallons of water tumble over the Horseshoe Falls in one minute.

—Ninety percent of the flow of the Niagara River tumbles over the Horseshoe Falls. Only ten percent flows over the American Falls.

—About 12,000 years ago, Niagara Falls was eleven kilometers (seven miles) downstream from its present position.

—The water depth of the pool at the base of the Falls is 170 feet.

—An estimated 300 million people have viewed the Falls since the white man arrive on this continent.

—There are actually three Falls: American (Rainbow), Luna (Bridal Veil), and Horseshoe.

—Today fifty percent of the Niagara River never makes it to the Falls; it is diverted for power. This percentage increases to seventy-five percent at night and in the winter months.

—The hydro potential of the Niagara River is 3.73 million kilowatts.

—Seven people have gone over the Horseshoe Falls in a barrel. Four lived.

clumsy steam vessel in 1846 to the present stream-lined cruisers. You are given a hooded raincoat, then a close look at the American Falls, and then into the center of the "Horseshoe." Foot of Clifton Hill. Runs mid-May till late October, about 9:45 A.M. to 4:45 P.M., longer hours in mid-summer and on holidays. Boats depart every fifteen minutes for a half-hour tour. Adults $3.25, children $1.75; five and under, free. Fifty cents for a ride back up the cliff on the incline railway.

"Maid of the Mist" Steamboats, 5920 River Road, P.O. Box 808, Niagara Falls, Ontario L2E 6V6. 416/358-5781.

Carnival with shops, dining, and entertainment. Observation Tower, giant • MAPLE LEAF VILLAGE Ferris wheel, bird show, puppet show, the works. 5705 Falls Avenue, Niagara Falls, Ontario L2G 7M9. 416/357-3090.

SKYLON • Sleek and soaring, 160 meters above the ground and 236 meters above the Falls. Outside elevators whisk you up to three levels of viewing from a lounge, dining room, and observation deck. The three-story base holds an international bazaar in one area, the world's largest indoor Ferris wheel in another. Open all year; adults $3.50, age 6-18 and seniors $2.00. Under five years free. The indoor amusement park operates weekends only during the off-season. Skylon, 5200 Robinson Street, Niagara Falls, Ontario L2G 2A3. 416/356-2651. Direct Toronto line: 416/364-1824.

TABLE ROCK HOUSE • This one's named for a limestone ledge that once hung over the gorge. The second floor houses a restaurant, first floor has souvenirs and entrance to the **Table Rock Scenic Tunnels.** You're given slickers and boots to wear after descending 38 m. (125 ft.) into the solid rock, from where you walk to observation decks near the base of (and behind) the Falls. Wow. Open all year, shorter hours in winter. Adults $2.75, children 6-12 75¢. Niagara Parks Commission, P.O. Box 150, Niagara Falls, Ontario. 416/358-3268.

Chock full of everything from a rare collection of open Egyptian mummy • NIAGARA FALLS
cases to a display of animal freaks and the Daredevil Hall of Fame. It's North   MUSEUM
America's oldest museum, 700,000 items deep, with a view tower, too. May
20 to October 9, 9:00 A.M. till midnight; closes at 6:00 P.M. the rest of the
year. Adults $2.50, students and senior citizens $1.50, children $1.00. Hours
and admission subject to change. Niagara Falls Museum, 5651 River Road,
P.O. Box 960, Niagara Falls, Ontario L2V 6V8. 416/356-2151.

The sprouting spot for most of the Parkway Flowers. Tulips, daffodils, • NIAGARA PARKS
mums, etc. in splashy spring shows, summer, winter, and fall blooms.   GREENHOUSE
Colorful and warm even when the snow is knee deep. One-half mile south   & CONSERVATORY
of Horseshoe Falls on the Niagara Parkway, admission free. P.O. Box 150,
Niagara Falls, Ontario L2E 6T2.

This super-view tower overlooking the Falls has dining facilities on three • PANASONIC CENTRE
floors near the 203 m. (665 ft.) level. Summer side attractions include a
Marine Aquarium and Waltzing Waters fountain. Open all year, longer
hours during the warm months. Tower only: adults $3.00, children 5-18
and seniors $1.95. Tower, aquarium, and Museum: adults $4.95, students
and seniors $3.95. Ten percent entertainment tax. Panasonic Centre, 6732
Oakes Drive, Niagara Falls, Ontario L2G 3W7. 416/356-1501.

One of the largest sets of tuned bells on the continent hangs in the tower at • RAINBOW TOWER
the Canadian end of Rainbow Bridge. One bell is actually the fifth largest   CARILLON
tuned bell in the world. Afternoon and evening concerts during the summer
months. P.O. Box 395, Niagara Falls, Ontario L2E 6T8. 416/354-5641.

Dolphins, with tolerant smiles, humor humans who want to watch them • MARINELAND
jump through hoops and things. Anything for a fish, or applause. Good
show, as killer whales, seals, and dolphins sing for their supper at this big
conglomerate of fun rides (long and scary rollercoaster), animal herds,
game farm, restaurants, gift shops, and more. An all-year attraction. Mid-
summer adult rate $9.25, children $3.25. Less in May or October, much less
in winter. Fee includes admission to all rides and attractions. 7657 Portage
Road, Niagara Falls, Ontario L2E 6X8. 416/356-8250.

Tussaud's Wax Museum, Ripley's Believe It or Not Museum, Lundy's
Land Historical Museum, the Movieland Wax Museum, Houdini Hall of
Fame; if it's strange, historic, or ever made it in the flicks, you'll find what
you're looking for here. Best to stop at an information booth and study
brochures.

THE MAN OF A THOUSAND TIGHTROPES

Through winter blizzards and summer heat a life-like effigy of Jean Francis Gravelet, better known as "Blondin," walks with his balancing pole on a tightwire above Clifton St. . . . a come-see-more for Toussaud's Wax Museum. The figure above the busiest street in town has been seen by millions.

The real Blondin would be pleased. Seldom has any human with a semblance of a right mind gone to such extremes to gain public attention and keep it.

Born in France in 1845, Blondin apparently was balancing on the clothes line in infancy because his family immediately packed him off to a school for acrobats; by age nine he had become known as the "Boy Wonder."

Fame, fortune, a contract with P. T. Barnum for a U.S.-Canada tour, and Blondin was big show biz by the time he announced that he would walk across Niagara Falls on a rope.

"You're nuts, Mister," was the general opinion, but Blondin had a 1,300-foot, two-inch manila rope with guy ropes strung from where Prospect Park is today on the American side to the site of the old Clifton House on the Canadian side. Thousands came to watch him fall into the foam; more thousands stayed home, even though bands were playing and the atmosphere was festive . . . as on hanging day in an old city square.

Tension built hour after hour and Blondin—to make the impossible even worse—waited until late afternoon when the sun was in his eyes to start walking. Half way, he stopped, lowered a thick string to the *Maid of the Mist* waiting (to catch him?) below, pulled up a bottle of wine, had a drink, and continued to the other side. It took fifteen minutes to go over, seven minutes to go back.

Blondin, like Caesar, Napoleon, or the Queen, became a household word. He was a hard act for himself to follow, so he started walking across blindfolded, then with his feet in chains, or on a bicycle, and many times pushing a wheelbarrow.

Once he worked a small stove to the center of the river and cooked an omelette, which he lowered to passengers on the tour boat.

More! More! Having "proved" repeatedly that he would *not* fall into the brink, ticket sales to cliff-side seats began to fade. Something was needed to revive interest. "Aha!" cried Harry Colcord, his manager. "The next time *I* will be riding across on his back!"

It was clearly a moment of sublime faith for the manager, who was no acrobat and on the day of the walk shook mightily with second thoughts.

The men, weighing nearly the same at 145 or so pounds, started off. The manager was told *not* to try to balance himself. *"You are me,"* warned Blondin. "All balancing will be done by me. Even if you think we are falling, do not try to adjust yourself." Blondin was confident but the manager's nerve endings were probably making medical history.

There are different accounts of the trip, but it is recorded that Blondin had to unload Colcord six times from shoulders to wire (and hold him there) to rest, then six times the wildly repentant Colcord had to climb back up. At one moment a guy wire broke and the main rope jerked to one side, but the Master Balancer took the unexpected motion in stride and went on (a gambler's sabotage was suspected). They made it, but Colcord swiftly left show biz.

More stunts and more fame for Blondin as the star attraction of the Crystal Palace in London followed. He grew rich (died poor), was given medals by Queen victoria, and lived to the age of seventy-three. Death came from an infection after slipping in the kitchen.

No medals recorded for Colcord.

Blondin's success ushered in an era of daring-do unmatched on earth. "Anything he can do I can do better," said the world's acrobats to themselves using every imaginable gimmick to add flair: firecrackers tied to the ankles, jumping from wire to waiting boat, wading and cavorting near the precipice on stilts. One lady, Maria Spelterina, walked across with her feet in peach baskets, then calmly walked back—backwards.

The idea of going over in a barrel started around 1886, with funny to tragic results. Flying under the Falls View Bridge was tried a few times, as well.

Finally it was decided that the Falls were not to be a platform for clowns, daredevils, and fortune seekers who kept coming up with new ways to show off. Too many were killed or died broke for all their trouble; not one came close to repeating Blondin's success.

Nature returned to star billing.

South (or upstream) from the Falls the road winds past one pleasant vista after another, a flower show in spring, a color show in fall; 2,800 acres of landscaping along the river between Lake Ontario and Lake Erie.

Dufferin Islands sends the river and road into a wide curve. Note the wreckage of a scow, which was once working near one of the power plants when it broke loose and headed for the Falls with two men on board. Thinking quickly, they opened up the bottom, sank it into some rocks, and were rescued. The hulk remains.

The showplace home of Sir Harry Oaks is right up the hill from here. Poor Harry died, the victim in a celebrated murder trial years ago.

Once a quaint rural schoolhouse with a logging wheel on the front lawn, it now teaches about first settlers and historic personalities. Open Victoria Day to Thanksgiving, weekends noon to 5:00 early and late in season, daily noon to 5:00 P.M. in mid-summer. Small donation. Niagara Parkway South L2E 6T2. 416/295-4036. • WILLOUGHBY TOWNSHIP MUSEUM

Town and military establishment. First the French fur traders built a post in 1750, then, when New France was given to Britain as a settlement in the Seven Years' War, the English built a fort on the riverbank, adjacent to the lake, their first construction in what is now Ontario. All in all they built three forts. In 1779 fort number one was destroyed by large masses of ice driven ashore in a storm; fort number two met the same fate twenty-four years later. A third fort was built—on higher ground—just in time to be invaded and taken over by Americans in 1814. The Yankees chased the British over to Lake Ontario, were chased back in a series of bloody skirmishes, then returned to Fort Erie, blew it up, and crossed the river to Buffalo. It was the last time U.S. forces marched on Canadian ground. • FORT ERIE

This reduced recap masks a sad truth; hundreds of brave men fought and died in swamplike conditions (one part of the fight saw thirteen days of continuous rain) far from their homes in a war that should have been fought at the conference tables.

In 1902 the Government of Canada erected a tall monument near the fort ruins. Six years later the Niagara Parks Commission started fixing up the lawns around it; fort repairs began in the late thirties, and a fully restored historic site opened to the public in 1939.

The fort, large and impressive, is entered across a drawbridge. You are allowed to climb up several strategic points to look around or watch the drill, the changing of the guard, and other duties performed in authentic nineteenth-century uniforms. Displays of military mementos, gift shop, refreshments. May 2 to mid-October, 9:30 A.M. to 6:00 P.M. Adults $1.50, children under 13, 35¢. Niagara Parks Commission, P.O. Box 150, Niagara Falls, Ontario L2E 6T2. 416/356-2241.

FORT ERIE • The city of 24,000 is an important gateway to Canada; more than eight million vehicles come over the Peace Bridge (the Buffalo connection) yearly.

There's a lot of "unsung" history here, like the white-pillared house on Jarvis Street where runaway slaves found refuge, and the fellow named Kraft who sold home-made cheeses from his horse and wagon. Did well, they say.

One of North America's older racetracks, the multimillion-dollar **Fort Erie Track** is a source of much local pride. Area counties are full of horse farms; the Prince of Wales Stakes, second gem in Canada's Triple Crown, is raced here. Summer meetings in June, July, and August. 416/871-3200.

The Ontario Coat of Arms has the red and white cross of St. George (patron saint of England) and the three maple leafs of Canada. The Ontario flag has the shield and the British Union flag.

Ontario's motto: *Ut Incepit Fidelis Sic Permanet* (Loyal she began, loyal she remains).

Once Ontario and Quebec were united, but there were so many English-speaking refugees coming north to get away from the American Revolution that the provincial leaders passed an act dividing Quebec into Upper (now Ontario) Canada and Lower Canada. Loyalists were free to settle in the new region and put down stakes along the St. Lawrence, on the Bay of Quinte, around Niagara, and at Detroit-Windsor. Further events reinforced the British influence and Canada took form as a predominantly English-speaking nation.

U.S. visitors, remember: You need *Canadian* stamps to send a letter home! Also, Ontario has a seat belt law: Buckle Up!

CHAPTER 4
LAKE ERIE

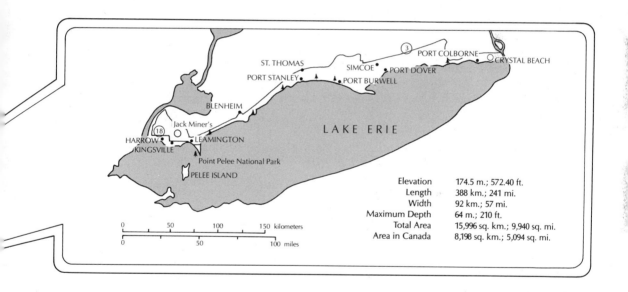

Elevation — 174.5 m.; 572.40 ft.
Length — 388 km.; 241 mi.
Width — 92 km.; 57 mi.
Maximum Depth — 64 m.; 210 ft.
Total Area — 15,996 sq. km.; 9,940 sq. mi.
Area in Canada — 8,198 sq. km.; 5,094 sq. mi.

THERE IS MUCH PRIDE and little trust in Lake Erie—long, shallow, and southernmost of the Great Lakes. The pride comes from the very people and communities who nearly killed the lake with pollutants but have managed to mend their ways to the extent that fishing is returning in full variety and the waters are bluer than they've been for years.

"Little trust" are words from the wise. The lake is shaped like a trough, averaging less than twenty m.

(sixty ft.) in depth and becoming extremely hazardous in a storm. Smart sailors will *not* ignore the weather warnings.

The first European visitors to the north shore of Erie were two Jesuit missionaries and their assistants. The men spent only the winter but saw enough evidence of abundant game, fruit trees, and mild climate to proclaim the region a "terrestrial paradise."

That should have started a rise in property values but it didn't. It took a wily opportunist named Thomas Talbot to really start the settlement process. In 1803, Talbot sold his army commission (a practice now defunct) and went off to collect the customary land grant given to field officers. It amounted to several thousand acres.

His next move was to get a government agreement that he would be given another 200 acres for every settler he brought in to work a 50-acre parcel. Prospective settlers, however, were not all that easy to find and after five years Talbot had placed only twenty families.

Part of the problem was isolation, so he built himself a road, the best in the province, connecting the prospective villages that Talbot hoped for. Each settler was required to help in its construction. It worked. By 1820 the road was nearly 300 miles long; by 1837 almost 50,000 people were settled on Talbot lands in twenty-seven townships.

In most accounts Talbot is described as a drunken, eccentric land baron who ruled like a feudal lord. He never married, put his own name on Talbotville, Port Talbot, and—it is suspected—St. Thomas, although records show few reasons for a halo.

Bygones are bygones; we have now the cheerful heritage of the Talbot Trail, a delightful way to explore the Erie coast. Signs marking the trail show a double-headed axe for the "T," and you are taken close to and away from the shore, sometimes looking at the long, blue horizon beyond a field of corn or tobacco, sometimes dipping into the valley at a river mouth and winding through pretty resort towns or agri-biz communities. There are eleven Provincial Parks along the route, a wealth of conservation areas, places to camp, and boating facilities. Sheet sailors especially, however, should be prepared for the long treks between ports Dover, Maitland, and Colborne.

One quarter of Canada's fruit produce and one half of Ontario's fruit come from Erie regions, and pick-it-yourself opportunities are as frequent as the roadside stands. The "terrestrial paradise" is a land flowing with apple juice and strawberry jam.

CRYSTAL TO HOLIDAY BEACH

There is a curious shortage of signposts for so extensive an establishment ... • CRYSTAL BEACH or perhaps I was too occupied with the idea of going down Sodom Road to an amusement park. Not *any* amusement park; Canada's largest fun park has the second largest roller coaster in the world. Crystal Beach's more than seventy-one rides and attractions include a four-run water slide that's *verrry* long and verrrry high. A quarter-mile beach goes with it. Clearly, someone disapproved mightily because the road to the park really is called "Sodom." If you're not of that ilk, pay $7.95 per adult, under four years free, seniors $3.00. The rides are in the ticket except for the coaster (75¢) and the water slide ($1.00 for each half hour). Refreshments, Big Top Restaurant, Cafe International. Write: P.O. Box 640, Crystal Beach, Ontario L0S 1B0. 416/984-2240, 984-1642. Note: Call ahead, as the park's future is uncertain as of this writing.

At the south end of the Welland Canal, facing the lake with a battery of • PORT COLBORNE marinas, pretty Port Colborne is Canada's flour-milling capital and home of the International Nickel Company's immense refinery. The Colborne lock #8 is one of the biggest on earth, and standing on the viewing platform south of Hwy. 3 gives you the best possible view of a freighter without actually going to sea.

The Historical and Marine Museum's tearoom serves tea and homemade biscuits in addition to the collection of early glassware and marine bric-a-brac, tying Port Colborne into the Lake Erie story. Museum grounds hold a log schoolhouse, barn, and the wheelhouse from the tugboat *Yvonne Dupre*.

South of Hwy. 3 on King Street, open April to November, noon till 5:00 P.M. Adults $1.00.

On Fridays, early morning till noon or thereabouts, there's a delightful Farmers' Market next to St. George's Park, at Charlotte and Catherine streets. Big annual event is Port Colborne's International Week, a wing-ding of parades, athletic events, fishing derbies, fish fries, and pancakes at breakfast. A gala that saturates the town.

For more P.C. information: Chamber of Commerce, 76 Main Street West, Port Colborne, Ontario L3K 3V2. 416/834-9765.

LONG BEACH • A long public access stretch of sandy shore with 300 campsites, boat
CONSERVATION AREA launch ramp, picnic tables. Firewood may be purchased, gas and other
supplies nearby. Superintendent: 416/386-6387.

ROCK POINT • Low on some facilities (no boat launch ramp, nearby rental, or campsites
PROVINCIAL PARK with electricity) but high on services (laundry, showers, and a store close
by). Very high on swimming, soaking up the sun. To reserve one of its 128
campsites, write Rock Point Provincial Park, Dunnville, Ontario N1A 2X5.
416/774-6642.

For big city escapees, Talbot Trail is as pleasant a drive in the country as
you'll ever find. Through tiny hello-goodbye communities with few facilities
but radiating quiet appeal.

SELKIRK PROVINCIAL • Swimming, a playground, and self-guided trails in a waterside beauty spot
PARK with 145 campsites, 44 electrified. R.R. #1, Selkirk, Ontario N0A 1P0.
416/776-2600.

PORT DOVER • Officially a town since 1879, and home of the world's largest *fresh*water
fishing fleet, this post-card-perfect little lakeside community has excellent
facilities for boats, trailer parks, and a neat park with wide sandy beach.

Harbour Museum, once a net-making shed, now houses artifacts relating
to the freshwater fishing industry. Open daily, all year.

Come, if you can, in August for the local arts and crafts show. Summer
theater throughout the season. Board of Trade, Harbour Street, Port Dover,
Ontario N0A 1N0. 519/583-2700. In winter, 583-0728.

SIMCOE • General John Graves Simcoe, first Governor of Upper Canada, was honored
twice on the map of Ontario, this time as the seat of Haldimand-Norfolk
County. The river Lynn runs through town, and the citizens have wisely
spread lovely parks along its banks. Simcoe's produce stands are cornucopias
of freshness. Excellent trout fishing streams are nearby, smallmouth black
bass and their cousins are hungry.

At 109 Norfolk Street South, the **Eva Brook Donly Museum of Art and
Antiques** backdrops a collection of 375 paintings of early area life, plus
Indian artifacts, fossils, and things that once growled in the night . . .
besides being an important source of Canadian genealogical information.
The house was built around 1843 (with new wing added in 1967), which
means the Museum in itself is an item. June to August, Tuesday through
Friday, 10:00 A.M. to 5:00 P.M., afternoons only on Saturday and Sunday. Rest

of the year, Wednesday to Sunday afternoons. Adults $1.00, students 50¢.
Eva Donly Museum, Simcoe, Ontario N3Y 2W3. 519/426-1583.

Housed in a gracious Greek Revival building that was designated an historic • LYNNWOOD
site in 1973, this museum has something for every art buff and even un-artsy   ARTS CENTRE
folk. Monthly shows of paintings, drawings, sculpture. Open all year, free,
but closed Mondays. Weekends afternoons only. Downtown, one block
east of main intersection, 21 Lynnwood Avenue. 519/428-0540.

For info on area events, stop at the Centre, 85 Pond Street, Simcoe,
Ontario N3Y 2T5. 519/426-6655.

Three Conservation areas are on our way south and west out of Simcoe:
Fisher, near hamlet of Fisher's Glen, on Lakeshore Road; Norfolk, just out of
Port Ryerse on Lakeshore; and Vittoria, Vittoria Road west of Hwy. 24. All
have fishing, only Norfolk has camping with 150 sites.

Wander the marked trails yourself or listen to the nature interpretive pro- • TURKEY POINT
gram (you should do both) at Turkey Point, a 194-site (none electrified)   PROVINCIAL PARK
camping park with swimming, laundromat, showers, boat launching, playground, and boat rentals nearby.

Three km. (2 mi.) north sits a 1798 mill, still producing flour by water • PORT ROWAN
power. In a new museum nearby and a reassembled barn are an array of
tools, farming machinery, and horse-drawn buggies. Sixty campsites with
swimming area, cider press, windmill, and other good reasons to investigate.
Backus Agricultural Museum Complex. Open April-November, Wednesday
and Saturday. Contact Long Point Conservation Authority, Box 525, Simcoe,
Ontario N3Y 4N5. 519/426-4623.

A finger of land reaching into the blue lake like a natural pier is "guarded" • LONG POINT
by the park. The 265 campsites (52 electrified) have showers, laundromat,   PROVINCIAL PARK
boat launching, Interpretive Building. Surf-swept and popular, the beach is
one of the best and fishing for bass, pike, muskie, etc. gets better every year.
Reservations can be made by contacting Long Point Provincial Park, Port
Rowan, Ontario N0E 1M0. 519/586-2133.

A hamlet astride Big Otter Creek, it's on the map but not in most tour • PORT BURWELL
guides. I suspect Burwellians like it that way. They do have marine services,
a long breakwater into Lake Erie, Sand Hill Park (*tall* dune), and a Provincial
Park with super beach. Old fire engine addicts, go to the firehouse for a
look at their vintage truck. It still works as a back-up vehicle.

TO SEE OR NOT TO SEE...

No question about it, the land between the lakes is a smorgasbord with Bard par excellence and Indian festival succotash. Samples:

CAMBRIDGE A meld of Galt, Preston, and Hesper, Cambridge is known for flour and woolen mills. In mid-July the Waterloo Regional Police Association holds **Highland Games** here, starring the Canadian National Pipe Band, sheepdog show, and dancing competition. For a wild time: **African Lion Safari,** a 500-acre drive-through park. R.R. #1, Cambridge.

WATERLOO–KITCHENER Twin cities with two universities and a lot of shared resources. One of the biggest **Octoberfests** in North America fills twenty festive halls with oompah and kraut und gut beer. Mid-October; don't miss the parade. The **Farmers' Market** has grown to a fifteen-million-dollar project in the middle of Kitchener, open all year, Saturday 5:00 A.M. till 2:00 P.M. Wednesdays also in warm weather. Enjoy **The Centre in the Square** (theatre, art gallery), **Waterloo Park and Zoo, Woodside National Historic Park** (boyhood home of William Lyon Mackenzie King), and/or the **Joseph Schneider House.** Take the children to watch the Glockenspiel's Snow White and the Seven Dwarfs; Canada's first, it has twenty-three bells, plays several times a day all year. King and Benton streets. For handmade bargains, come to the Mennonite Relief Sale in not-far New Hamburg, last Saturday in May.

BRANTFORD Where Pa Bell (Alexander) made the first long distance call on his invention, the telephone, to the town of Paris, nine kilometers away. Bell's modest home with assorted gadgetry is open all year, daily except Monday. In summer, Mondays too. The **Brant County Museum**'s treasures include a Six Nation Indian collection; **Her Majesty's Chapel of the Mohawks** (world's only Royal Indian Chapel); the oldest Protestant Church in Ontario; the **Woodland Indian Cultural Educational Centre and Museum;** the **Art Gallery of Brant** (Arts Place); **Glenhyrst Gardens**; the **Octogon House** . . . ; there's more. On Friday and Saturday evenings during the first three weekends in August, the Six Nations Indians reenact their history and culture in an amphitheatre among the trees. **The Indian John Archery Tournament** is one to aim for; in nearby Alberton, Saturday and Sunday, third week in June.

LONDON Big and busy and on the Thames, but all accents are Canadian. London supports an exceptional symphony orchestra, a dozen museums, theatres, et al. Try: the **Royal Canadian Regiment Museum**, the **London Regional Art Gallery**, the **Centennial Museum**. **Springbrook Park** flows with flowers, lawns, and **Storybook Gardens** for the young 'uns. They also like the **London Regional Children's Museum.** Well done. **Ska-Nah-Doht Indian Village** depicts Iroquois life; the **Lawson Museum** is an 1853 Gothic houseful of old odds and interesting ends. Try **Fanshawe Park and Pioneer Village**, a conservation area project. The large village holds pioneer craft demos in summer, with fishing and picnic tables, too. Big London event is the **International Air Show**, air and ground display of military craft. The Canadian Snowbirds and American Thunderbirds do their atmospheric gymnastics. First weekend in June.

STRATFORD Shakespeare is alive and well and even provided with a river called Avon plus swans playing their serene roles. Stratford's **Shakespearian Festival** deserves its glowing reputation. Although W. S. runs the season, operas, ballets, and even bluegrass folkfests have been added. June to October.

There's so much more, but lest we never get back to the coast, I refer you to the bountiful racks of information at the Visitors Bureaus or consult Chapter 10 for addresses and numbers.

A summer city with more population than its sponsoring town on warm • IROQUOIS BEACH
days; 232 campsites, none with electricity. Showers, laundromat, SWIM-   PROVINCIAL PARK
MING, but go back to launch your boat. Self-guided trails and interpretive
program. Reservations: Iroquois Beach Provincial Park, P.O. Box 9, Port
Burwell, Ontario N0N 1T0. 519/874-4691.

The road dips into a valley at the mouth of Catfish Creek, tree-water setting • PORT BRUCE
for tiny Port Bruce. Marine facilities are on Lake Road. 519/773-9599.

A day-use only park, popular for swimming, waterskiing, fishing. No fee.   • PORT BRUCE
                                                                            PROVINCIAL PARK

Lord Stanley decided to name this port after himself in 1823, not too • PORT STANLEY
modest a gesture, but after all, Lord Stanley *was* the one who saw how
valuable this north shore port would be for the goods of London. The Port
Stanley Marina Ltd. (519/782-3482 or 782-3481) is one of several places to
dock and gas up in a thick cluster of docks. Resort town with vacation
homes and excellent bathing facilities.

Named because Talbot's first name was Thomas or for a true saintly soul? • ST. THOMAS
You'd have to be a die-hard futurist not to enjoy the wealth of Victorian
architecture and nostalgic streets of St. Thomas, on Hwy. 3 half way between

Windsor and Buffalo. There are roads by-passing the town for those following the coast, but don't.

Called "flower city"—the evidence sprouts from hanging baskets and curbside beds—there are two florally flamboyant parks: Waterworks and Pinafore. Pinafore has a little lake and wildlife sanctuary and a narrow-gauge steam train the kids will love. Waterworks' lagoon grows gigantic water lilies, and neat little bridges arch over the goldfish-filled ponds. Pick ideas (but not bouquets) for home.

Southwest on R.R. #16 to

JOHN E. PEARCE • Day use only, picnic tables and self-guided woodland trails. Excellent place
PROVINCIAL PARK   to watch the hawk migrations.

Hwy. 3 rolls through rich and gentle farm country. Watch for slow-moving vehicles.

RONDEAU • A large park with sand for eight km. (five mi.) to stretch out on. Marsh and
PROVINCIAL PARK   meandering waterways are great for canoes, fishing (pike, perch, and sixty-two other species recorded caught here), and checking up on the birds. Wander through the woods, listen to the naturalist (on duty from May till September). 226 campsites, only 12 with electricity. No showers or laundromat, or playground. Interpretive Building and a lot for imaginative kids to do. Reservations, R.R. #1, Morpeth, Ontario N0P 1X0. 519/674-5405.

BLENHEIM • The Jesuits who visited here in 1620 were the first recorded white men in the region. Ask about the Charal Winery and Vineyards, and their tasting room; just one of the fruit products in an area where growing, canning, . . . and fermenting are the main business.

ERIEAU • Down the road a bit from Hwy. 3, on Rondeau Bay. The wide, shallow bay has been a fisherman's haven for many years and Erieau is the main supply depot, boat stop. Two marinas facing Lake Erie, two facing the Bay. Erieau Marina Ltd., for example, has 660 cm. (22 ft.) draft at the dock. No rentals but full facilities. 519/676-4471.

WHEATLEY • A freshwater fishing port where the building and repairing of commercial fishing boats is a traditional business. Big event is the Old Boys Reunion early in July. Parade, fireworks, etc. for old and not-so-old; girls, too.

WHEATLEY • Fun spot, 206 campsites, none with electricity. Swimming, playground, etc.
PROVINCIAL PARK   Big advantage is its nearness to Jack Miner's, Colsanti's greenhouses, Point Pelee, etc. Good for canoes. P.O. Box 640, Wheatley, Ontario N0P 2P0. 519/825-4659.

Once called Wilkinson's Corners, referred to by some wags as "Heinzville" • LEAMINGTON
in reference to the large cannery where fifty-seven varieties of pickles and
lakefuls of tomato soup are cooked. For lovers of geographic trivia, Leamington (remember, this is Canada, kingdom of the deep north) is on the
42nd parallel shared with Northern California and Rome, Italy.

Nice town, its information booth is appropriately shaped like a large
tomato. More than 1,200 campsites in the area: golf, tennis, and butterfly
watching (see Point Pelee). Important point of entry for Americans coming
via the Pelee Islander from Sandusky, Ohio. For a schedule of trips, events,
etc., write Chamber of Commerce, Box 321, Leamington, Ontario N8H
3W3. 519/326-2721 (summer) or 326-5479.

When 25,000 or so people show up semiannually to watch the birds show • POINT PELEE
up semiannually, one questions whether the watchers are being watched . . .   NATIONAL PARK

or which is the watchee. However, aside from the seasons of vast migrations, Point Pelee is a living museum of natural history, flora and fauna, sounds and silences. Smallish as National Parks go, there are still over 1,011 hectares (two squares miles) of marshland with a mile-long boardwalk to observe some 330 species of birds, plus a woodland with a happy botanist's list of trees and shrubs along self-guided trails.

This stalactite of sand and gravel dripping from Erie's north shore is the southernmost point of the Canadian mainland. Since the public use area is relatively small, no individual camping is allowed and visitors enter then transfer to a trackless train rather than drive all the way to land's end . . . also giving the naturalists a chance to explain local ecology. A swimming beach runs almost continuously along the west bank and part way up the east side, but no dipping at the point because of dangerous currents.

Fishing seasons vary from year to year (you must have a National Park Fishing Permit); private concessionaires sell food, rent canoes and bikes during the summer.

Ask about the monarch butterfly migration when you call or write Superintendent, Point Pelee National Park, R.R. #1, Leamington, Ontario N8H 3V4. 519/326-3204.

PELEE ISLAND • Half way between the Ohio and Ontario shores is the largest island in Lake Erie, home to a permanent population of less than 300 souls. Six km. (four mi.) across and about thirteen km. (nine mi.) long, there are good roads, a garland of beaches, and even an airport on Pelee with Ford Trimotor service to Sandusky.

The fishing has been written up by experts as among the best, so naturally the island is ready for visitors with rods and reels. A few good motels; cottages and cabins to rent.

Getting there is half the fun—on one of the frequent ferries from Leamington, Kingsville, or Sandusky. Boats sail from the foot of Jackson Street in Sandusky and head for Leamington via Pelee Island on Tuesday, Wednesday, Thursday, and Friday, or head for Kingsville Monday, Saturday, and Sunday. Round trip, $14.00 adults, children $7.00, under six years, free; autos $28.00. June 15th to September 7th. Call 519/724-2115 for information, toll free in 519 area: 1-800-265-5683.

Big event in the fall is the International Pheasant Hunt, drawing hunters from each side of the lake at $110 per-day license fee. There are two shoots, each limited to 600 participants who apply far in advance for the chance. To deal yourself in, call Town Clerk, Pelee Island, Ontario N0R 1M0. 519/724-2931.

Cacti, calla lilies, clay pots, ice cream, and even a llama (at the writer's • RUTHVEN visit) under the glass roofs of Colasanti's, an imaginative greenhouse that kept adding attractions . . . like tropical birds, goats, and that creature from the Andes. Bargains for gardeners, refreshments, little red wagons to tote your plants or kids around in.

Like so many lakeshore towns, winter Kingsville and summer Kingsville is a • KINGSVILLE study in contrasts that goes beyond a change in the weather. In summer the population quadruples and the party is under way: the Lion's Carnival, the Band Tattoo, or the fall Migration Festival. Good place to rent a cottage or buy fresh fish at dockside.

Kingsville has reached a goodly measure of fame as the home of Jack Miner's Bird Sanctuary, a project so unique and a man so ahead of his time that kings, queens, and presidents have paid him honor. The sanctuary is just north of town, easily found with direction signs.

Those with veggie plots who want to raise their level of expertise would • HARROW do well to make an appointment and tour the multimillion-dollar Harrow Agricultural Research Station, part of the Research Branch of the Canadian Department of Agriculture. Tour wagons are provided for the fifty-four-minute trip, a film is shown, and visitors can view some of the on-going experiments. Of great interest is the weed garden containing more than 100 species. If farmers spot the weed that is giving them trouble they can then request the data on controlling the pest. Varieties are tested for disease resistance, which are best for canning, etc. Printed brochure and pamphlets at no charge.

November until April, inside tours only, 8:15 A.M. to 4:45 P.M. In July and August, inside and outside tours Tuesday and Thursday only, 2:00 P.M. No tours in May or June.

For an appointment (only), Harrow Research Station, Harrow, Ontario N0R 1G0. 519/738-2251.

In the Fox Creek Conservation Area is a rare (for Ontario) Greek Revival- • COLCHESTER style farmhouse right on the edge of Lake Erie and backed by barns, an ice house, a blacksmith shop, and such supporting structures. John Richardson

WILD GOOSE JACK ... A GIANT IN THE REEDS

Jack Miner's name should ring loud, clear bells—like Magellan or Edison—but beyond his home regions it is seldom recognized. He explored new environmental territory, lit the bulb of the waterfowl conservation movement. Unlike the romantics and poets who only expounded on the beauties of the plain, unvarnished world, Jack Miner did something about enlarging and protecting it.

At thirty-five, Miner, an illiterate farmer-brickmaker and hunting guide, was one of the sharpest shooters in Canada. Twenty years later he had put aside his guns forever, and had done so much to improve the habitat and survival rate of ducks and geese that bird hunting today is alive and well, not lying with the carcasses of the carrier pigeon or dodo bird.

Miner's first step was to turn a large part of his farm into a bird sanctuary in 1904, first of its kind in the world, where waterfowl could not be shot. Canada Geese had become so rare by then that it was four years before a wild one flew down to roost near Miner's four winged decoys. Of course the neighbors thought he was a little tetched because of his idea that the same birds flew back to the same places in their migrations. In 1909 Miner put a crude band around the legs of several ducks, asking any hunter who shot the bird to send him a notice of where it was taken. For a start he banded mallards, widgeon, and other surface-feeding ducks, then began to put bands on the legs of Canada Geese. Hunters shooting these birds got an unexpected message from the Lord at the same time because the deeply devout Miner (who learned to read and write from his wife and children) included a Bible verse on the tag. More than one hunter was moved to write to J. M. and thank him for the reminder.

Over 150,000 birds have been banded at the Miner Sanctuary, where meticulously kept records reveal patterns of migration. It became evident that massive overkill in some areas could wipe out birds completely . . . and that "bird brains" were smarter than supposed. When the winged dinners "learned" they would be safe at Miner's, for example, ducks and geese flew at altitudes too high for guns, then came circling down into his fields on an invisible spiral staircase for a secure stay. They had to be sure of the spot because hunters for miles around flocked to the next-door acreage to shoot any birds that missed the right real estate. By 1917, however, the Ontario Government had been enlightened about Jack's cause and voted unanimously to create a Crown Game Preserve, prohibiting hunting for more than a mile into adjoining properties.

Directly because of Miner's efforts, laws were passed regulating hunting and more than 200 privately owned, federal, and local sanctuaries (the number grows yearly) were established in the U.S. and Canada.

As son Manly Miner put it, "Remember that Canada Geese, while they are referred to as waterfowl, are upland feeders and roost on bodies of water, then go inland during the day to feed on pasture fields and fields where the farmer has harvested his corn.

"When our human population was only half the size, there was plenty of space (and fewer hunters), but today if it were not for the sanctuaries and refuges, where could a goose alight and not have a gun pointing at it?"

Miner was a handsome, ruddy man whose growth in fame did not shrink his gentle, steadfast nature. He spoke to full houses at Carnegie Hall, was guest speaker when kings, tycoons, and presidents were in the audience; the Order of the British Empire was bestowed on him, yet he never lost his curiosity about birds and plants, or was ever known to show arrogance when "nobodies" crowded into his precious time. To honor the man and his cause, the Canadians have designated the week of April 17 (Miner's birthday) as National Wildlife Week.

A beloved Canadian son to whom we are all indebted.

* * *

There is no charge to visit Jack Miner's Bird Sanctuary, open October 1 to May 1. Closed on Sunday. During the summer months the fowl are in the Hudson Bay region nesting and the sanctuary is closed. End of March, early April is best for watching spring migrations; then the last of October, early November. Best time is 3:00 P.M. till dark to see late evening flights . . . and *hear* them. Box 39, Kingsville, Ontario. 519/773-4034.

"Wild Goose Jack," a beautifully photographed film biography of Jack Miner, is available to groups, television stations, etc. Produced by Clear Horizon Films, 2 College Street, Suite 108, Toronto, Ontario M5G 1K3. 416/927-1724.

Park purchased the site in 1833, built a house soon after, married, and raised six children. He was the brother of the Parks in Amherstburg, a family of successful merchants, sawmill operators, and dealers. The schooner *Erie and Ontario* was the first vessel in the Park fleet. John's country house reflects an above-average prosperity with fine walnut trim, large stairwell, gracious living room. Today the visitor will probably find someone cooking in the kitchen fireplace or making candles or spinning, all part of the daily routine of nineteenth-century life. Open all year, but closed weekends during the winter, closed on Saturdays during spring and fall. Summer hours: Monday to Friday, 9:00 A.M.-4:00 P.M., Saturday and Sunday, 11:30 A.M. to 5:00 P.M. Adults 50¢. Watch for Arts and Crafts Festival in August, Harvest Festival in early October. Write Curator, c/o Essex Region Conservation Authority, 360 Fairview Avenue West, Essex, Ontario N8M 1Y6. 510/738-2029.

More history with a fun twist is at the Southwestern Ontario Heritage Village, right in the middle of Essex County on fifty-two acres and carefully kept lawns. There are twelve buildings in the village complex, restored and refurnished with items from ancestral attics. A furnished one-room schoolhouse, 1854 railroad station, transport museum, and little honeymoon house built in 1865 are part of the grouping.

Directly north of the Park Homestead on Co. Rd. 23, eight km. (five mi.) south of Essex. Call 519/776-6909.

HOLIDAY BEACH
PROVINCIAL PARK • Inviting, green, relaxed. A grand place to hold a family reunion . . . with enough picnic tables to seat the whole town of Amherstburg. During September and October thousands of migrating hawks gather in the area, and a waterfowl sanctuary is right next door. Long beach, boat launching ramp, forty-six campsites, none with electricity. Reservations, P.O. Box 128, Amherstburg, Ontario N9V 2Z3. 519/736-3772.

CANADIAN HOLIDAYS

The *Canadian Thanksgiving* is the *second Monday in October.*

Christmas, Easter, Labour Day same as in the United States.

Canada Day (formerly Dominion Day) comes on *July 1.*

Victoria Day Weekend is closest to *May 24.*

A Civic Holiday is declared the first *Monday in August* in four Canadian provinces including Ontario, making a long shut-down weekend.

Remembrance Day is on *November 11* (Armistice Day).

Boxing Day December 26.

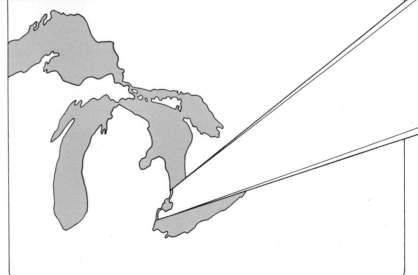

CHAPTER 5
GREAT CONNECTIONS
The Detroit River,
Lake St. Clair, The St. Clair River

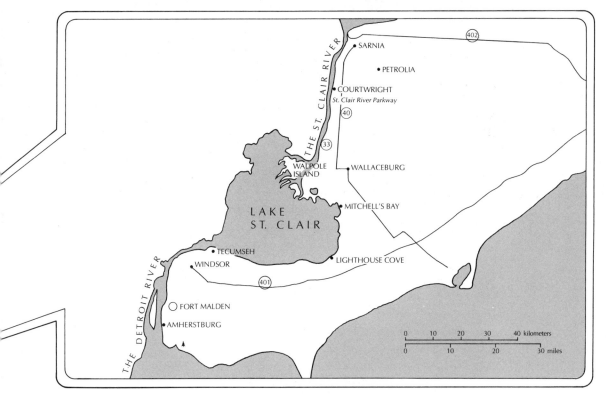

FROM AMHERSTBURG TO SARNIA we follow two memorable rivers and a lake that would be considered one of the *Great* Lakes if the others weren't such giants. Just why Lake St. Clair isn't included may rightly puzzle anyone who sails out into its glistening expanses.

The rivers aren't really rivers, either; they are conduits between basins and are considered *straits* by the sticklers for accuracy. We'll brush such minutiae aside and note that both rivers have been—in peak economic periods—the busiest channels in the world, carrying more traffic than the Panama Canal, Suez, and Rhine combined.

Area history went into its recorded stage when the Frenchman, Antoine de la Mothe Cadillac, suggested that a settlement be built where downtown Detroit now stands. In the course of time the growing community went from French to British to American hands until the border line was properly set. Canoes gave way to sails and steam, and riverfront farms on both sides were pushed back for industry, although the Canadian side of the border retains parcels of rural companionship with the water's edge that are long gone on the American side. Canadian farms still touch the Detroit River and Lake St. Clair, much as they did a century and more ago.

Lake St. Clair spreads like a shallow bowl, never more than eight meters (twenty-four ft.) deep, and averaging only about three meters (around ten ft.)—not much for a surface thirty-five km. (twenty-four mi.) long and nearly as wide. It is undoubtedly one of the favorite fishing lakes of the world, a pasttime once threatened by the lamphrey, pollution, overkill, and the like, but now returning to something of its old status.

On any sunny summer weekend the number of sailboats out on the lake will out-count the mayflies on a screen door. Add wind surfers, motor boats, fishermen, freighters, and more; everyone had better know what he or she is doing, wear a life jacket, and obey the rules. Classes in small craft handling are given in *many* places; don't let your pride or bravado (or lack of time) keep you from learning a little more.

The St. Clair River Parkway is one of the coastline's best. You'll soon see why.

AMHERSTBURG TO SARNIA

AMHERSTBURG • It may be only twenty minutes from Windsor and thirty-one minutes from metropolitan Detroit, but pleasant Amherstburg is a sweet light-year from either one. Quaint but not cutesy; historic but not facing squarely backward.

The town started off in a kind of colonial arms race, in the discontent over boundary lines left by the American Revolution. When the English were summarily kicked out of Detroit in 1796 they picked this site near Lake Erie to establish a fort (first called Fort Amherstburg) as headquarters for the British Right Army Division in Canada and branch office of the

British Indian Department. It was a good spot to guard against Americans coming across the river or up from Lake Erie; just as good for launching possible future offensives.

Therefore, a navy yard was built next to the fort, soon turning out armed vessels meant to give no-nonsense messages to the Americans. With Indian support, the British regained Detroit for a year in the War of 1812 . . . until the Battle of Lake Erie turned everything around again.

The original Fort Amherstburg became Fort Malden, burned to the ground • FORT MALDEN during the struggle, was rebuilt, and long after animosities faded, became an Ontario lunatic asylum until its recognition as an historic site. Much of the original earthworks, their atrophied cannons pointing at passing freighters and pleasure boats, are still found on the four and a half hectare (eleven-acre) grounds. Along a wide spread of lawn, trees, and benches, there's a restored barracks, a cottage built for military retirees, and a pair of excellent museums. Young men in Redcoat uniforms guard, parade, and drill during July and August—and even fire their muskets.

Your tour of Amherstburg *must* start here. Open June 1 to Labour Day, 10:00-6:00; 10:00-5:00 the rest of the year. P.O. Box 38, Amherstburg, Ontario N9V 2Z2. 519/736-5416.

It wasn't just the troops who vacated the west banks of the Detroit River in 1796; Loyalist settlers followed suit. One merchant with a new house on the Rouge River took it apart and floated the sections to Amherstburg rather than switch allegiances. The **Park House**, oldest within 250 miles, is now a museum with furnishings of life in the 1850s (slight modernization). See demonstrations of early domestic duties, tinsmithing, a hand operated press, and the building's unusual construction. 214 Dalhousie Street, June 1 to August 31, 10:00 A.M. to 5:00 P.M. daily; March 21 to May 31 and September 1 to December 21, 1:30-4:30 Sunday, 12:30-4:30 Tuesday-Friday. 519/736-2511. Small donation.

The Park House is on one corner of the King's Navy Yard Park, a pin-neat place to watch freighters pass like silent fortresses (unless they need to toot) up the river. The Boblo boats are the largest craft you'll see going downstream at this point, because that land directly across from Amherstburg is Boblo Island and downriver shipping passes on the far side.

Seventeen houses and stores were built before 1850 and many others before 1900. Ten of the heritage architectural sites face Dalhousie Street

NORTH AMERICAN
BLACK HISTORICAL MUSEUM
& CULTURAL CENTRE
OPEN- WED. FRI. 10AM-5PM / SAT-SUN.1PM-5PM

parallel to the river; a folder describing them is available at the Park House Museum.

Over on King Street (roughly between Simcoe and Richmond, five blocks east of Dalhousie) are three buildings belonging to the **North American Black Historical Museum, Inc.** An 1848 church, Nazery A.M.E., built by former slaves who found refuge in Amherstburg via the Underground Railroad, and the new Museum and Cultural Centre Building are situated exactly where the original Black settlement was located. Exhibits show Black history from slavery to freedom in Canada, in a display that enlightens on many subjects while telling its own story. Open 10:00-5:00 Wednesday to Friday, 1:00-5:00 Saturday and Sunday. Donations appreciated. 277 King Street, Amherstburg, Ontario. 519/736-7353.

BOBLO ISLAND • Bois Blanc ranks as one of the most durable and beloved amusement parks on the continent, set on a 300-acre island and accessible only by boat. In bygone days (eighty years' worth) the huge dance pavilion was considered the finest of its kind in North America; the sturdily housed merry-go-round was a landmark in fun. Old timers who come around for a dose of nostalgia will find that the dance hall is now an echoing shell, but the carousel still turns, the dock has been remodeled; everything has fresh paint. Boblo has never been more inviting.

More than fifty rides and attractions are offered, along with scenic picnic places, a small zoo for the kids, live stage performances, and huge lawns to stretch out and do nothing.

You can take the excursion boats from Detroit (five times daily) or the ferry from Amherstburg, south side of town every fifteen minutes, beginning at 11:00 A.M.

Cruise, island admission, and shows: Adults 12-61, $8.50 (from Detroit), $5.00 (from Amherstburg); children 4-11, $7.50 (from Detroit), $4.50 (from Amherstburg); seniors, $6.50 (from Detroit), $4.00 (from Amherstburg). Or unlimited rides, $6.00 per person (purchased on island only). Reduced rate for complete package. Children under 4 free. Visa and Mastercard accepted; group rates available. For information call 313/964-5775 or 313/962-9622; in Windsor 519/255-1271. Island of Boblo Company, 151 W. Jefferson, Detroit, Michigan 48226.

Ministry of Transport docking is available at Amherstburg, and a large marina at Duffy's has all facilities.

I endorse the Navy Yard Restaurant, the remodeled Salmoni Hotel (1849) at the corner of Navy Yard Park. Excellent—save room for dessert.

More information at any of the museums or Tourist Information Centre, Navy Yard Park, Amherstburg, Ontario N9V 2C7.

King's Highway 18 rolls north, past a certain amount of roadside fishing near the Canard (Duck) River. To the west you catch glimpses of the huge industrial complexes on Michigan's side of the Detroit River, a study in contrasts against the Canadian side's marshes and farms.

• LASALLE Strung along the road with no particular town center, its roadside stands have made the community a favorite stop for city cooks who want fresh-from-the-fields produce.

• SANDWICH Unpretentious little Sandwich, now a part of the City of Windsor, has the Ambassador Bridge to form the skyline and its share of historic constructions. Of the 100 buildings in a four-block area, nearly two-thirds were built before 1900. History buffs will find a walking-tour guide sheet at the Ontario-Windsor Information desks.

Windsor

What Canadian city is south of the U.S.? Windsor, curving **under** Michigan at the tip of Canada's "sun parlor." This bit of geographic trivia can be verified by standing in Windsor's Dieppe Park on the Detroit River, a grand site for ship watchers, breeze seekers, and travelers who want their picture taken against a big skyline. Face the gleaming towers of Detroit and look at your compass. North!

Windsor, with a population around 200,000, is Canada's southernmost large city and sixth largest industrial center—Ford of Canada, General Motors, chemicals, machinery, and the distilleries of Hiram Walker. For all of that, it's an exceedingly pleasant place with good shopping, a large university, cultural savvy, and enough fine restaurants to lure steady customers across the border.

When Europeans were first coming into the region more than 300 years ago, it may have seemed as though Detroit would spread on both sides of the river. Aerial photographs still reveal the outlines of the long, narrow "ribbon" farms stretching back from the shores; their owners looked to Fort Pontchartrain (Detroit) for protection. Two wars changed everything.

The Battle of Quebec on the Plains of Abraham lasted fifteen minutes, part of a war that was seven years long, and switched Canada's destiny from French to British. In the colonial revolt, the British had a turn at losing, and Detroit-Windsor unity was severed by a new boundary. Sir Isaac Brock recaptured the American Fort Detroit in the War of 1812 and held it for a year, then had to clear out. Mutual distrust took a long time to fade.

For Americans, a brewing storm within their own land eventually pushed worries about invasion from Canada aside, while Windsor became terminus of the Underground Railway and offered an open door to freedom for thousands of runaway slaves.

Post-Civil War years saw great growth, commerce, genuine friendship, and the shared agonies of a World War . . . followed by a new era of illegal traffic. Liquor from Windsor, Amherstburg, and points between made waves of its own before U.S. Prohibition laws were finally repealed.

The Detroit-Windsor relationship gets special attention at the **Hiram Walker Historical Museum,** formerly the Francois Baby House. Tucked in behind the Cleary Auditorium on Pitt Street, one block south of the river, the Museum shows bits and pieces of working life from earliest settlement days, such as furniture, tools, maps, and newspapers. Open Sunday 2:00 to 5:00 P.M.; Tuesday to Saturday 9:00 A.M. to 5:00 P.M. Free. 254 Pitt Street West, Windsor, Ontario N9A 5L5. 519/253-1812.

On Riverside Drive, close to the new Windsor Hilton, with twelve galleries, • WINDSOR
a sculpture court, and children's gallery. Collections lean heavily on Cana-   ART GALLERY
dian artists but spotlight work from every era and area. Restaurant, gift
shop. Check for special events. 445 Riverside Drive, open all year, free.
Tuesday through Saturday 10:00 A.M. to 5:00 P.M.; Wednesday 10:00 A.M. to
10:00 P.M. Closed Mondays. 519/258-7111.

Sunken Garden rates an *aaahhh*. Not just flora in abundance, but special • JACKSON PARK
lighting after dark, fountains, picnic area, bowling greens, a ball park, and
more. A World War II Lancaster bomber flies in memory only from the
adjacent Lancaster Memorial Rose Test Garden, a peaceful spread of 12,000
rose bushes (500 varieties) from all over the world. Is a rose is a rose is a
rose? Find out. Tecumseh Road and Ouellette Avenue.

More flowers and a fountain are on Riverside Drive where **Coventry
Gardens** and **Reaume Park** skirt the river with a wide swatch of green
grass and red roses. In a shallow inlet, North America's largest floating
fountain, called the Peace Fountain, goes through endless spray ballets
daily (with floodlights when the sun goes down). And you get to watch the
long freighters at the same time.

This Tudor mansion, built by a son of Hiram Walker and designed by famed • WILLISTEAD
Detroit architect Albert Kahn, could easily inspire a few Gothic romance   MANOR HOUSE
novels. Hand carved details in stained white oak, Great Hall and dramatic
staircase; lovers of elegant dwellings will relish a tour. The surrounding
lawns are known as Willistead Park, scene of a popular Art-in-the-Park fest
on the first weekend in June. Walker and Niagara streets, then one block
west. Open July-August, Sunday to Wednesday 1:00-4:00 P.M.; May and
June, Sunday only, same hours; September to April, first and third Sunday,
also 1:00 to 4:00 P.M. 519/255-6545.

A Detroit River shoremark and the oldest industry in town, the **Hiram
Walker Canadian Club Distillery** offers tours—but no free samples—
most weeks of the summer. Except for the first three weeks in July, there's
a tour each day, Monday through Friday at 2:00 P.M. Reservations required.
510/254-5171.

On Wednesdays, and Saturday mornings especially, downtown between • WINDSOR
Chatham and Pitt, find a two-story milieu of fruit, vegetables, flowers,   PUBLIC MARKET
poultry, pastry, and people. Fresh and cheap. Italiaphiles should go to Erie

Street for pastas and sauces; the Ouelette Avenue Mall for china and woolens, or the Lambton Plaza. Good shopping in Windsor.

The **International Freedom Festival** is a whoopee celebration shared by both countries to commemorate Canada Day (Dominion Day) and the U.S. Fourth of July. Tugboat races, air and water shows, a carnival, and *gigantic* fireworks display headline about fifty different events.

In 1959 four Detroit girls paid their fifteen-cent bus fare to Windsor to sing in the annual Emancipation Day talent contest. They won. They called themselves the Supremes and went on to make music history. The Day continues to be marked by Miss Sepia contest, barbecue, marching bands in parade; the high-stepping works. First weekend in August. Contact the

OVER AND UNDER: BORDER CROSSING

The Ambassador Bridge—There is a special bond between the writer of this guide and the Ambassador Bridge. My father used to take his two youngsters for walks on the bridge, one and three-fourths miles long. Higher and higher with each exciting step, higher over the houses and railroad tracks on the Detroit side, then over the gleaming water, freighters, and finally over Assumption College on the Windsor side.

The wind blows strong and cool and the city seems wondrous from that vantage point. We made a ceremony of planting one foot in Canada and the other in the U.S., and I've never recovered from thinking that a border isn't a border unless it has a river to mark it. A plaque on the international line reads, "The Visible Expression of Friendship in the Hearts of Two People with Like Ideas and Ideals." One of the hopeful achievements of the race . . . and a space walk for the groundbound.

To drive across: One dollar for passenger cars (as of this writing), more for trailers. You will be asked what your citizenship is, where you are going, how long you plan to stay, etc. Be ready with a birth certificate or voter's card if there is any question. Naturalized citizens should have

their naturalization papers. Aliens require an alien registration receipt upon returning from a visit to Canada of less than six months.

The Detroit-Windsor Tunnel—The only underwater international vehicular tunnel in the world took two and a half years to build, is 5,160 feet long.

No pedestrians, but you can ride a bus (depot just east of 500 Ouellette Avenue). Prices and questions are the same as for the Bridge. The Tunnel is a wee mite closer to downtown, will take you directly to Detroit's Renaissance Center, Hart Plaza, Greektown, the boats to Boblo, etc. Of course, any visit to the Detroit area has to include a trip out to Dearborn and the Henry Ford Museum–Greenfield Village where the American-Canadian life-styles and ingenuity are given a classy showcase.

Follow the Travel Information signs at the Tunnel exit.

For Tunnel Bus information: 944-4111.

Windsor-Detroit Area Immigration Information:
Canadian: 1-519/253-3006
U.S.: 1-313/226-3290

See U.S.-Canadian Customs, Chapter 10.

Canadian-American Black Brothers of Ontario or the Travel Information desk.

Windsor and Essex County Tourist and Convention Bureau, 80 Chatham Street SE (in the block north of the Tunnel entrance). Open Monday through Friday 8:30 A.M. to 4:30 P.M. 519/255-6530. Another information station is on Huron Church Road not far from the Bridge. Open same hours most of the year, but from May 15 to Labour Day until 8:00 P.M. 519/151-7612.

Ask about events at Cleary Auditorium, Windsor Light Opera, the Windsor Symphony, and Essex Hall Theatre, or tours through the Canamec Scientific Glassblowing Plant.

High apartments and quiet streets, a community named for the Indian chief • TECUMSEH who was given the title of Brigadier General in the British forces and met death at the battle of Moraviantown during the War of 1812. Chrysler of Canada and the Jolly Green Giant are at home in Tecumseh; the annual Cornfest is *the* big event. Corn . . . sweet, juicy, and on the cob . . . parade, the Windsor Police Pipe Band, everything they can throw into the fun list.

Marina and lighthouse, as you now edge the south side of Lake St. Clair.   • LIGHTHOUSE POINT

Very pleasant little park on the lake with off-shore fishing and camping.   • BELLE RIVER

An 1818 lighthouse and tiny park three km. (two mi.) from Hwy. 2. Look • LIGHTHOUSE COVE carefully or you may miss the sign. The Thames, one of the area's widest streams, flows past its guardian light into the lake and bears a lot of pleasure boat traffic. Paved launching ramp, gas, boat facilities, restaurant. The lighthouse is open to the top window, but not to the light.

Hwy. 2 becomes 36, then suddenly it's 35 you're following to 34 . . . closest to the lake. *No* road along the shore.

Panfish, largemouth bass, northern pike, pickerel; the fish population of • MITCHELL'S BAY Lake St. Clair keeps the humans coming to tidy little places like Mitchell's Bay. A 280-boat marina, launching ramps, etc. Swimming and camping are nearby at Marine Park on Mitchell Bay Road. Write: Box 20, Dover Centre, Ontario N0P 1L0 or call 519/354-8423.

"Glasstown of Canada," "Lacrosse Capital of North America," "Biggest Little • WALLACEBURG Town in North America"—whatever the name, it's certainly one of the

most enthusiastic. Two forks of the Sydenham River meet in town, deepest stream in this part of the province. Boats can dock downtown, close to shopping and restaurants. Need some bowls, tumblers, and general glassware? The Libbey St. Clair firm and L. E. Smith of Pennsylvania have a factory outlet on Forham Street. Baseball, slo-pitch lacrosse, and soccer games almost every day; pick-your-own orchards and boat rentals easy to come by. 519/627-1141 or 627-1603.

WALPOLE ISLAND • Five islands—Walpole (largest), Seaway, Squirrel, Basset, and St. Anne's—make up the St. Clair River delta known as "The Flats" where fishing in the marshy streams runs from good to fabulous. Declared an Indian Reserve in 1850 by Queen Victoria, Walpole is the scene of a major annual pow-wow held in mid-July. Chippewas, Potawatomi, and Ottawa tribesmen dance, demonstrate game and craft skills in big family get-togethers. The public is invited.

Guides for hunting and fishing can be engaged by calling the Band

THE REALITY OF FICTION

Harriet Beecher Stowe was already an ardent abolitionist when she met Josiah Henson, heard of his struggles, and wrote the powerful *Uncle Tom's Cabin*, a book that did more to open eyes to the evils of slavery than any number of graphic speeches.

Henson was born into slavery on a Maryland farm, was brutalized, cheated, and separated from his family. When he could take no more, and with occasional help from sympathetic whites, he reached safety in Canada. It was an early stage of the Underground Railway, by which more than 75,000 escaped blacks found freedom.

Bright and articulate, Henson's fame grew; he was asked to tell his story many times, was even greeted by Queen Victoria.

Henson's inspiring life and related events are told at the **Uncle Tom's Cabin Museum** (six buildings), one mile west of Dresden, Ontario, not far from Wallaceburg. Open May 1 to October 31, 10:00 to 6:00 daily. Adults $2.00, senior citizens and students with cards $1.50, children 6–12 75¢. Subject to change.

Picnic tables and refreshments available, handicap ramps for two buildings.

Uncle Tom's Cabin and Museum, R.R. #5, Dresden, Ontario N0P 1M0. 519/683-2978.

Office, 519/627-1481. Since the Reserve does not come under the usual provincial jurisdiction, you'll need a special permit. Call the above number or write Walpole Island Band Office, R.R. #3, Wallaceburg, Ontario N8A 4K9.

Don't leave till you've visited the handsome new craft store on the north end of the big island in Highbanks Park. Some camping at Evergreen Acres next door. 519/627-3814.

History note: the Monument on Hwy. 32 as you drive over is said to contain the bones of Tecumseh, famed Indian leader.

Three small, speedy ferries carrying about four cars a trip churn back and forth across the St. Clair River, Walpole Island to Algonac, Port Lambton to Robert's Landing, and Sombra to Marine City. Cars, $2.50; pedestrians, 40¢; trailers, $2.00 to $2.50; motor homes, $3.00 to $3.50; motorcycles, $1.00; bikes, 50¢. Prices subject to change. Remember, there's a Customs officer on the other side; be prepared to offer identification, show purchases.

The **St. Clair Parkway** skims along the river, past one park after another, through little towns of the present tense without the present tension. In spring when the fruit trees and lilacs are in bloom you might want to pull over to the curb and stay forever, watching the long ships pass, picnicking on the tidy lawns. A road to treasure.

Parks come so thick and fast that if you pass one, don't fret; the next is within walking distance up the road. All have fishing, boat-watching benches, and shade. South or north of town, they're listed with the community they are closest to.

PORT LAMBTON • Great view of the river, space for the docking of nearly any size boat. Ferry to Michigan's Robert's Landing comes and goes at frequent intervals. Marshy Creek Park, Port Lambton Park, and Brander Park are the guest rooms of town. At Brander you'll find bike trails, playground, barbecues; all the basics.

SOMBRA • Another place to catch the ferry. The Sombra Township Museum is filled to the joists with everything grandma ever laid eyes on or wore or threw at grandpa. Indian items and Great Lakes marine pics for seaway buffs. Open 1:00 to 5:00 most days.

Reagan. Sombra, Cathcart, and Lambton-Cundick parks are very close. Cathcart and Lambton-Cundick, a kilometer apart, have launch ramps and at least fifty campsites each. Showers, flush toilets, and recreational activities.

COURTRIGHT • The MASSIVE Lambton Generating Station of Ontario Hydro is the conspicuous biggie in a tree-filled community with a small hotel and riverfront park. At Seager (where's the drinking water?) and Willow Park boats can be watched and fish caught, or books read and poems written. Drifter's choice.

If you round up fifteen to fifty friends all over twelve years old and phone the office two weeks in advance, you may be able to tour the Hydro plant. It should be quite interesting. Write: Ontario Hydro, 1075 Wellington Road, London, Ontario N6E 1M1. 519/867-2663.

MOORETOWN • Golfers can take a greens break on the St. Clair Parkway Course, a 6,700-yard challenge. The township has a Sports Complex with a pair of ice rinks, indoor swimming pool, health spa, the works. The campgrounds on Emily Street have 110 sites with most of the amenities. 519/867-2951.

A former high school has been turned into the **Mooretown Museum,** a growing project with a log cabin on the site, a giant new display shed, and

114

Victorian house that will be open soon. Open daily 1:00 to 5:00 P.M., May to October.

We are in an area dubbed "Chemical Valley" now, where the Shell Canada • CORUNNA dock can load three tankers at a time. Barbecues, boat watching, and shore fishing in Guthrie Park.

A sparkling spectacle of lights at night; by day the oil refineries and agri-chem plants of the Sarnia southside present the neatest, shiniest grouping in big petroleum.

The oil business and how it came to Sarnia is a story by itself (see feature on pp. 118-19).

In Port Huron, across the river in Michigan, you can watch the river traffic • SARNIA till the sun goes down, then feast on the lights of Sarnia, a panorama of sparklers on velvet. Or cross the Bluewater Bridge and drive through them on the St. Clair Parkway . . . King's Highway 40. Every view is popular.

Sarnia is the largest Canadian city touching Lake Huron, an area including Point Edward, Sarnia Township, and Moore Township within its name coverage. A companion of LaSalle, Father Hennepin, is said to be responsible for the earliest settlement, but the discovery of oil in Lambton County put Sarnia on the map in heavy type.

It was 1858 when the use of kerosene for lighting was in the discovery stages and the first commercial oil field in North America began to flow in southern Ontario. Refineries and shipping docks sprang up almost before the roads did. Teams of horses brought barrels to Sarnia (only one or two barrels at a time in summer when they had to haul through mud and thick trees; more in winter when barrels on sleds slid easily over the ice); later, pipelines carried it to port.

From the first crude experimental refineries have grown today's petro-chemicals, synthetic rubber, resins, and even feed stock plants that under-write Sarnia's economy. Close to shipping and supply, other manufacturers gravitated to the area as well and Sarnia turns out everything from school furniture to auto parts.

It's a true crossroads city. Lake Huron meets the St. Clair River, Hwy. 402 meets the Blue Water Bridge and U.S. Interstate 94, travelers go from VIA

Rail to Amtrak, and the airports offer regularly scheduled flights to Toronto, Cleveland, etc. Unless there are major conventions, it's very easy to find a room. At least 300 campsites are listed in the district.

The **Sarnia Public Library and Art Gallery** on Cristina Street at Wellington has Canadian paintings worth a thousand words and *plenty* of printed syllables to help you see and know the Sarnia-Canadian story more completely. Rotating art exhibits supplement the home collection. Open 9:00 A.M. to 9:00 P.M. Monday through Friday, till 5:30 P.M. on Saturday, 2:00 to 5:00 P.M. Sunday. Free.

The *Duc d'Orleans* is the aristocratically named tour boat available for river cruises starting from the dock south of Centennial Park, downtown. Regular tours, Sunday brunch cruises, etc. . . call 519/337-5152 for specifics, or walk to the riverfront and ask. It's an enjoyable place to stroll anyway, to smell the flowers and watch the boats. In 1981, 2,137 ships stopped at Sarnia to transfer cargo. The number is down a bit now, but there is a lot of action.

Under the Bridge Park is the most popular spot in town on the third Saturday morning in July when sailing participants in the Port Huron-to-Mackinac races come out of their berths in Port Huron's Black River to assemble at the starting line in the big lake. All manner of boats take part, and with the morning sun gleaming on the sails it's a sight to remember . . . and photograph. Check out the date, then come early to get a good spot. Bluewater Bridge crossing toll is fifty cents per *car* at this moment. Rules, customs same as Ambassador Bridge. See Windsor.

Canatara Park, on the shores of Lake Huron, is a large, rambling beauty. The name is Mohawk for "big lake." Wide beach, windsurfing, swimming, barbecues, covered pavilions, ball diamonds, and even a Children's Farm. Buildings are child size, kids can pet the creatures, all for free.

The Bluewater Anglers Association sponsors an extremely lively competition over salmon during the last week in April. In 1982, 1,200 fisher-types took away thousands of dollars' worth of prizes, with the largest catch weighing in at eighteen pounds. For Salmon Derby (other categories for brown, rainbow, and lake trout) information, contact the Sarnia Visitors Bureau.

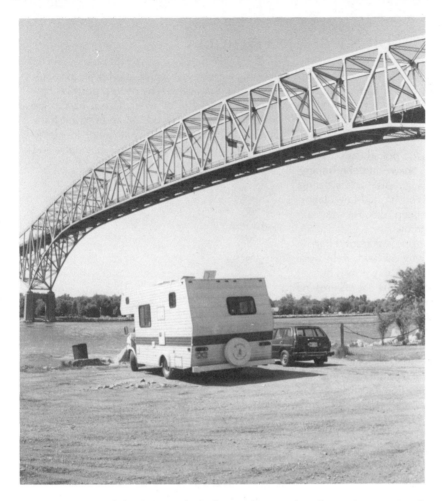

Canada Day Celebrations include fireworks, parades, shows, international food booths, and all else.

The Sarnia and District Visitor and Convention Bureau, 224 North Vidal Street, Sarnia, Ontario N7T 5Y3. 519/336-2400.

Canada's name is thought to have come from a mistaken interpretation of what an Indian chief was saying to explorer Jacques Cartier. The word used was referring to a collection of huts, "Kanatata," but Cartier thought it meant the whole region and wrote it down in the records.

OIL'S WELL IN PETROLIA

Scene: Oil Springs, Ontario, a little backwoods boom town just east of Sarnia, south of Petrolia.

Time: January 16, 1862.

January can be colder than a polar bear's sitzplatz in Ontario, but Hugh N. Shaw—in debt, hungry, and called crazy by his neighbors—was sweating, obsessed with the long rod he had been laboriously screwing into the deep rock. He was making his last attempt to find oil.

There was reason for hope. All around him, in the world's first developing oil field, wells were producing 50 to 800 barrels a day. It was not yet the era of the automobile, but the use of kerosene for lighting had advanced, along with the age-old need for lubricants. Oil was money and a rush was on.

However, Shaw had been digging and drilling for six months and his starting capital of $50.00 was long gone. One more day and he would lose the title to the acre of land he had managed to purchase, and go down in defeat. He broke rock at 155 feet . . . 156 feet . . . 157 feet. . . . Suddenly, there was a thunderous cracking sound and seconds later a geyser of thick, black crude spouted up to the tree tops, breaking the wooden rig and raining muck on a cold, white world.

The world's first gusher!

There was glee and anguish as hundreds of barrels of oil, day after day, spewed out onto the ground with no way to stop it! A phenomenal fountain that called for on-the-spot advances in technology.

Suggestions for plugging the mess got nowhere until a pipe standing twenty feet in the air was installed. By that time, three weeks later, a lake of oil was spreading across the county, darkening the creeks and even starting to slick over Lake St. Clair.

The oil rush turned into a stampede with speculators getting rich, going broke, sending the price of commodities into the stratosphere. Barrels for

shipping were always scarce and horses for hauling mostly unavailable. The nearest port was Sarnia, and to get the oil over there it had to be hauled through the woods on an unpaved track sludgy with mud. Things went better in winter when barrels could be loaded on sleighs and scooted over the ice.

The story of towns like Oil Springs, Petrolia, and others in these regions is well told (no pun intended) at the Oil Museum: the first refineries at Petrolia, the soaring and sudden drops in the market, rags to riches to rags, a town with the best plank roads in the country, to a town broke. The discovery of oil in many other places put the early local refineries out of business, but Sarnia was permanently keyed in to the petroleum industry.

Seven nitro plants in Petrolia are spoken of in the Museum, with the cryptic comment: "They all blew up."

Those who understood the first commercial oil well to be in Pennsylvania are partly right. The Ontario rigs were hand-turned and primitive. Edwin Drake's well near Titusville, PA was the first to use a steam-powered cable-tool drill and the first casing use recorded. He barreled ten to thirty-five barrels a day, and was the first U.S. commercial producer.

More of the story at the Oil Museum, Kelly Road, R.R. #2, Oil Springs, Ontario N0N 1P0. 519/834-2840.

Petrolia today is a pretty town, proud of its old houses and halls. They've got a map for those who'd like to wander and know something about what they're seeing.

If you're here around the third weekend in August, stop and watch the fun at the Steam Threshers Reunion in Brigden. Flea Market, too. On 80 east of 26.

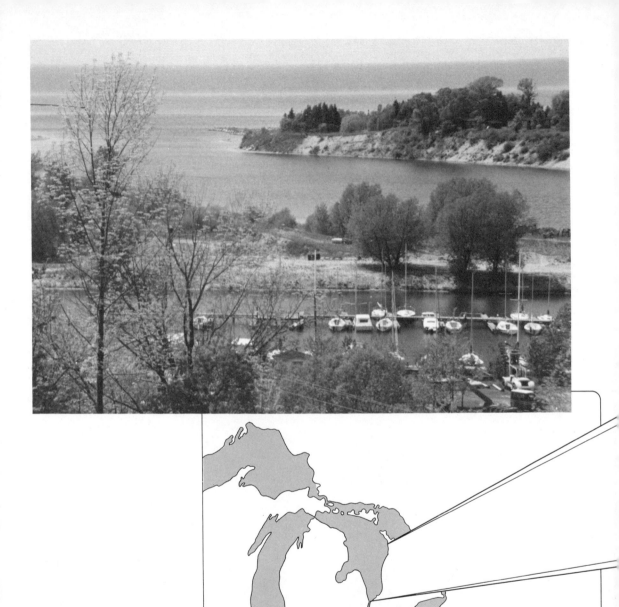

CHAPTER 6
LAKE HURON

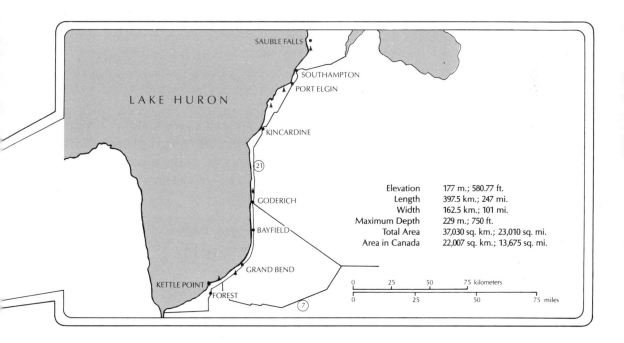

SAUBLE FALLS

SOUTHAMPTON
PORT ELGIN

LAKE HURON

KINCARDINE

GODERICH

BAYFIELD

Elevation	177 m.; 580.77 ft.
Length	397.5 km.; 247 mi.
Width	162.5 km.; 101 mi.
Maximum Depth	229 m.; 750 ft.
Total Area	37,030 sq. km.; 23,010 sq. mi.
Area in Canada	22,007 sq. km.; 13,675 sq. mi.

GRAND BEND

KETTLE POINT
FOREST

0   25   50   75 kilometers
0   25   50   75 miles

THE SECOND LARGEST of the Great Lakes, Huron appears on the earliest maps as "La Mer Douce," the Sweet Sea. Sweet or not, its wide and wondrous horizons didn't seem to excite much interest at first. After stepping over to the west side of the Bruce Peninsula and paddling around a bit, notes were made of it but more attention was paid to the channels to the north. For one thing, it was safer for canoes emerging from the French River into Georgian Bay to follow the shore and stay in the comparative shelter of Manitoulin Island rather than risk the long onslaught of waves from what seemed to be an open sea.

La Salle's ship, the *Griffin,* first sailing vessel to be built on the Great Lakes, came up Lake Huron in 1679 on its voyage of exploration, stopped on the far side of Lake Michigan for a load of furs, and vanished without completing a single round trip. Traffic remained sparse until the founding of Detroit in 1701, increased very gradually during the next century, but boomed with the discovery of copper, as the lumber mills and fisheries grew, with the coming of steam, and the opening of the Sault Locks and Lake Superior to shipments of iron ore and midwest wheat. Traffic on Lake Huron rates high in comparison with any water body in the world.

Saginaw Bay on the Michigan side has Bay City and the southern tip of Lake Huron can claim Sarnia, but otherwise the communities have remained small, low-keyed—and they like it that way. Although Goderich exports salt and sees long ships come into its port, Ontario's golden strand is a vaca-tioner's dream domain; marvelous beaches, pretty towns, and glorious sunsets with the best of fishing to boot.

Caution must be part of your deck gear when venturing out to fish. As Ishmael says in *Moby Dick,* the Great Lakes are "swept by Borean blasts as direful as any that lash the salty wave." The worst storm in Huron's history sank ten freighters, drove twenty others ashore, and took 235 lives.

That said, may you eat your fill of coho.

Kettle Point to Sauble Falls

The southern end of our second largest Great Lake is lined with private property. Take Hwy. 402 out of Sarnia and follow Hwy. 21 through Forest.

FOREST • Once a dense, dark woods, it still wears a canopy of green. Brake at the sound of an oomp-pah-pah, for the Forest Excelsior Band may be perform-ing—the oldest continuously playing band in Canada.

An old duplex house has been turned into the Forest Lambton Museum, where an extensive doll collection and some ancient camera equipment are part of the fun. Open May 24 till Labour Day.

Big farm produce country, so fill your baskets with freshables.

An Indian reserve, it's rimmed with cottages and enormous round "kettle" • KETTLE POINT
stones here and there. Of great interest to geologists, but too big to carry
off . . . which is now against the rules anyway.

Splendid acres of sandy beach, on a shore that tapers gently into the deep • IPPERWASH
blue yonder. Very safe place for a swim. Besides the main park, along a road   PROVINCIAL PARK
to the west are public beach access points and parking lots between
sections of private property.
   Ipperwash offers 283 campsites, 114 of them with electricity. Some are
in an open area near the beach, others in the forested "back rooms" of the
park . . . closer to the trilliums, sphagnum moss, pitcher plants, and rare
(and *tiny*) orchids. Good bass and perch fishing nearby, boat launch ramp,
park store. P.O. Box 1085, Forest, Ontario N0N 1J0. 519/243-2888.

Popular little summer bloomtown between the two big parks, P.F. has at • PORT FRANKS
least four restaurants, some stores, and a motel. The Ausable River meets
the lake here; canoe rentals and marine services available.

Set in one of the largest forests in southwestern Ontario with a ten km. (six • PINERY
mi.) beach, this huge spread of a park has eighty km. of roads (fifty mi.), a   PROVINCIAL PARK
canoe and paddleboat concession on the old Ausable Channel, and enough
bogs, wildflowers, animal life, and birds to keep any naturalist investigating
. . . or pointing. A park nature schedule of slide talks, skits, live demonstrations, guided hikes, etc., plus information center with flora-fauna info.
   One thousand campsites in three camping areas, boat launch, concession.
P.O. Box 490, R.R. #2, Grand Bend, Ontario N0M 1T0. 519/243-2220.

I give this place a rave notice. For a county museum it is top-notch and • LAMBTON
modern with a prize collection of pressed glass pitchers well displayed; old   HERITAGE MUSEUM
prints, clocks, toys, furniture, tools. . . . They have special annual features
(Antique Auto Rally, Antique Engine Fest, Collectors' Day, etc.) plus a
bulletin board with notices of any and every local event. You might find just
your thing happening soon.
   Lambton Heritage Museum, Grand Bend, Ontario N0M 1T0. 519/243-
2600.

Has success spoiled Grand Bend? The beach is so beautiful and the facilities • GRAND BEND
so complete that it has suffered eras of overdose. You can golf, play tennis,
bowl, roller skate, ride horseback, sail, fish, shop, slither down a giant slide,

or eat your way through town. Aspiring skydivers can even take a day-long course *and* their first jump at the airport. There's a Village Daycare Program for parents who'd like a day to themselves (inquire at clerk's office).

The Huron County Playhouse, professional summer theater, is three km. (two mi.) east of Grand Bend off Hwy. 81 on the Stephen B. Line. The summer season goes from June 19 through September 11 (or thereabouts), tickets ranging from $5.50 to $8.00. Contact Huron County Playhouse, Grand Bend, Ontario N0M 1T0. 519/238-8387.

One popular event is the annual Sandcastle Day, a newcomer to the calendar. The '83 competition was held in late August, probably a precedent. Burgerfest, a June spree, has live music, bathing beauty contest, and burgers.

Grand Bend Chamber of Commerce, Box 248, Grand Bend, Ontario N0M 170. 519/238-2001.

BAYFIELD • A leading American magazine noted for its photos declared that Bayfield, Ontario, had the world's second most glorious sunsets (Hawaii's evening skies won first place). I'm not sure how they measure such things, but you can sit on top of the bluff in Bayfield's Pioneer Park and observe for yourself. Lovely.

Bayfield is a genteel place with class-A boutiques and art shops, a bank, two small hotels, and a harbor. Not exactly set up for the tourist trade, one hotel appropriately called the Little Inn (the people who established the inn were named Little) is hitting the guide books as a charmer. Have lunch there if you can.

The Bayfield River forms a big dip in the terrain on the north side of town as it wanders to the lake. Log pier for fishing . . . and watching sunsets.

GODERICH • Queen Elizabeth dubbed Goderich the "prettiest town in Canada," a compliment quoted daily and twice on Sunday by the town fathers. She has a good eye. Goderich is the largest Canadian community completely on Lake Huron, located on a high bluff overlooking the lake and the mouth of the Maitland River . . . and is most certainly pretty.

In the first quarter of the 1800s the land-grant policies in Upper Canada were a jumble. Every township had to set aside a large chunk for the crown and clergy, the rest was often sold to absentee buyers who were simply speculating and had no intention of settling. Then there were all those

124

victims of the War of 1812 whose homes and possessions were lost in battle; they were promised compensation but funds were short. A Scotsman named John Galt was a leader of a scheme to buy up unused Crown Land, turn some of the proceeds over to these folks—and make a profit besides. The Canada Company was formed, a huge area of land called the Huron Tract obtained, and Galt with a friend, one William Dunlap, came over to survey, lay out towns, and make the "bush" easier and more tempting to settle.

Thus Goderich, chosen as site for company headquarters, was born. It didn't turn out to be the great port city as hoped, but it flourished when a huge deposit of pure rock salt was discovered (they were really drilling for oil) 160 m. (700 ft.) below their fruit cellars.

Exploring Goderich must begin in the unique octagonal town "square," with the courthouse at the center, surrounded by lawn and trees; the hub of eight streets like spokes on a wheel. To the casual comer, it's a successful arrangement, and a pleasant place to shop or spend the night. The old Hotel Bedford, on one of the sixteen square corners, has been refurbished with new comforts and appeal. The dining room avoids the standard restaurant blahs very nicely.

Down by the lakeside are a small park, the **Marine Museum** (a ship's forestructure), beach, playground equipment, refreshment stand, and pier. Maybe one of the big lake freighters will come in to dock beside the huge grain or salt elevators—a show in itself that takes place a couple of times a week. A steadier parade of small craft in and out of the river marinas shows the popularity of Goderich as a mooring site.

A chief attraction is the **Huron County Jail** (the old one), now a museum. At 140 years of age, the hexagon-shaped "gaol" (the older English spelling) is the senior public building in Western Ontario and represents a step forward in prison reform. An earlier prison in the district was so insecure that inmates left at night and returned in the morning; criminals, debtors, the aged, and insane were all lumped together. Not only was *this* jail harder to escape from, some effort was made to separate prisoners by severity of crime, sex, and age. But tough! Grass cutting, for example, was done with one prisoner's leg chained to another; one carried the ball weight of the leg iron while the other did the cutting . . . *inside* the walls. The last public hanging in Canada took place here, half a mile from midtown . . . considered too inconveniently far out when it was built.

A totally different side of local history, it's open May to Labour Day, daily,

10:00 A.M. to 5:30 P.M.; from Labour Day to the middle of November, Saturday and Sunday noon to 5:00 P.M. Adults $1.50, seniors and students (13-18) $1.00. Huron Historic Jail, 181 Victoria Street North, Goderich, Ontario N7A 2T8. 519/524-6971.

The **Huron County Pioneer Museum** focuses on the story of motive power from the horse to the tractor to the locomotive. A floral clock and log house are also on the premises. However, with twenty-three rooms and 40,000 square feet of floor space you know the collection is going to be *in depth.* 110 North Street, open all year; May 1 to October 31 Monday through Saturday, 9:00 A.M. to 4:30 P.M., Sunday 1:00 P.M. to 4:30 P.M. Adults $1.50, students and seniors $1.00. Pioneer Museum, Goderich, Ontario N7A 2T8. 519/524-9610.

More than 2,000 campsites are within a dozen miles of Goderich, summer theater at Blyth, great dining at Benmiller's, golf, salmon and trout fishing, harness racing at Clinton.

Big events: Founder's Day and Friendship Days in the last half of June, annual Festival of Arts and Crafts and Sidewalks Days in late July. Write or call the Goderich Tourism Office, 519/524-6600.

• POINT FARMS
PROVINCIAL PARK

The Baron de Tuyle (*where* is Tuyle?) decided that this glistening shoreline was just the place for a splendid European-style hotel. After a few setbacks, a fine hotel with clientele from Toronto and London prospered then dwindled into decline as habits of vacationing families changed. The building is totally gone, but the park boasts an Activity Centre, playing fields, fitness trail, and two campgrounds with a total of 200 sites, 74 with electricity. Reservations taken: R.R. #3, Goderich, Ontario N7A 3X9. 519/524-7124.

The road skims pleasantly northward, mostly out of sight of the lake beyond the trees to the west. Follow the signs to Port Albert, however, through this place that is more a suburb than a town, down into a valley, across a bridge . . . aha! A pretty waterfalls, tiny park, and sign telling how many trout have been caught there so far in the year. There's even a shed for cleaning fish.

On your road map it looks as if turning at Amberly is going to let you drive along the shore, but what you get is the backyards of private property. Turn at the sign for the lighthouse restaurant and you'll find a tiny lakeside park with the Clark Point lighthouse standing guard.

Kincardine is not far ahead.

THE BRUCE PENINSULA

A narrowing finger of land that seems to be trying to poke off contact between Lake Huron and Georgian Bay: a well-watered world with a split personality. The west coast is sandy beaches and low fields; the east side is high with rugged cliffs and rocky shores. No single road runs around the edge and some spots of coast are hard to reach, yet none of it is without interest. Hwy. 6 to Tobermory is side-trip boulevard and worth every detour.

Geologically, this is a continuation of the Niagara escarpment, an arc of limestone that goes from Lake Ontario (the Niagara River flows over part of it) up and around Lake Michigan (see it again along the Garden Peninsula) and down the Door Peninsula into Wisconsin.

The canoes of Champlain and Brulé were probably the first European vessels to be pulled up on the coasts; they didn't stay. So the land was ignored, a jagged out-cropping of stone covered with dense forest, until Captain William Owen of the British Navy charted the long inlet that bears his name. Settlers came in slowly, but they were hampered by laws against cutting down trees. They were allowed to cut for their houses and barns but not to clear a field for planting, which made no fair sense at all. The tallest and best trees went to timber barons with government contracts to supply ship decking and masts, and there was tremendous waste. The settlers eventually won the battle against big timber interests, and local entrepreneurs went after such lumber as was left. Records show more than forty mills between Owen Sound and Tobermory sliced hundreds of thousands of board feet each year, mostly for the expanding railroads who needed ties by the millions.

Fade out those rough days, fade in the present: the Peninsula as vacationland par excellence and one of Nature's favorite showcases.

In its eighty km. (fifty mi.) of length, you are never more than eleven km. (seven mi.) from the big water, that is, the lake or bay. More than 1,600 km. (1,000 mi.) of shoreline; 7,000 campsites, three wildlife sanctuaries, hundreds of shipwrecks in the locality for scuba divers to search out, some top-notch museums, and splendid hiking . . . all for your enjoyment.

One naturalist reported seeing sixty-five bird species within a three-hour time period at Inverhuron Provincial Park during the mid-May migrations. Bluejays, nuthatches, cardinals, buntings, phoebes, herons, gulls; the resident bird list reads like an avarian catalogue. Try to plan an evening at a Provincial Park film presentation or a day walking on a guided tour for some bird lore from an expert.

If you can't tell a viper's bugloss from common mullein (I can't), pick up a wild-flower guide for your walking pack. Everyone spots woodland trilliums, Ontario's provincial flower, but you will be surprised at the number of orchids, at the marsh-land pitcher plants (they live on the carcasses of insects) and—amid the mosses—hepaticas and pasque flowers waiting to have their picture taken. Botany clubs come from far places for that express purpose.

Boat rentals, bait shops, and advice on just what is swimming where and which ones are hungry that day are readily available. (Fishing licenses are required for nonresidents.)

All this largess is called the Grey-Bruce area for the two counties that form the peninsula and its base. More information at every town along the way. Also see Chapter 10.

The Saturday-night special in this tartaned community is the sound of • KINCARDINE
pipers marching from Victoria Park up the street for a few blocks and then
back. Bagpipes and Scottish ancestry everywhere in the town named for
the Earl of Elgin and Kincardine. In the 1870s Kincardine was a busy
grain-shipping port with warehouses full of farm produce, but when the
railroad came, taking cargo more quickly and directly to market, the shipping business faded away. Today only pleasure boats are seen in the harbor.

The white and red lighthouse once held a distillery. No whiskey could
be bought legally on Sunday, but where there's a thirst there's a way. The
owner set a pail outside the door with a tin cup next to it. (Whiskey was
five cents a cup back then.) On Monday morning the cup was full of
nickels and the whiskey gone.

Biggest of all Kincardine events doesn't happen very often. The first Old
Boys' and Old Girls' Reunion took place in 1907 and was such a hugging
success that it was repeated every few years, is now on a ten-year cycle.
Church services, Highland games, dances, dinners, a beauty contest. . . . The
party has won fame far beyond the city limits and draws nonclansmen from
all over.

The Chamber of Commerce has an office in the old town hall, an interesting structure in a community of well-preserved vintage buildings. Kincardine, Ontario N0G 2G0. 519/396-2731.

A day-use only park with no camping, no fees charged. Choice place for a • INVERHURON
picnic, nice beach, boat launch. PROVINCIAL PARK

This is one of the world's largest nuclear power plants. A visitor center is • BRUCE NUCLEAR
open daily from 10:00 A.M. to 5:00 P.M. during July and August. Free public POWER DEVELOPMENT
tours, programs, a film, exhibits, and a bus tour of the development. Write:
Information Office, BNPD, Box 1000, Tiverton, Ontario N0G 2T0. 519/
368-7031, Ext. 3011.

1,150 hectares (over 2,500 acres) of woods, shores, and scenery. Some • MACGREGOR POINT
beaches are sandy, some rocky and rough. There is a bluff marking the edge PROVINCIAL PARK
of the glacial Lake Algonquin and extensive wetlands with all the variety of
flora and fauna such areas incubate. There're 360 campsites, not too many
with electricity; showers, laundromat, self-guided trails, Interpretive Building, and program. For reservations write MacGregor Point, P.O. Box 539,
Port Elgin, Ontario N0H 2C0. 519/832-9056.

PORT ELGIN • The Earl of Elgin and Kincardine might have a Guinness item here; two towns with different names named after the same man. A beautiful beach put P.E. in the resort business long ago, but a golf course, lawn bowling, horseback riding, and band concerts in the park draw visitors, too.

The biggest Scottish Festival in Bruce County starts around June 20 with all things dear to a Scot's heart: Highland Games, dancing competitions, pipe band, et al. Voyageur Days, fishing derbies, Agricultural Fair, Harbour Hi-Jinks . . . you're almost certain to run into something going on.

Spreading maple trees splash Port Elgin with vibrant color in the fall. How beautiful for Kodak!

Port Elgin Chamber of Commerce, Box 69, 515 Goderich Street, Port Elgin, Ontario N0H 2C0. 519/832-2332.

SOUTHAMPTON • A powerful automated beacon of the Chantry Lighthouse on an island one half mile off the public beach marks the approximate half way point for vessels traveling between Sarnia and Sault Ste. Marie: At the mouth of the Saugeen River, Southampton has achieved fair fame for salmon fishing, and for canoeists paddling the ninety-two km. (fifty-five mi.) distance to Hanover (Hanover Park to Denny's Dam). The river is placid in many stretches, has small rapids and eddies in others; a good place to learn.

BRUCE COUNTY • Started in a stately old schoolhouse, then added a modern wing with a
MUSEUM large central gallery featuring major exhibits, both touring shows and items from its own collections. A two-story log house and 1873 log school building are also on the grounds. Very good show. One block north and a block east of Hwy. 21, mid-May and June, open daily 1:00 to 5:00 P.M.; July and August, Monday through Saturday 10:00 A.M. to 5:00 P.M., Sunday doors open at 1:00 P.M. Closed January. 519/797-3644.

Southampton Chamber of Commerce, P.O. Box 464, Southampton, Ontario N0H 2L0. 519/797-2215 or 797-2015.

A **Chippewa Indian Reserve** stretches between Southampton and Sauble Beach, so the highway bends inland. Turn at Hwy. 6 and take Co. Rd. 8 to the coast. The **Sauble Beach** beach is a wide, wide highway of its own; an eleven km. (seven mi.) long pleasure zone of sand between the trees and the blue horizons. Surf-hikers' heaven.

SAUBLE FALLS • The Bruce Peninsula does not deal gently with those who want to get past
PROVINCIAL PARK its treacherous rocks, and an old short-cut has been through Colpoys Bay

across the narrow part of the peninsula and into Lake Huron. Along the route Sauble Falls was a spot requiring portage.

The Falls, a long flight of watery steps, once powered a lumber mill, then the Hydro Power Company, but now it's pure recreation. Areas next to the Falls' fishing sanctuary are popular for chinook salmon and rainbow trout, pike and smallmouth bass. Boat ramp and canoe rentals nearby.

Of its 152 campsites, none has electricity. Self-guided trails, interpretive center and program. For reservations: P.O. Box 789, Wiarton, Ontario N0H 2T0. 519/422-1952.

The coves of Oliphant and Howdenvale show a change in the character of the landscape . . . lakescape. The woods are full of resort lodges and fishing sites, while the waters of Pike Bay and Stokes Bay center around small boat marinas, sailing, fishing, and boating in general. From Stokes to Tobermory only occasional service roads go in; largely undeveloped.

CHAPTER 7
GEORGIAN BAY

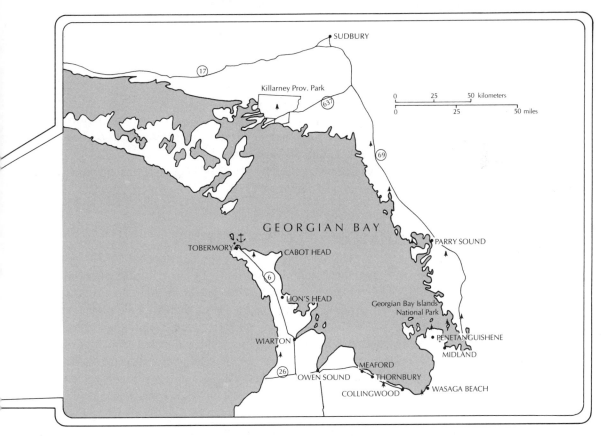

SUDBURY

17

Killarney Prov. Park

637

0   25   50 kilometers
0   25   50 miles

69

GEORGIAN BAY

TOBERMORY

CABOT HEAD

PARRY SOUND

6

LION'S HEAD

Georgian Bay Islands National Park

WIARTON

PENETANGUISHENE

MIDLAND

26

MEAFORD

THORNBURY

OWEN SOUND

COLLINGWOOD

WASAGA BEACH

GEORGIAN BAY is, technically, an enormous annex to Lake Huron, but if the Bruce Peninsula reached to within wading distance of Manitoulin, it would have been labeled the sixth Great Lake. In fact, it was named Lake Manitoulin once by Captain William Owen of the Royal Navy, the Englishman who made the first modern charts of its waters with his own name winding up on one of the Bay's bays.

Renamed after George IV, 190 km. (120 mi.) long and 80 km. (50 mi.) wide, the Bay lies on a southeast to northwest axis with incredible variety along its shores. On the north are pine forests and white calcite hills, nubs of a mountain range once higher and more extensive than the Rockies. Here is wilderness, regions without roads or the sound of motors, where huge scoured rocks guard the shores against intruders. The south shore is a different world, wearing a garland of soft, inviting beaches and hills covered with fruit trees and farms.

On the Bruce side, a rugged wall of limestone, part of the Niagara escarpment, goes right to the peninsula tip; up from the marshlands of the southeast corner, thirty thousand rugged islands characterize the Bay's eastern coast.

The summertime bay is frequently smooth and serene but not to be trusted. Anyone who thinks that because it's a "bay" storms are less severe, is taking a large chance. Georgian Bay is strewn with wrecks; too many of them are twentieth-century pleasure boats.

A dozen provincial parks, historic treasures, long bluffs that give way to gentle villages; to these delights we turn.

TOBERMORY TO SUDBURY

TOBERMORY • Sunsets over Lake Huron, sunrises over Georgian Bay, two harbors swishing with the boats of summer and a submerged Provincial Park. You have reached St. Edmund's Township on the tip of the Bruce Peninsula, and Tobermory, where Hwy. 6 must ride the ferry before continuing north.

The village, named for Tobermory, Scotland, and called "Tub-er-murry" by the locals, has two bays. Business action surrounds "Little Tub," a small inlet of large charm, while "Big Tub" (big in comparison only) is lined with homes and cottages and holds several old shipwrecks below its placid surface.

This was a tough place to settle, even as late as 1870 when the first pioneer paid eighty cents an acre for land. Soil was poor, food was short; there were droughts and fires. The most reliable source of income was lumber, on which the community inched ahead and came to a measure of prosperity. As the woods faded, fishing grew strong and tons of lake trout were taken by commercial fisheries until the 1940 invasion of lamprey eel, lethal scourge of trout. A business that began with sailing craft (the first steam fishing tug was called "the contemptible sea skunk" by its wind-dependent rivals) never recovered.

Ill winds, however, have turned out to be Tobermory's good fortune. Before radar and sonar, with virtually no buoys and few land lights, a ship in a storm was as helpless as a sock in a washtub. At least two dozen vessels broke against the limestone outcroppings and now lie in cold, clear water near Tobermory, inviting thousands of divers each year to come and see their remarkably preserved hulks. Renting and selling diving equipment is part of the village's stock-in-trade.

What nature would preserve man would filch for rec room souvenirs, so Ontario wisely turned a large area into an underwater provincial park and called it **Fathom Five.** The park includes four major islands, a mainland base, nineteen shipwrecks, and underwater caves. **Flower Pot** Island, within the F.F.P.P. perimeter, is part of the **Georgian Bay Islands National Park** system. Those with credentials to prove competence will be able to get information regarding the wreck sites, etc. at the Visitor's Center on Little Tub, open from May till the end of September.

There's more than one way to scan a hulk, however. Nondivers can see the wrecks via the movies at the **Crowsnest Theater-Craftshop-Print Gallery** on Little Tub. Open 9:00 to 9:00, late May till Canadian Thanksgiving in October.

Or they can peek through the thick plates of the new glass-bottom boat, M.V. *Seaview III,* a double-deck touring craft with a schedule designed to fit the comings and goings of the Manitoulin Island Ferry.

The *Seaview, Captain Ahab* Cruise and the *Island Mariner* also take sightseers to Flower Pot Island, where a number of layered rock formations look like the aforementioned, all because the softer bottom rock has worn down at a faster rate than the top layers. Full of trails and caves; a choice place for picnicking and hiking.

Pride of the Canadian ferry fleet is the M.S. *Chi Cheemaun,* largest ever built for this type of service. The name means "big canoe," a fun sort of understatement since the boat holds 600 cars, trailers, trucks, campers, or whatever, and provides a delightful two-hour change of pace for those headed toward Manitoulin. Bus tour service is available for anyone wanting to see the big island sans car (information at Ferry Terminal) and just going for a ride has unwind value. Cafeteria, cocktails. One way, adults $7.00, children under 11 $3.50, and toddlers free. $15.00 for your car, $8.00 for motorcycles; trailers and trucks more, depending on size. Two to four sailings daily, late April to mid-October. Contact Ontario Northland Marine Services, Tobermory, Ontario (519/596-2212) for complete schedule.

As you mosey around Little Tub waiting for the ferry, look toward the tip of land on the north side of town. Wireless Point was the first radio station on the Great Lakes, transmitting and receiving its messages in code from lake vessels. It was, sadly, one of the few stations to pick up distress signals from the ocean liner *Titanic* in those last tragic hours. The station building still stands.

Tobermory is the northern terminus of the Bruce Trail, a hikers-only path that coils its way up from Niagara Falls. The stretch of trail from here to Owen Sound is the crown of the whole scenic walk, especially the Wiarton-Lions Head-Tobermory segments. The Bruce Trail Association begs you to respect the rights of landowners who have given permission to WALK through their property; no fence climbing, flower picking, littering, etc. (Too bad these things have to be mentioned.) If you are able to put one foot in front of the other, put film in your camera and *GO!* Early morning will give you good lighting on the spectacular cliffs and coves. Inquire: Bruce Trail Association, Box 857, Hamilton, Ontario L8N 3N9.

Boaters: Tobermory's docking facilities, listed in Ontario boating guide, include one dock with a draft of thirty-five ft. (ten and a half km.); two others at nine and twelve ft. All have gasoline and diesel fuel, electricity, pump out, etc. For more marine information call or write: Georgian Lakes Travel Association, Simcoe County Building, Midhurst, Ontario L0L 1X0. 705/726-9300.

Special event: Big Canoe Day, third Sunday in June.

Down Hwy. 6 a short piece, the St. Edmunds Museum occupies an old schoolhouse and a log cabin. The rudder of the *Grand Rapids,* a steamer sunk in 1907, sits on the lawn, a reminder that more legacies and legends are within.

CYPRUS LAKE • There was a time in the Earth's history when all the Great Lakes' area lay
PROVINCIAL PARK beneath a warm sea and teemed with living coral, primitive sea creatures, and plants. Eons later great sheets of ice came, retreated, came back three more times, bringing the rock debris of other places, grinding, carving, slicing the face of North America. Cyprus Lake Park is a geologist's textbook

FATHOM FIVE SAMPLER ... AND A WARNING

(Park charts show exact locations)

City of Grand Rapids Steamer, built in 1879. 122.5 feet long, sank in 15 ft. (4.5 m.), October 1907 in Little Tub.

John Walters Schooner, built in 1852. 108 feet long, lies 15 ft. (4.5 m.) deep. Wrecked around 1899. An excellent site for snorklers and novice divers; a lot to see and touch.

W. L. Wetmore Steamer, built in 1871. 213.7 feet long, lies 30 ft. (9 m.) deep. Wrecked in a storm, November 1901. In addition to large amount of timber wreckage, some of the machinery including boiler is still in place.

James C. King Schooner/barge, built 1867. 175 feet long, lies 25 to 95 ft. (7 to 30 m.) deep. The *King* was wrecked while under tow to the *Wetmore* in November 1901. This site good for advanced levels of experience; not for novices or trainees.

Newaygo Steamer, built in 1890. 196 feet long, lies 25 ft. (7 m.) deep. Wrecked during a November 1903 storm. Wreckage scattered, although the main portion lies flat on the bottom. Excellent site for all levels of diving experience.

Philo Scoville Schooner, built in 1863. 139 feet long, lies broken 25 to 95 ft. (7 to 30 m.) deep. Not for novices.

Charles P. Minch Schooner, built in 1867. 157 feet long, lies 20 to 50 ft. (6 to 16 m.) deep. Driven on to the rocks of Cove Island, the wreckage is spread around, some close to shore. An excellent site for all levels of expertise.

Forest City Steamer, built in 1870. 216 feet long, lies 60 to 150 ft. (18 to 46 m.) deep. The F.C. struck Bear's Rump Island in a fog, slid off and sank, June 1904. Recommended for highly advanced divers only.

WATCH IT!
This buoy indicates a restricted boating area:

—You MUST NOT go into these areas without a permit. Permits are given for sport diving, some fishing, and authorized research. Tell the Park people your plans.

WHEREVER YOU DIVE:
—No vessel may anchor into a wreck site . . . a quick way to wreck the wrecks. Use the lake bottom or mooring buoys only.

—All diving must be indicated by use of a clearly visible dive flag flown within 100 ft. (30 m.) of the action.
—No vessels may be anchored unattended. An adult with boat know-how must be on board.
—All Federal and Provincial laws must be obeyed at all times or your next jaunt may be to jail.

For more information about Fathom Five Park and general area diving rules, regulations, lessons, equipment, etc., write Fathom Five Provincial Park, P.O. Box 66, Tobermory, Ontario N0H 2R0. Phone area code 519-2503. (That's right. As of this writing Tobermory still has four-digit telephone numbers!) Call toll free from Canada 1-800-268-3735; from continental U.S. 1-800-828-8585.

and a hiker's glory. There's a well-developed nature program with films and guided walks all summer long. Canoeing, fishing, swimming, and 242 non-electric campsites. Reservations taken. Cyprus Lake Provincial Park, R.R. #1, Tobermory, Ontario N0H 2R0.

CABOT HEAD • Beauty spot. Half the joy is the water's edge scenic drive to reach it.

DYERS BAY • Tiny settlement on the bay of the same name. Look for the Devil's Chimney Pot rock formation.

CAPE CHIN • A bit of England here in the shape of St. Margaret's Church, meticulous replica of a British stone country house of worship. On East Road, north of Lion's Head in Lindsay Township.

Note: There aren't any roads that follow the coast completely, and you are quite apt to go for long stretches seeing nothing but thick foliage and the back side of private homes. The roads that run high along the top of the escarpment will offer you more distant scenic views. Hwy. 6, however, is too far inland for views of either coast.

LION'S HEAD • A population of 530 enjoys the crème de la crème on an ultra-scenic coast. Shopping, a waterfront park, swimming, children's playground, camping, motels, and a good yacht harbor. A 450 cm. (15 ft.) draft at the dock, gas and diesel fuel, launch ramp, mooring space, repair facilities, and more available. Lion's Head Park, P.O. Box 208, Lion's Head, Ontario N0H 1W0. 510/797-3731.

Fly-ins will find a grass runway; scuba divers plenty to go for.

Site of a natural rock bridge.   • BARROW BAY

A large Ojibway settlement that welcomes visitors. Reconstructed Indian • CAPE CROCKER
fort, camp sites, fishing, hiking; admission charged.   INDIAN RESERVE

When the trees were still thick and tall, Colpoy's Bay was brown with • WIARTON
floating logs. Seven sawmills lined the shores, three furniture factories
were located here, and the railway came to Wiarton. There seemed no end
to such prosperity . . . a common delusion. The towering forest giants have
long since been turned into sailing masts, the train station abandoned then
reclaimed as an endearing relic in **Blue Water Park**, and only one furniture
maker is still plying his trade. Modern Wiarton enjoys new life as host to
divers, flyers, boaters, and vacationers of all persuasions. The shopping is
good, camping is available in the park next to beaches and a playground,
and there's a dock to fit your bobbing barge.

Contact Wiarton Yacht Basin, 873 Bay Street, P.O. Box 764, 519/534-1301
or Wiarton Outboard Marine, 771 Bay Street, 519/534-1800. Wiarton's zip
is N0H 2T0.

Wiarton's Golf and Country Club, open to the public, has rentals and
sales. R.R. #4, Durham Road. 519/881-0709.

Visitors are invited to see the facilities of combined **Coast Guard/Flight
Service Station** at the Wiarton Airport—responsible for *all* marine and air
traffic control in the Georgian Bay-Upper Lake Huron area.

It's a busy field. Over 20,000 private and charter flights a year have used
Wiarton's 5,000- and 3,000-foot runways and the Wiarton Flying Club
sponsors an annual "Fly-in" breakfast, attracting upwards of 100 planes.

Part of a warming trend: On Mary's Street a lovely old Wiarton home has
become Glenbellart House, bed and breakfast. There's hardly a better way
to learn about any town than to sit down and be friendly with the home
folks at breakfast.

Annual events: the Rotary Village Fair and Frog Jumping Contest in
August, and the Wiarton Fall Fair in September.

For information call the Clerk's Office, 519/534-1400, or write Box 310,
Wiarton, Ontario N0H 2T0.

ISLAND VIEW DRIVE • Co. Rd. 26 from Wiarton curves south around a nubby peninsula between the cliffs and Georgian Bay, then joins Co. Rd. 1 into Owen Sound. There's a catch. The view is mainly of the trees (just as I said!), although a small

Tune Up a Spring Salad with Fiddleheads...

You'll spot them among the cedars, near the riverbanks, along the paths in the May woods; unopened ferns, still tightly wound and looking like the tuning end of a violin. This tender, edible moment is short, but if you pinch off the coils with only an inch of stem, rinse to remove the brown "paper" outer cover, you can add them to a salad with your favorite light dressing. Or steam and serve with fish, butter and lemon sauce.

However, park rules may forbid picking anything within their boundaries, so check first. The fiddleheads are abundant everywhere and you'll have no trouble finding a place to forage.

township park has picnic tables and access to the Bay. If you hope to swim wear beach shoes. For more of a view, turn at Big Bay (pause for a cone of *homemade* ice cream at the little store), then drive uphill, pulling the car over now and then to look back. Beautiful.

Remember this straight-across road if you're coming from the other direction.

Doorkeeper for the Bruce Peninsula and major center for Bruce and Grey • OWEN SOUND counties. A grain elevator, three and a half miles of docks, plus a long freighter or two indicate a shipping port; a couple of fine museums tell you more. The Pottawatomi and Syndenham rivers wind their way through town toward the Bay, mecca for scuba divers, summer sailors, photographers, and those with an urge to set up an easel and paint.

Tom Thomson, who grew up in Owen Sound, did a lot of that, and in the course of time helped to steer Canadian art to a vibrant realism. Though closely associated with an influential Toronto art fellowship called the Group of Seven, Thomson worked alone and died while on a solitary canoe trip through Algonquin Park in 1917. The **Tom Thomson Memorial Gallery and Museum** tells his story while displaying choice Thomson paintings along with works by the Group, Emily Carr, and other Canadian artists. (See additional Thomson pieces in the McMichael Museum near Toronto.) Open daily in July and August, closed on Mondays the rest of the year when Wednesday and Friday hours are reduced to evenings only, 7:00 to 9:00 P.M. 840 First Avenue West (on the west bank of the Syndenham, next door to the library). Admission.

The **Grey-Owen Sound Counties' Museum** brings together log buildings, wampum belts, farm tools, and prehistory in a first-class exhibit. Demonstrations of the crafts and folk arts of pioneer life—things they did for survival and we do for fun—continue throughout the summer, More fun and nostalgia at the Spoke and Bustle weekend; high bikes, horseless flivvers, and dresses with wondrous backings. Early in August. Write 975 Sixth Street East, Owen Sound, Ontario.

Owen Sound boasts fifteen parks and playgrounds to spread out a picnic lunch, including **Inglis Falls,** with benches, tables, and tumbling water waiting; **Harrison Park** (five minutes from mid-town), with camping, two swimming pools, tennis, wild fowl display, paddle boats, and lawn bowling.

Moppets are certain to like **Story Book Park.** A little train, merry-go-round, animal farm, and fairy tale friends. Picnic tables, campsites. South of Owen Sound, about three km. (two mi.) off Hwy. 6 (10) on Storybook Road. 519/376-2291.

The Owen Sound Marina, Ltd. lists pump out, fuel, laundromat, chandlery, rentals, and storage among its services. 519/376-3999. For other marinas and boat information, contact Owen Sound Chamber of Commerce, 808 Second Avenue East, Owen Sound, Ontario N4K 2H4. 519/376-6261.

Antique sale, usually first week in July (Thursday-Saturday) in Owen Sound Arena. Ask about the Cycle Races in July, the Summerfolk Festival in August, and the Owen Sound Fall Fair in September.

PICNIC AREA • Just east of Woodford on the road to Meaford.

MEAFORD • If all the towns in the Great Lakes area that began with a lumber mill were suddenly to vanish, the map would be nearly blank and Meaford among the missing. Soon after the establishment of that first mill, the streets were platted and "St. Vincent" was the given name. Now changed to Meaford, emphasis has gone from pines to apple trees—7,000 acres of orchards. Even the travel information booth is shaped like a big Georgian apple.

A dog, gone, gets honors at **Beautiful Joe Park**, a serene wooded area on Big Head River with campsites and picnic tables (but not many fire hydrants), and dedicated to a pooch made famous by the writings of Margaret Marshall Saunders. Joe lived in Meaford, is buried (dug his last hole) here in B. J. Park.

What may look at first like city hall also encloses the restored 700-seat opera house, an item of much town pride. Professional dramas and musicals can be seen during July and August, sponsored by the Laughing Water Festival, and extremely popular. Call ahead. Meaford & District Chamber of Commerce, P.O. Box 1298, Meaford, Ontario N0H 1Y0.

THORNBURY • "An apple a day. . . ." Thornburians want to see the old prescription stretched to two or three, since this is the home of the Northern Spy and a locale where the blossoms of May turn the landscape pinkish white. If you can't make it to the spring flower show, come at harvest time for fresh fruit at its succulent best.

The Beaver River runs through Thornbury, and has given rise to an annual homemade boat race, an event described as being low on class, high on fun. That's in late April.

For a pleasantly scenic, bucolic ride, turn down the Beaver Valley Road toward Kimberly. It winds up 305 m. (1,000 ft.) or more, giving you occasional wide views of everything from another segment of the Niagara Escarpment. About ninety m. (100 yd.) west of the road in Eugenia is a lovely park with waterfall and picnic tables. Glorious in the fall!

Coming or going on this excursion, stop in Clarksburg (Thornbury's south suburb) to examine the **Beaver Valley Military Museum** in the former town hall. It houses Grey County's military units of the past 120 years; maybe great-grandpa's regiment. Open all day in July and August, afternoons only May 26-June 30, Labour Day to early November.

The Thornbury Fish lock, only one of its kind in Ontario, allows migrating rainbow trout to get up past the Thornbury Dam and then on to the Beaver River to spawn. The fish are taged, weighed, and measured as they go through, a procedure that can be watched if you make a reservation. No charge. Write to the Ministry of Natural Resources, Fish & Wildlife Division, 611 9th Avenue East, Owen Sound, Ontario N4K 3E4. 519/376-3860.

Beaver Valley Chamber of Commerce, P.O. Box 477, Thornbury, Ontario N0H 2P0. 519/599-3342.

• CRAIGLEITH PROVINCIAL PARK

Shoreside spread offering 170 campsites (12 with electricity), handicap facilities, and something special for a province park: windsurfing rentals and lessons. An Interpretive Building and program fills in on flora, fauna, and fossils . . . trilobits, nautiloids, gastropods, and other creatures stamped forever into the ancient rock.

For information and reservations: Craigleith Provincial Park, R.R. #3, Collingwood, Ontario L9Y 3Z2. 705/445-4467.

• COLLINGWOOD

A zesty town that certainly did well to change its original name, "Hen and Chickens." Boundary wars were long over before the first small cabin was erected near a cove with an island and several tiny islets. Those projections, like a frozen bird with chicks, identified the spot. However, "Hen and Chickens" would not have looked properly dignified on the schedule of the train that finally put a growing community in touch with the world. Collingwood was renamed to honor a British admiral.

The town's history points up some legal messes of the past. During the first half of the nineteenth century, plots of land were granted to people who never came near them. Retired military men, the grandchildren of United Empire Loyalists, and those who had given heroic service were given deeds along with thank-you's. Much of the land near Georgian Bay, called "The Queen's Bush," was held by these persons who wouldn't sell, wouldn't settle, and wouldn't pay their taxes on the ground that the land *really* belonged to the Crown; they were merely the ones solely able to use it. No taxes, no roads, no grist mills, no progress. It was very difficult for legitimate settlers to obtain even a lease, and if the newcomer was poor or uneducated, he was at the class-conscious "mercy" of the courts.

Such legal struggles must have been depressing along with the cold winds and isolation, but the influx of Scots, Germans, Irish, and ex-slaves didn't slow down. The first wood-burning locomotive of the Northern Railroad chugged into Collingwood in 1855; the first paddlewheel steamer, the *Algoma,* came in 1864. Train-to-boat traffic and shipping gradually brought Collingwood prosperity and power.

A builder of versatile boats called skiffs, William Watts, moved into town, launching Collingwood as a shipbuilding center. His first products were about twenty feet long with one of two spritsails, and they became very popular with the commercial fishermen, who kept ordering longer and longer versions with more sail. Steam trawlers took over that operation, but Collingwood was eventually producing lake freighters, tankers, patrol boats for World War II, the ferry *Chi Cheeman,* etc. New innovations to ship design have been their forte, along with loading equipment, winches, and all the hardware needed for a hard-working deck.

There are no tours of the shipyards, but you can stand in a parking lot and see the sterns of giant freighters in drydock, sometimes with their hulls peeled back for repairs.

The hills giving shelter to this stretch of coast are the Blue Mountains, with one 541 m. (1,775 ft.) summit near Collingwood being *the* **Blue Mountain.** In winter its slopes are alive with the sound of schussing; skiers enjoying Ontario's top winter sports area. In summer one of the chairlifts stays busy hoisting visitors to the top for lunch, a super view, and maybe a slip down to the base via a Giant Slide. Take Hwy. 26 to Blue Mountain Road (the pottery of that name is on the corner), follow to the lift by Blue Mountain Lodge, pay a fee, and enjoy. Or just keep driving up, past the Scenic Caves, to the top. A summit cafe is open along with the lift from July 1 to Labour Day, Mondays excepted.

Paths in and around the **Scenic Caves** offer something of a workout, depending on how far you want to go. Natural, fortress-like walls and niches

were used by the Tobacco and Petun Indians to defend against Iroquois raiders; rare fossils and ferns give modern botanists and geologists an intriguing outdoor study hall. Open from May till the end of September, morning till evening. Admission charged.

Concerts under the stars near the Blue Mountain Ski Resort are put on by music students of Georgian College, Barrie. Frequent summer treat and free. Call 519/445-0231 for program information.

Using a fine local clay and simple, pleasing designs, Collingwood's **Blue Mountain Pottery** turns out enormous numbers of vases, bowls, mugs, and general tableware. Somehow, no two pieces emerge from the potters' hands and the 2,000°F. ovens looking exactly alike; the company is happy to have you tour their plant to see how it's all done. Factory and retail outlet, with seconds, on Hwy. 26, just where you turned to go up the mountain. 705/445-6530 or 445-3000.

Across the road the sweet business of candy making goes on in full view (but behind glass). Build up the need for a sugar fix as butterscotch, peppermint, and chocolate are cooked, twisted, and dripped into irresistible morsels. A collection of antique candy-making equipment and sweets parlour is part of the lure, every day from 9:00 A.M. till 7:00 P.M.

Poke awhile through the **Collingwood Museum.** Ancient and recent Indian lore, arts and crafts of the pioneers, lots of marine history. Located in Memorial Park, First and St. Paul streets.

Sunset Park has camping for tents and trailers, picnic space and beach, a municipal recreation site. There's a Collingwood airport, two golf courses, charter boat rentals, go-carts, etc.

For more information: Collingwood Chamber of Commerce, 101 Huronatio Street, Collingwood, Ontario L9Y 2L9. 705/445-0221.

WASAGA BEACH • Fourteen km. (nine mi.) of beach sandwiched between businesses and bay, PROVINCIAL PARK carefully sectioned so that natural areas, picnic and playground places, and the near carnival spots are decently away from each other. You can do a lot with nine miles. No camping, but not to worry; the park border is lined with resorts, private campgrounds, and motels.

Endless sand dunes, playgrounds, boardwalks, bike trails, hike trails, and all that blue water. Excellent spring and fall fishing for rainbow trout; nature center, guided hikes.

Gets *crowded* on summer weekends, but midweek, mornings, and spring-fall days are most inviting.

WASAGA BEACH • *Everybody* comes to Wasaga Beach and that can be a little much on a hot day, but there are things here you wouldn't want to miss. The **Museum of the Upper Lakes** is one of them.

Occupying its own island, the Upper Lakes Museum is sure-fire, and that includes the cannons that go off periodically. An unusual theater gives vivid electronic lessons on the War of 1812 and the supply schooner *Nancy*'s revenge against U.S. forces. Over in the Museum are cutaway models of Great Lakes vessels from La Salle's *Griffin* (the first "European" vessel lost on the lakes) to freighters and modern yachts.

Wander among anchors, buoys, etc. along the paths and footbridge to Tower Island to inspect the model lighthouse.

The Museum is part of the Heritage Project of **Huronia Historical Parks.** As you follow the coast eastward, you'll come to others.

At Wasaga Beach leave Hwy. 26 for #92, then turn up Co. Rd. 29 if you want to follow the exact contour of the Bay. It's beach-beach-beach for twenty and more communities on the east coast of Nottawaga Bay, an area thick with cottages and resorts. I suggest cutting over to Co. Rd. 6 and continue to Thunder Bay, Thunder Beach, and a public wharf. The islands you see on your Ontario road map are part of an Indian reservation.

Awesome Awenda's **Nipissing Bluffs,** deep woods, and scenic views might • AWENDA
keep you hiking and taking pictures till dark. Fishing, canoeing, 150   PROVINCIAL PARK
generous-sized campsites (no electricity), handicap facilities, showers,
laundromat, and swimming, too. Make a reservation early. P.O. Box 973,
Penetanguishene, Ontario K0M 2B0. 705/549-2231.

P.S. *Don't, DON'T* stay on a trail until dark. That's dangerous and dumb.

Hard to spell and discouraging for visitors to pronounce at first; a simple • PENETANGUISHENE
"Pen-tang" will do. It means "Place of Rolling White Sands."

At the south end of this pretty town of 5,400 souls are two angels
representing harmony between the region's French and English cultures . . .
a happy irony. Scrutiny of the facts reveals fairly nasty Anglo-French tension
(many of the French were descendants of the Voyageurs and their Indian
wives). Angels they weren't and harmony didn't come overnight. It's nice
to know, however, that some hatchets are finally buried and today there is
much genuine mutual pride in all contributors to area history.

The naval and military establishments at Penetanguishene (follow the
signs to the end of Church Street) were built by the British after the War of
1812. It seemed ideal; an almost hidden harbor that was big enough to
moor the "inland" fleet, serve as supply base and repair dock. One forgets
that such posts ran on short supplies, rigid routines, and months of bore-
dom. Lumber had to be cut, the stores restocked, fires built, and someone
had to stand sentry, regardless of the cold. The officers had small, comfortable houses but lowly sailors were jammed into one-room barracks with
hammock beds. In reconstructed buildings the Navy tale is told, aided by
costumed guides who explain as you wander.

The Army joined the Navy for a couple of years. At their end of the
Establishment site, Redcoats put on a musket-firing demonstration, ex-
plaining that half the strategy was to look so splendid in uniform and
bearing that any enemy would be overcome by the sheer brilliance of the
show. These and other quaint ideas are shared. Visitors' Center, docking,
picnic tables, etc., but no refreshments. Wear comfortable shoes for this
excellent display. Open daily 10:00 A.M. to 6:00 P.M., Victoria Day weekend
in May to Labour Day. Last admission 4:30 P.M. Small charge. Write: Huronia
Historical Parks, P.O. Box 160, Midland, Ontario L4R 4K8. 705/526-7838.
Ask about Liberty Days in July, Descendants' Day in August.

Housed in an 1875 office and general store, the Penetanguishene Centennial Museum concentrates on the *town's* side of area history. A horse-

drawn fire wagon stands in the village's original firehouse; other bygone paraphernalia in abundance. Open daily from Victoria Day to Labour Day.

From Penetang's town dock the M.S. *Georgian Queen* leaves daily at 2:00 for a three-hour cruise among a sprinkling of Georgian Bay's 30,000 islands. Champlain's landing, points of military interest, snacks, and sunshine. July and August, $6.00 adults, $3.00 children. Argee Boat Cruises, Ltd., P.O. Box 205, Penetanguishene, Ontario L0K 1P0. Summer phone 705/549-7795.

MIDLAND • Ontario's first community started as home base for the Jesuits; a tiny morsel of the Old World in a vast, devouring wilderness. For this counterclockwise Bay Tour the eastern edge is the wrong side of town to begin, but chronologically that's where "knowing Midland" starts.

"Saint-Marie Among the Hurons" was the mission intended as headquarters and a retreat where priests and lay workers struggling in lonely forest outposts could find a few creature comforts half a world from home . . . plus companions who spoke French. It was a site that influenced the exploration and development of the whole continent, while bringing cruel martyrdom to its founders, Fathers Brebeuf, Lalemant, and Daniel.

Visitors to the reconstruction see a film on the ten-year life of the enclave, a film ending with the French setting their buildings on fire before fleeing to evade the ferocious Iroquois.

The end, as always, turns out to be a new beginning. In moments you are walking into the painstakingly authentic reconstruction, complete to black-robed priest, Indian traders, and pigs in a rough log barn. The stockade fence seems fortlike, but this was a totally peaceful project with the first hospital ever to care for Indian patients.

Next to the Church of Saint Joseph (used for public services today) is a wigwam and longhouse for visiting nomadic hunters and Hurons. It's the real thing: bent saplings tied with vines, covered with bark. The longhouse accommodated several families and one wonders how their eyes coped with the darkness and smoke.

Wait for a guide or wander through the three-acre village and museum on your own. Costumed craftsmen show how everything used was made on the spot with materials culled from woods and waters. You may want to

try a few ideas yourself or buy samples from the shop in the Visitors' Centre.

Sainte-Marie is about five km. (three mi.) east of Midland; follow "Wye Valley Heritage" signs to Hwy. 12. Open daily, Victoria Day in May (around the 26th) to Labour Day, 10:00 A.M. to 6:00 P.M. and to Canadian Thanksgiving 10 A.M. to 5:00 P.M. Admission $1.50 adults, 25¢ children, 75¢ students. Special family rate. Groups need a reservation. Write Huronia Historical Parks, P.O. Box 160, Midland, Ontario L4R 4K8. 705/526-7838.

WYE MARSH WILDLIFE CENTER • Should be part of your Ste-Marie day. Self-guiding nature trails and a floating marsh boardwalk take you into a border world between marine and land life. Indoor theater display hall and wild-wise folks will answer questions. Hwy. 12, next to the Village, open Victoria Day to Thanksgiving.

MARTYR'S SHRINE • Remembers victims of the struggles between Iroquois, Hurons, and French. Three of the eight men honored, Fathers Brebeuf, Daniel, and Lalemant, were first in North America to be canonized by the Roman Catholic Church. Pilgrimages are conducted to the twin-spired Shrine Church; grounds open and services held from 9:00 A.M. to dusk, from late May to Canadian Thanksgiving in October. Write: Director, St. Mary's Shrine, Midland, Ontario L4R 4L3. 705/526-6121.

Closer to the heart of town and Little Lake Park, the **Huron Indian Village** is full scale, straight from the source, and better than a dozen books on the subject. A film entitled "The Huron and How He Lived" fills in details not readily visible.

An adjacent museum has a generous display of Indian and pioneer tools, pottery, clothing, etc., plus photos and models of ships . . . an extensive record of Great Lakes maritime history. The Gallery goes into the prehistoric past, 500 million years of Georgian Bay geology, and the works of artists, sculptors, and map-makers reflecting first impressions of the region. Huronia Museum and Gallery of Historic Huronia and Huron Village, Box 638, Midland, Ontario L4R 4P4. 705/526-2844.

On the light side of Midland history, it must be told how the British-American Lumber Company took a leap into the future when it built its own electric plant in 1881 and lit up the mill and work yards with arc lamps. Excursion steamers and special trains brought folks into town just to see the night wonders.

There's a lot of charm to this little city; pretty houses and shady streets.

Stroll down King Street, stopping at 345, the **Artisan's Market Place,** where over 100 local craftspeople sell a variety of nifty products. Photographers should check into the Budd Watson Gallery, a large, privately owned showplace for displays of top lens work. Watson has had one-man shows at the Kodak Gallery in New York and other prestigious backdrops.

"The Castle" on Balm Beach Road is a storefront as rare as a magic sword stuck in a rock. Turrets, drawbridge, even a dragon at the walls breathing fire now and then. Wicker, brass (magic wands?), and a dungeon within.

The harbor has enough marinas for a summer navy; berthing for hundreds of transients, all the facilities. About once a week a long lake freighter pulls in, and generally the dockside area is a good place to sit and boat watch.

Or take a ride. 30,000 Islands!? By geological survey count there're more than 50,000 islands in eastern Georgian Bay, one of the highest concentrations of islands in the world.

Miss Midland and *Lady Midland* leave the town dock three or four times a day for one- or three-hour island viewing cruises—as long as thirty or more passengers show up. On a clear day nothing could be more pleasant. $8.50 for long rides, $5.00 for short ones. Children about half. Reservations suggested. Write R. J. Frames & Sons, Ltd., Box 546, Midland, Ontario L4R 4L3. 705/526-6783.

If you like to see it all by air, rides are available at the Huronia Airport. $25 for a fifteen- to twenty-minute trip; flight routes open to discussion. Contact Box 256, Perkinsfield, Ontario L0L 2J0. 705/526-8451.

Shondecti is a Huron word for "they returned to such a place," and it's the name of an unusual celebration that's become one of the most popular special events in the area. Meant to commemorate the arrival of canoe flotillas from "Kebec" (Quebec) three centuries ago, the schedule includes a reenactment of the complete voyage in canoes, a canoe portage parade, canoe races, canoe regattas, etc. Around the second weekend in July.

Find out more from the Midland Chamber of Commerce, 298 First Street North, Midland, Ontario L4R 3N9. 705/526-7884.

The slender peninsula at the north end of the village was Ontario's first • PORT MCNICOLL stone quarry. Surrounded by cottages. Public boat ramp on Hog Bay.

On Hwy. 12 between Port NcNicoll and Victoria Harbour. • PICNIC AREA

VICTORIA HARBOUR • A public wharf at the point of this village-peninsula, where fishing for rainbow trout is the business of the day.

In short order you are around Sturgeon Bay and will leave Hwy. 12 for 69 . . . northward. Public wharf and boat ramp available at Waubaushene, before you cross the bridge at Matchedash Bay.

WAUBAUSHENE • A nature preserve unique for its clear record of prehistoric lake levels.
CONSERVATION AREA

PORT SEVERN • Western end of a meandering and positively pleasant water link between Lake Ontario and Georgian Bay that stretches for 384 km. (240 mi.) along streams and lakes with names like Lovesick and Sparrow. At least forty locks, one named for Glenn Miller. Biggest pond along the way is Lake Simcoe, a goal for most of the boaters entering at this point. Over near Severn Falls, about twenty-six km. (sixteen mi.) away, is Big Chute Marine Railway, a gadget you can hardly find anywhere. Boats are put on railcars and hauled up to the next water level . . . the easy way.

Lock #44 at Port Severn is the only manual lock left in the system.

HONEY HARBOUR • Sweet name for a pretty little spot (population 240) buzzing with summer visitors, many of them here to hail a water taxi to Georgian Bay Islands National Park for camping and hiking.

GEORGIAN BAY ISLANDS • More than sixty-five islands or parts of islands, mostly in the southeastern
NATIONAL PARK part of the Bay. The largest is long, angular Beausolel Island, popular with those who can tote their own gear. Pickerel, pike, perch, bass, whitefish lure anglers; nesting and migrating waterfowl lure the bird watchers. Or go just to sit and stare at the trees.

No charge for day users, $5.00 per day for semi-serviced campsites, $3.00 for primitive sites. Overnight boat docking $3.00 to $9.00, depending on the length of your boat.

Park Superintendent, Georgian Bay Islands National Park, Box 28, Honey Harbour, Ontario P0E 1E0. 705/756-2415.

SIX MILE LAKE • If you've never paddled your own canoe, maybe this will get you started. A
PROVINCIAL PARK canoe skills program is part of the facility, along with 192 rustic campsites, swimming, boat ramp, interpretive program, and self-guided trails. Reservations taken. Six Mile Lake Provincial Park, Box 340, Coldwater, Ontario L0K 1E0. 705/756-2746.

MUSKOKA LAKES

Pine-filled islands and shimmering blue lakes; reasons for Muskoka popularity are as clear as the crystal air.

The district reaches from Algonquin Park to Georgian Bay, from Gravenhurst to a bit north of Huntsville. In the halcyon days before World War I, wealthy vacationers built palace-cottages on Muskoka Lake, on Joseph or Rosseau, while those who couldn't afford their own posh layouts could stay at luxury resorts. Even the New York crowd came up. In 1903 eight lake steamers, swarms of lesser launches, and supply boats were loading the lakes with traffic. There is still a lot of class around.

The best way to see the grand old houses is by boat, as they were built to face the water and the road-side views aren't quite as elegant.

The area has a zillion resorts, campgrounds, boat rentals, etc. and still, by the very nature of the water-land ratio, almost everything seems fairly secluded and uncrowded.

Gravenhurst The town focal point is an elegant old opera house where you might check on the offerings of summer theater. The restored birthplace of **Dr. Norman Bethune,** famed medical missionary to China, is open, along with a Visitor's Centre and exhibit of Chinese gifts. 235 John Street. Free. Call 705/687-4261 for hours. *Lady Muskoka*, a 200-passenger cruiser, makes a gentle way to spend two and a half hours, seeing the palaces of the past. Muskoka Bay Dock, Sagamo Drive. Adults $8.00, children $4.00. S.S. *Segwun*, elegant passenger ship from Victorian days, is carefully restored and offers a variety of cruises, dining, cocktails, and snacks from May to Thanksgiving. Government Dock, call 705/687-8185 for reservations or more information.

Bracebridge The moppets in your car will love **Santa's Village.** I'm not always keen on these cutesy attempts but this succeeds far better than most. Pet farm, paddlewheel boat, Candy Cane Express, and those kid rope bridges, etc. that any lively adult will have a hard time resisting. Open late May to Labour Day. Follow the signs or call 705/645-2512. Around $2.00 adults, $1.00 children, rides extra. The **Woodchester Villa**, an octagonal house reached by following the signs from the south end of Manitoba Street, was built in 1882, way ahead of its time. Poured concrete, indoor lavatories, water pressure system, etc. Open from early June to Labour Day, weekends in the fall. Next door to the first Presbyterian church in Bracebridge, now a museum. Small admission. 705/645-8793. Or look into the **Port Carling Cruise,** Port Carling locks. 705/765-3307.

Huntsville More cruises are available on the *Britannia*, Lake of Bays Boat cruises (705/635-2443) forty km. (twenty-five mi.) southeast of town, or the *Miss White Pine*, a tour of Fairy Lake, Lake Muskoka canal and river, etc. Government dock, in town; call 705/635-2443.

The **Muskoka Pioneer Village Museum** will tell you more about the local history than any number of volumes. Three pioneer homes, store, barn, church, sawmill . . . the early works. In **Huntsville Memorial Park**, adjacent to the arena. Exit at Muskoka Rd. 3 to Brunel Road. Late May to Labour Day, 10:00 A.M. to 5:00 P.M.; reduced hours the rest of the year. Small admission. 705/789-4657.

It's a stunning area during the fall color show, last two weeks in September. To find out more write to the Muskoka Lakes Tourist Association, Box 58, Gravenhurst, Ontario P0C 1G0.

Yes, Audrey Hepburn, there really *is* a Moon River, more given to fish than • MOON RIVER romance, however. Canoe route between the Bay and Lake Muskoka.
Foot's Bay, MacTier (hospital), Lake Joseph, Gordon Bay. Going toward Parry Sound the tiny communities zip past before you know you've

arrived. Summer supplies everywhere; boats to rent, cottages to call your own for awhile, resorts in large supply. Outdoor people have a hard time leaving a lovely district.

Public picnic facilities just off Hwy. 69 on 169 or near the road to Hamer Bay.

OASTLER LAKE • People come to hike, swim, and catch the next canoe. O.L.P.P. has 150
PROVINCIAL PARK campsites (none with electricity), and an excellent beach—the kind that can get fairly crowded on a hot day. Great at off-moments. Reservations taken. Oastler Lake Provincial Park, 4 Miller Street, Parry Sound, Ontario P2A 1S8. 705/378-2401.

PARRY SOUND • Young William Beatty was a steady Methodist when he came with his father and brothers in 1863 on a timber search—and he never really left. After finishing school, Beatty returned to become resident manager of the company mill and the town that was laid out by the family as their firm grew. Eventually William bought out the others' interest and focused his zeal on being a model patron-tycoon-landlord, banning all liquor and demanding church attendance.

Parry Sound established road connections with the Muskoka district, a steamer tie with Collingwood, and prospered. For those who lived up to Beatty's rules, it was a good place to live. The casual visitor could guess that it still is. On **Tower Hill** a lookout platform puts viewers at bird level; another good place to look around is from **Rose Point Swing Bridge.** A high trestle over Bay Street brings freight and VIA rail passengers to town, a marvelous way to come. At the end of the street you board the *Island Queen* for a three-hour cruise among a few hundred of the 30,000 islands. Heated boats with snack bars, wheelchair facilities, etc. Only sleet, hail, and dark of night could spoil a cruise . . . in which case it's no go. From June to mid-October; mid-summer, two trips a day. Adults $8.00, children under 12 $4.00, under six free. Contact Mr. Roy Anderson, 30,000 Islands Cruise Lines, Inc., 9 Bay Street, Parry Sound, Ontario P2A 1S4. 705/746-2311.

Alligators, plainly out of their home swamps, are the subject for discussion at the **Reptile House and Craft Shop.** Also lizards and snakes. (It does not seem to make the beasts nervous to have folks nearby who *could* easily turn them into shoes and purses.) Students from Guelph University act as tour guides, will explain everything except why reptiles are so strangely fascinating. Picnic area, too. Adults $1.50, children and seniors 75¢. Reptile House, R.R. #2, Parry Sound, Ontario P2A 2W8. 705/378-2475.

A memorable musical event attracting world-renowned artists—popular and classical—is Parry Sound's Festival of the Sound, a July-August special. In late August, a merrie Highland Fling, bagpipes, tossing the caber, highland dancing, and Scottish pageantry.

Earlier by four months is a festival of a different kind: when the smelt are running the two-legged dippers (who threaten to outnumber the fish) turn the time into a full-fledged jamboree. Walleyes and yellow pickerel start biting at the river mouths about that time.

The Ojibways have a reservation, **Parry Island,** also on the Bay, and hold a fall Indian Fair featuring Indian dances and sale of handicrafts.

Boat docking, launch ramps, rentals, resorts, and campsites; Parry Sound Resort Association, P.O. Box 401, Parry Sound, Ontario P2A 2X4. 705/746-5621.

A rugged peninsula jutting into the Sound's clear waters; the stuff scenic postcards are made of. Swimming, scuba diving, sailing, hiking. A whopping 893 campsites for those who don't need their electric blankets; rustic facilities, interpretive program. Make a reservation. Killbear Provincial Park, P.O. Box 71, R.R. #1, Nobel, Ontario P0G 1G0. 705/342-5312. • KILLBEAR PROVINCIAL PARK

Snug Harbour, Snug Haven, Dillon, Carling. Ignored by the guidebooks but the life of any region are the tiny centers where friendly people are ready to help you dock your boat, point to the best eateries, and offer advice on fishing. Stop, gaze, and listen to the talk in the lore-loaded spots for information unavailable to your advisors back in the visitors' centers. . . . On the other hand, ever notice how the things visitors come miles to see are ignored by local folks?

Fishermen will like this smallish spread with access to Georgian Bay, boat rentals and docks nearby. There are eighty-two campsites, but no electricity, no playground, nor interpretive center. Reservations. Sturgeon Bay Provincial Park, Pointe au Baril P.O., Pointe au Baril, Ontario P0G 1K0. 705/366-2521. • STURGEON BAY PROVINCIAL PARK

Learn to canoe and then go on a group outing. It's just one of the opportunities offered along with hiking, swimming, etc. Two colonies of Great Blue Herons are nested here, making bird watchers especially happy. Pine woods, • GRUNDY LAKE PROVINCIAL PARK rough terrain, lakes, and 520 nonelectric campsites. Reservations. Britt P.O., R.R. #1, Britt, Ontario P0G 1A0. 705/383-2286.

THE FRENCH RIVER AREA • Up from Montreal on the Ottawa River, across Lake Nipissing, along the French River (first called the River of Sorcerers)... then out into the wide sweet waters of Georgian Bay came Champlain, Brule, voyageurs, trappers, missionaries, Indians; the French River, the westward connection, is one of the most historically important rivers on the continent. Today it wins new popularity as a recreational stream and a test for canoeing skills.

Picnic area where the highway crosses, but keep an eye on your tots. Steep, sleek, and stony banks.

KILLARNEY PROVINCIAL PARK • A long detour down Co. Rd. 637 (a picnic area about half way on Tyson Lake) to the park and little village of the same name. The community was once a fur trading post, now deals with supplies for campers in the huge wilderness park.

The "Group of Seven" artists were inspired in Killarney and you'll see why. Sixty km. (forty mi.) of trails traverse the quartzite mountains, turquoise lakes, and hidden waterfalls. Demonstrations are given in canoe safety, camping skills; guided hikes available. The 110 interior campsites are *primitive,* there's lots of splendid canoeing, *no* motors.

Come again in winter with your cross country skis! Killarney Provincial Park, George Lake, Killarney, Ontario P0M 2A0. 705/287-2368.

For a "civilization break," I recommend dinner at the Killarney Mountain Lodge in the village. You'll want to check in.

The surprise city. What's all this doing up here? Theater, parks, museums, • SUDBURY horse racing . . . and houses built tightly against huge rocks.

As the result of some unknown ancient trauma (volcano? meteor?), the Sudbury basin has unusual mineral treasures close to its surface, producing gold, silver, copper, cobalt, platinum, iron, and about eighty-five percent of the world's nickel.

The first comers, however, "mined" the trees. In the early 1870s, disastrous fires in Chicago, Wisconsin, and Michigan, plus the expanding railroads' insatiable need for ties, brought lumbermen to the northern forests where they cut and hauled away logs like hungry hordes looting a food bin. The supply couldn't last; in ten years the land was bleak and stripped, left to the wolves and winter winds.

Meanwhile, far away on the Pacific coast, British Columbia was saying, "Yes, we will join the Dominion IF you bring us a transcontinental railroad." Thus began the Canadian Pacific Railroad's great push to the west and to the accidental discovery of the Sudbury mineral wealth. Due to an error in surveying the right-of-way, the track builders came around Lake Nipissing in a wider arc than intended and a metalwise blacksmith on the construction crew hit a chunk of nickel-copper ore with his pick. The copper rush followed instantly . . . but seemed destined for a quick fade-out until technology came to the rescue. Ores turned out to be poor quality and it was not worth the expense of extracting the "worthless" nickel mixed in with the copper. Then new techniques and the discovery that nickel added to iron made a much stronger grade of steel put Sudbury in the mining business. "Poor quality" transformed into a $7,500,000,000 (that's *billions*) nickel-copper deposit.

At **Copper Cliff,** six km. (four mi.) west of Sudbury's heart, is the world's highest freestanding smokestack, a 637-footer (194 m.) that can be seen far out of town and marks the site of the International Nickel Company of Canada Ltd.'s smelter. The **Copper Cliff Museum's** collection of antiques fills an authentic, original settler's cabin. More of the Sudbury story, from logs to mines, it's on Balsam Street, open July and August six days a week.

Across town the **Falconbridge Nickel Mines, Ltd.** has tours of their mine smelter complex during summer months; visitors are advised to contact hosts in advance. It's free, but no one under twelve is admitted. Contact Public Affairs Dept., Falconbridge Nickel Mines, Falconbridge, Ontario P0M 1S0. 705/693-2761.

The Sudbury Science Centre's **Big Nickel Mine** is a top-notch show. Visitors can descend a twenty m. (sixty-six ft.) "mine shaft," get next to the machinery, watch men prepare for blasting, and learn what a tope is or what mucking is all about. *Big* attraction is the nine-meter (thirty-foot) high stainless steel replica of the 1951 Canadian commemorative five cent piece. Numismatic Park, Lorne Street, off Hwy. 17 West. Open daily from May till mid-October. 705/673-5659.

Crossing town is in itself an experience for those used to cities built on flat places or even "ordinary" hills. Sudbury is a city on a rock pile (the Canadian Shield in the geology books), and enormous boulders seem to be jutting out of everyone's backyard. The rocks and unusual outlying terrain have a stark look, so much like the moon that the first astronauts were brought to Sudbury for lunar landing practice. The bareness comes from years and years of smelter fumes. Happily, through an all-out citizens' effort, the condition is being corrected . . . green is coming back to heal the scars.

One of the most spectacular free sights around town is the late day slag-pouring operation, seen from Hwy. 144. Like watching a lava flow in a landscape, nothing short of eerie.

They managed to find enough flat space for a horse track; harness racing is every Wednesday and Saturday, all year round, at **Sudbury Downs.** Or try the theater-in-the-park, **Bell Park**, where programs of band concerts, rock festivals, and plays are presented during the summer. Harris and York streets.

Bilingual guides (French is a prime language in Sudbury) are available in the **Flour Mill Heritage Museum,** full of antique furniture, tools, weapons, etc., at 514 Notre Dame Boulevard, mid-June to Labour Day, Monday through Friday. The **Museum and Arts Centre,** ensconced in a 1906 home and coach house, has a lovely setting for its treasures and continuously changing exhibits. St. John Street at Nelson Street; open all year, daily afternoons and Tuesday and Friday evenings. Closed Mondays.

For a list of inns, eateries, parks with camping, etc., stop at the Sudbury

Convention & Visitor Services Bureau on Civic Square, or write to the above, Box 1000, 200 Brady Street Civic Centre, Sudbury, Ontario P3E 4S5. 705/674-3141.

Heading west on Hwy. 17, Fairbank is near enough to serve the purposes of this guide. The park is located on what is called the Sudbury Nickel Irruptive (basin . . . earth dent). A pleasant family recreation site on Fairbank Lake, it boasts hiking trails and a pocket of southern trees (sugar maple and yellow birch) that you can hardly find hereabouts. Fishing is good, swimming is cold. The 160 campsites have tables, a fireplace, and space, but no electricity. Reservations taken. Fairbank Provincial Park, P.O. Box 3500, Station "A," Sudbury, Ontario P3A 4S2. 705/522-7823.

• FAIRBANK PROVINCIAL PARK

THE REMARKABLE INDIAN CANOE

... the forest's life was in it,
All its mystery and its magic,
All the lightness of the birch tree,
All the toughness of the cedar,
All the larch's simple sinews;
And it floated on the river
Like a yellow leaf in autumn,
Like a yellow water lily.
—*From Longfellow's "Song of Hiawatha"*

While Indians in other parts of the continent were scooping out log canoes in the same manner used by primitive Goths an ocean away and centuries before, the northern tribes of the big-lake country were producing what George Catlin called "perhaps the most beautiful and light model of all water craft that ever were invented. . . ." Catlin had a sure eye for works of art. He was a painter who traveled the Northwest before there were many settlements, leaving us a legacy of Indian portraits and a valuable record of native life.

The canoe was the earliest form of lake transport; portable, strong, and easy to build. Construction began with a lengthwise incision made along the trunk of a birch tree and the bark peeled off in one great sheet, about a quarter inch thick. Ends were sewn up with the small ropelike roots of spruce or tamarack—*wat-tap*—and the length strengthened with splints of cedar, cedar rib cross braces between the gunwales. (Sometimes the bark was sewn over a preconstructed frame.) Boiled pine pitch did the waterproofing. Since sharp rocks or underwater logs were a constant hazard, every prudent canoeist carried extra bark, *wat-tap*, pitch (gum), and an axe . . . in case disaster hit and a whole new construction was called for.

The average "household" canoe was over three m. (twelve ft.) long and could carry two men, but there were canoes of twelve-meter (forty-foot) lengths and longer capable of transporting ten to twenty men *and* a ton of freight. In "Schoolcraft's Travels," the trapper-settler writes of fur company canoes, each "calculated to carry sixty packages of skins weighing ninety pounds [per package] and provisions to the amount of one thousand pounds. This is exclusive of the weight of eight men, each of whom is allowed to put on board a bag or knapsack of the weight of forty pounds. In addition, a quantity of bark, wat-tap, and articles necessary for repairs . . . the aggregate weight of all this may be estimated at about four tons. Such a canoe, thus loaded, is paddled by eight men and carried empty by four men across portages, is easily repaired and is altogether one of the most eligible modes of conveyance that can be employed upon the lakes. . . . Nothing that has been contrived to float upon water offers an adequate substitute."

High praise, but learning to paddle his own canoe was a definite paleface problem. Again Catlin: "They lean gracefully and dodge about under the skillful balance of an Indian, but like everything wild are treacherous and timid under the guidance of a white man, and if he not be an experienced equilibrist, he is sure to get two or three times soused in his first endeavors at acquaintance with them."

Another writer noted, ". . . the Indian canoe seems to need an Indian for its most facile use and guidance . . . [white man's] timidity and anxiety furnished a constant source of ridicule and banter to the native pilots. The merriment was loud and unsympathizing when the passenger tipped himself into the waters. . . ."

Indians of both sexes handled canoes as part of their growing up, so they did most of the paddling while their employers suffered stiffly. The best position for occupants was to be flat on one's back, or to rest on bent knees if he was to help paddle . . . for endless hours at a time. One careless stirring could flip the boat and make the natives terribly grouchy, especially if wage-earning cargo was lost in the drink. Life depended on keeping steady. Among those who expressed loud disgust at the rigid positions was Count Trontenac,

Governor of Canada for Louis XIV. Even the long-suffering Jesuit missionaries wrote of the constant risks and discomforts in the tricky transport; their precious sacramental vessels had to be protected at all costs and there were piteously nervous moments.

Nevertheless, the Europeans took canoes along the shores of the Great Lakes, up a labyrinth of streams as far as the Arctic, across Wisconsin and Illinois to the Mississippi. They were to lake country what covered wagons were to the West, portable life-centers and conveyance-keys needed to unlock the secrets of a water wilderness.

CHAPTER 8
MANITOULIN ISLAND and THE NORTH CHANNEL

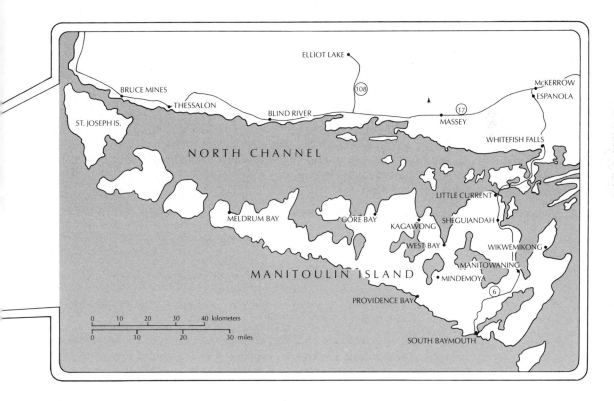

COMING OUT OF THE FRENCH RIVER into the wide blue waters of Georgian Bay, the canoes of Brulé and the Voyageurs stayed close to the north shore, thus going through the North Channel and into Lake Superior before venturing far into Lake Huron or Lake Michigan. Missionaries, *coureurs de bois,* et al. made much use of this broad passage on the north side of Manitoulin; consequently it was the first Great Lake area mapped with any accuracy.

In geologic terms the North Channel is new-born, left when the last glacier melted into the far north, leaving the pits and hollows it had engineered to fill with the drainage of its incredible mass. Yet the rocks on which the forest spreads and the water flows are among the oldest on the planet, part of the Precambrian shield.

Sailors love the Channel for its abundant nooks and bays when shelter is needed. For the landsman, the scenery, fishing, historic stops, and crystalline air make a compelling combination. There is also that knowledge, as you drive Hwy. 17, that you are at the edge of *the* North; places like Timmins and Hearst, a couple of highways and railroad tracks, but mostly it is wilderness from here to the Arctic. That fact won't leave your brain alone.

The south side of the Channel, Manitoulin Island, is as beckoning as a garden with paths. The Great Spirit, the Manitou, lives here, said the Indians. We of European stock don't feel any differently. "God's country," you'll hear again and again.

The island is about 160 km. (100 mi.) long and 60 km. (40 mi.) wide at the widest part. Like jewels strewn at random, the more than 100 lakes on Manitoulin are amply populated with trout, pickerel, and pan fish. Excellent hiking and camping, bird watching, rock hounding; botanists love it.

The great indoors is there when you need it most. Shopping, restaurants, resorts. Manitoulin is a delight.

MCKERROW • Turning point for those headed toward **Manitoulin Island;** a gas stop for going to **Sault Ste. Marie.** In this two-part chapter we will do both, turning south first to tour the world's largest freshwater island.

ESPANOLA • Spanish references are as rare in this part of the world as English titles in Japan, but you'll note a spot called Spanish down the road, a long stream called the Spanish River, and Espanola, gateway to Manitoulin Island. Rumor speaks of an Indian raid down the Mississippi and a Spanish woman prisoner who became the wife of a brave and taught her children her own language. Sounds reasonable.

Big paper mill, new shopping mall if you're running low on supplies, and the only nine-hole golf course between Sudbury and Sault Ste. Marie.

"HISTORIC" TIDBIT • A marker on Hwy. 6 at Birch Island reads: "Franklin Delano Roosevelt, thirty-second president of the United States of America during his vacation in Canada immediately prior to the historic Quebec Conference fished these waters August 1st to August 8, 1943." Erected by Department of Highways, Ontario 1946. Sorry, it doesn't say what he caught.

Between Whitefish Falls and McGregor Bay.   • PICNIC AREA

If there's a waterfall it must be upstream a bit, but this picturesque little • WHITEFISH FALLS
village lining the river bank has fishing supplies, information, and marinas.

MANITOULIN ISLAND

Called by the Indians *Wabejong* ("place where the water starts to run"). In • LITTLE CURRENT
Physics 101 you learn that air or water going through a narrow place picks
up speed (the Venturi effect), and that's just what happens in the narrows
between Manitoulin and Great Cloche Island, a favored waterway of Indians,
traders, fleets of fishermen, and the burgeoning boating public. Entrance-
exit to the North Channel, hello-goodbye town for the north side of Manitoulin, the island's largest community hums merrily with summer commerce. A quarter-mile: long dock bobs with end-to-end boats (sometimes
two or three a-beam). Shops and groceries bustle in the two-block downtown. The Travel Information Center is on Hwy. 68.

Little Current had logging and sawmills in its history, and a thriving
fishing industry that was killed off by the lamprey. Much of the coal used in
Northern Ontario is unloaded here, then transferred by truck and train to
other destinations. Fishing is back but now the seekers are sportsmen
trying to match the whopping 8-foot, 275-pound sturgeon (nearly 50 lbs.
of caviar) that was caught in 1914.

Big event is Haweater Weekend, a homecoming fest with carnival and
fun. Early islanders had to eat the bitter berries of the hawthorn tree to
survive, and folks born here have been called Haweaters ever since.

Travel Information on Hwy. 6, Little Current mid-June through Labour
Day. Other times write to the Rainbow Country Travel Association, 1543
Paris Street, Sudbury, Ontario P3E 3B7. 705/368-2150.

Highways 6, 542, and 540 rise and dip past old farms, scenic views; tiny
villages dot the deeply indented shores. Since there is no single road that
makes a tidy loop, we meander and zigzag, finding points of interest in all
directions and backtracking when needed.

THE INDIANS HAD A WORD FOR IT . . .

Manitowaning . . . "Den of the Spirit" . . . supposedly the home of the Great Manitou.

Wikwemikong . . . "Bay of the Beaver." Some will tell you it is "Bay with a Gravel Bottom."

Abejewung . . . "Where the water rises" . . . Indian Point Bridge.

Bebekodawangog . . . "Where sand curves around the water" . . . Providence Bay.

Sagradawawong . . . "The Outlet." Now South Bay Mouth.

Takibiwikwet . . . "Cold Water." Now Spring Bay.

Pushkdinong . . . "The Barren Hill." Now Gore Bay, and no longer barren; one of the beauty spots of the Island.

Kagawong . . . "Where mists rise from the falling waters."

Manitoulin . . . originally *Manitouminis;* minus meaning island . . . Manitou or Great Spirit.

Waiebegewung . . . "Where the waters flow" . . . the Indian name of Little Current.

Sheguiandah . . . "Home of the Stork," "Place of the Grindstone."

Assiginack . . . "The Blackbird" . . . name of a township . . . named after an Indian Chief . . . John Baptiste Assiginak.

Tehkummah . . . "Rays of light flashing in the sky" . . . lightning?

Sheshigwaning . . . "Place of rattlesnakes." No more!

Mindemoya . . . "The Old Woman."

On Hwy. 6:

SHEGUIANDAH • Eleven km. (seven mi.) south of Little Current, the well-stocked **L. C. Howland Museum** has a working replica of a nineteenth-century grist mill, some log houses, a barn, blacksmith shop, and displays. Open from May 1 till late October, 12:00 to 5:00 P.M., a little earlier during July and August.

Archeologists have found evidence of a settlement on this site dating back at least 3,000 years, making it one of the oldest sites in North America.

Gardens, an old quarry, and exceptional muskie fishing for those who plant, gather stone, or want a reel challenge.

TEN MILE POINT • A well-trained car will put on its own brakes. Beautiful scenic vista.

MANITOWANING • Bright button of a town with an old church, an interesting lighthouse, museums, tennis courts, and a race track. You seldom find a spot this small *and* this diversified. The **Assiginack Museum** complex started in a jail on Main Street, now includes a house, log cabin, and transportation shed; then down at the dockside the S.S. *Norisle,* first Manitoulin ferry, turned into a

marine museum, along with the **Burns Wharf** and **Rolling Mill.** Open June 1 to August 31, 10:00 A.M. to 5:00 P.M., 11:00 to 4:00 in September. Small admission charged.

St. Paul's Anglican Church has more years on it than any other in the Manitoulin-Algoma districts. Built in 1845 by local Indians, there's a mural in the basement depicting the structure's history.

One meet a year for the track, a fine course for harness racers. The rest of the time it's used by trainers. Come on Canada Day, July 1.

Docking facilities and a sandy beach; camping not far.

Ever see a greased pig contest? Horse pulls, fish fry, calf riding, a midway, and dancing at Summerfest in mid-July.

Turn east from Manitowaning to reach North America's only *unceded* • WIKWEMIKONG Indian Reserve (i.e., this is *theirs*), a mix of ancient names and modern life-styles. You're invited to come around and watch the annual pow-wow on Civic Holiday Weekend and let your feet tap to a different drummer. Colorful costumes and dances attract tribes of photographers, too.

The island's segment of Hwy. 6 ends here (or maybe it begins there), dock • SOUTH BAYMOUTH of the *Chi-Cheemaun,* ferry to Tobermory. Visit the **Little Red School House Museum,** then go hiking on one of the nature trails. A municipal camping park for those who don't need a lot of fixings; some nice motels for those who do.

On Hwy. 542:

Find out what researchers are trying to learn and what they already know • SANDFIELD about hatching and feeding trout and smallmouth bass. Pretty little park   FISH HATCHERY below the dam.

On one of the crystalline inland lakes. Would you believe a creamery where • MINDEMOYA 100,000 pounds of butter is processed annually? Cattle hold a fair share of Manitoulin's economy, as the yearly auction at Little Current—biggest one-day sale in the world—indicates.

Remember the Red Cross Hospital at Mindemoya if an emergency comes up. Golf course, motels, cottages, and lodges; new sneakers, hawberry jam, tackle. Supplies, supplies.

PROVIDENCE BAY • Down road 551, a sandy beach, Great Lakes fishing boats at their docks, and some unexpectedly fine shopping. A large amount of Canadian wares and a fall fair that brings in more craftsmen.

On Hwy. 540:

The long road to the end of the island is a beautiful winding route through the inland lakes district, where there are a lot of places to fish. However, there are seasons and sanctuaries; check with the authorities for specific fishing regulations.

MELDRUM BAY • The western entrance to **Manitoulin,** a timeless village now a yachting favorite, customs port, and supply depot. The **Net Shed Museum** on the waterfront has a fine collection of trapper and farmer tools and other gadgets used in past island life.

The lighthouse on Mississagi Strait has another museum, a popular pilgrimage, judging by its loaded guest book. The life of a lighthouse keeper is brought into focus, also tales of the skeletons once found and pieces thought to be from the *Griffin,* lost in 1670. Open June to September, 10:00 A.M. to 9:00 P.M.

GORE BAY • Seat of Manitoulin District, chinked between high cliffs, the second largest town on the island. "Large" is certainly relative; 750 people call it home year-round, tending the lovely old houses, courthouse, and jail-turned-museum in this main port of entry for U.S. pleasure boats cruising the North Channel.

The town, named for the *Gore,* a ship caught by the winter ice long years ago, grew as a fishing port. Remnants of the past survive at **Elliot's Flea Market and Pool Hall,** ensconced in one of Gore Bay's former hotels. Visit the impressive courthouse and **Gore Bay Museum,** then take a picnic hamper to **East Bluff Lookout Park.** (Turn right at Flower Triangle Entrance to Gore Bay, follow the road up.) Lookout spots in multiple choice.

An all-weather airport (radio, lights, 6,000-foot runway) with a customs official, Provincial Police, brewer's retail warehouse; Gore Bay keeps up. The very appealing Gordon's Lodge is open all year, and a new sailboat charter has bareboat rentals to experienced sailors (Canadian Yacht Charters), or you can cruise on a forty-two-foot ketch for a week via Chemong Charters. Both companies work from the government dock.

The Gore Bay Museum helps put on the "Summer Fun Weekend," usually the third weekend in July.

Golf addicts can get their fix at a new nine-hole course, one and a half km. (one mi.) south of the 540-542 intersection. Lounge, snacks, rentals, etc. New camping grounds at Janet Head Park, four km. (two and a half mi.) from town. Electricity, showers, dumping station, boat launching, a lighthouse, beach, and swimming, too. Reserve a site by contacting the town office, Gore Bay, Ontario P0P 1H0. For other spots to spread your canvas, write: Manitoulin Tourist Association, Box 357, Gore Bay, Ontario P0P 1H0 (mid-June through Labour Day) or Rainbow Country Office (see Little Current).

KAGAWONG Doesn't need a museum; it *is* one, unconsciously wearing the look of a thousand tiny settlements with histories dating back a century or more. A small white church has a pulpit made from the wreck of an old boat; the hotel may or may not be doing business, but it adds flavor. Government dockage, charter boat cruises, and weekly dances in the dockhouse.

The Kagawong River takes a tumble nearby and a new wildlife park runs from Bridal Veil Falls to Kagawong Bay. Make it.

WEST BAY Nobody can quite explain why the places with Indian names seem to have English citizens and the places with English names have Indian residents. West Bay has the only all-Indian gift shop around. Go visit the Church of the Immaculate Conception, even if you're non-Catholic. When the original Gothic "traditional" church burned; they rebuilt for the Indian congregation. Twelve sides (for twelve tribal councils) around a pitlike structure, wooden beams, and wide steps down to the altar for seats.

The **Ojibway Cultural Foundation** has displays of native culture and art, is also open to visitors.

CUP AND SAUCER LOOKOUT Worth it, worth all of it. Worth coming north, bringing your sturdy shoes, climbing the stairs and climbing some more. There are railings and other helps the first part of the trail, but it takes a mildly adventurous spirit to tackle the steeper slopes. On a clear day you can see to Lake Huron, or way into the "near north."

These side roads, such as the one to Honora Bay, lead to cottages, campgrounds, and resorts in hospitable abundance. The Silver Birches tucked down on this bay may be better than typical; a consultation with the travel people a little ahead of time will assure you of deluxe or humble digs in a scenic setting.

Two miles west of Little Current, 540 rolls to a real high; follow signs to **McLean's Mountain Lookout.** Picnic, *view.* A left-hand turn on a country road will bring you to Hwy. 6, not far south of Little Current.

Back to McKerrow and on to the Soo.

THE NORTH CHANNEL

WEBBWOOD • Population under 600, some small businesses and churches.

CHUTES • Slightly north of Massey, 100 campsites and handicap facilities in the wash-
PROVINCIAL PARK rooms. More than half the sites have electricity; showers, swimming, boat launching ramp. If you have no boat to launch, they'll rent you one nearby. Meanwhile, hike around the self-guided nature trails. P.O. Box 1340, Espanola, Ontario P0P 1C0. 705/869-1330.

MASSEY • If you don't talk fishing you'll find a lot of polite silence in Massey, a prime spot for advice, directions, rentals, supplies. A fine ten-room historical museum too, open June 1 through Labour Day, 9:00 A.M. till 7:30 P.M.

In early August Massey puts on a humdinger County Fair that is reported to be happily behind times in its down-home approach.

Walford, Spanish, Cutler, Serpent River, Spragge, and Algoma Mills. Now you approach them, now you pass. Two roadside picnic areas; one west of Spanish, the other west of Cutler. Hwy. 108 comes in near Serpent River, the road to Elliot Lake, once an almost ghost town, now catering to the fishing-hunting trade.

BLIND RIVER • The Hudson's Bay Company had a fur-trading post here when the first lumber mill was built. The fur business faded into history around the turn of the century, but by that time seven logging operations were floating huge log rafts to their mills. One outfit, McFadden's, was reputed to be the largest sawmill east of the Rocky Mountains, and operated until 1969.

Tree biz gets full tribute at the **Timber Village Museum** on the eastern edge of town. Scale models, full replicas, and Joseph Brier's intriguing wood carvings are part of the display. 10:00 A.M. to 6:00 P.M. late June until

ELLIOT LAKE

Gold! Silver! The news leaks out, there's a stampede of prospectors, a boom town of shanties, saloons, charlatans, loan sharks, and shady ladies. Lucky diggers build fancy houses, the unlucky (who are lucky enough to survive) go muttering off into the hills. If the lode of metal holds out long enough the shanty town can turn into something respectable, but never too respectable to forget the wild-wooly-naughty beginnings, all traces of which are put on display in local museums.

Meet Elliot Lake.

When the atomic era made uranium *the* sought-after element and some geologic detective work led to a source forty-eight km. (thirty mi.) north of Blind River, Elliot Lake was established. This strike, however, was no stampede of random individuals, but a carefully maneuvered coup led by a financier who already had some choice gold mines. When John Hirshhorn sniffed uranium in the wind he flew employees into the area to stake claims and wound up with billion-dollar holdings.

Mining and processing had to begin immediately. A town was needed, but the shanty-town sequence didn't follow. Elliot Lake was planned hurriedly and thoughtfully, and from the beginning resembled a southern suburb more than a northwoods throw-together. It had class.

Things looked dark for E.L. five years later when the Americans who were buying most of the output decided not to buy any more uranium. Most of the mines closed, the nice houses went begging on the market, and people moved away. Then suddenly—just when phrases like "ghost town" were circulating—England ordered uranium, Canada built a nuclear power plant, and the mines opened again.

Elliot Lake is alive, well, and looking good. Over at the **Elliot Lake Mining and Nuclear Museum** they explain what they're all about, show the processing of uranium into nuclear power, as well as display wildlife, logging history, and not much that is wild, wooly, or naughty. June 20 to Labour Day, 8:30 A.M. to 5:00 P.M. Monday through Friday. Adults 50¢. 45 Hillside Drive North, Elliot Lake, Ontario P5A 1X5. 705/848-2287. Ask about the mine tour.

Shopping, motels, restaurants in the midst of 200 nearby lakes. Write to the Chamber of Commerce, Box 1, Elliot Lake, Ontario P5A 2J6. 705/848-3974.

Labour Day. Small charge. Picnic area on the grounds. P.O. Box 628, Blind River, Ontario P0R 1B0. 705/356-7544.

First class accommodations in town, good shopping, and a hospital, if you need one.

Docking and a launching ramp are available at the Blind River Marina, but (as of this writing) the full range of services for boaters is not quite ready.

About that name: the earliest Voyageurs couldn't see the mouth of the Mississagi River from the lake and gave the spot a label that stuck.

Pretty place to picnic by the riverside.   • MISSISSAUGA

Sturdy title for a town once named Tally Ho, a reference to the times when • IRON BRIDGE loggers came out of the woods to tally up the number of days they had worked and to receive their wages. The town of 800 plus maintains a small

Historical Museum and large grasp on the current fishing situation. Rentals and equipment; motels for staying around extra days.

THESSALON • Better to say **"Thessalon *and* the Mississagi Valley,"** because the side trip up Hwy. 129 is something that shouldn't be missed. Go at least as far as Aubrey Falls along a road that generally follows the curve of the river, winding through splendidly rugged hills. The Falls are about 100 km. (63 mi.) north (Ranger Lake Road), a 30-m. (100-ft.) cascade into a gorge. Gas stop near.

Consult your map for a circle route back to Thessalon, a town that began with logging and is still turning out wood products. At the **Birchland Veneer Mill** visitors can watch logs meeting the cutting blades—from a safe distance, of course.

A twenty-three-acre trailer park and fine sand beach are on Thessalon's waterfront along with a large Government Wharf and deep-water docking facilities with full services, including repairs for cruisers and yachts. Plenty of resort and restaurant accommodations in and near town.

BRUCE MINES • A touch of France, a smattering of England, on this rocky north spot where the first copper mine in Canada opened for business. The **Bruce Mines Museum** and **Library** are housed in a former Presbyterian church with a "Norman" bell tower. Inside are mostly Victorian-Edwardian souvenirs, household wares, and work tools; more than 2,500 items. Prize possession is a doll house once belonging to the Marchioness of Queensberry, whose gentlemanly husband set down firm rules for boxers. Open from mid-May until mid-October, 10:00 A.M. to 4:00 P.M., longer hours in July and August. Small charge. There's a tourist information booth and washrooms as well. On Hwy. 17. Bruce Mines Museum, Bruce Mines, Ontario P0R 1C0. 705/785-3705.

ST. JOSEPH ISLAND • Western end of the Manitoulin Island chain, about forty-two km. long and twenty-seven km. wide (twenty-eight by fifteen mi.); once called *Anipich* by the Ojibways, meaning "place of the hardwood trees." The maples and birch turn St. Joseph into a fall color carnival, but it's scenic and pretty any time, with Co. Rd. 548 offering a fairly complete circle tour.

The British built a fort here in 1786 when Drummond Island was awarded to the United States after the American Revolution and English forces had to establish a new site. In the struggles over boundary lines and

172

which island belonged to which power, a band of Redcoats and Indians from Fort St. Joseph captured Mackinac Island, a cold spot to spend the winter... especially with a shortage of coats among the troops. So Captain Charles Roberts summoned his British ingenuity and ordered blankets to be turned into overcoats. Men have been wearing "Mackinaws" ever since.

The Americans set fire to the old fort, but today they are among the chief visitors to **The Fort St. Joseph National Historic Park,** viewing the ruins and taking the guided tours. Modern display hall, picnic area on the shore, 800-acre wilderness area and bird sanctuary. Open Victoria Day to Canadian Thanksgiving, 9:00 A.M. to 6:00 P.M. No charge.

Pause at Hilton Beach and Richard's Landing, stop in at the St. Joseph Island Museum at Richard's Landing. Open 10:00 A.M. to 5:00 P.M. July and August; shorter hours in June and September.

Rockhounds combing these shores generally go home happy. Those "just sitting" types can watch the parade of ships going to and from the ports of Lake Superior from Sailor's Encampment, a lovely wooded section on the St. Mary's River. Off-shore waters attract fishermen with surpluses of pike, walleye, perch, and bass.

Big annual event is the Algoma Maple Festival. Watch the modern way to "sugar-off" a tree, then pig-out on maple everything from ice cream to pancakes. Flea market too; weekends in mid-April. For resort, boat rental, and other information, write Algoma Kinniwabi Travel Association, 616 Queen Street East, Suite 203, Sault Ste. Marie (AO), Ontario P6A 2A4. 705/254-4293.

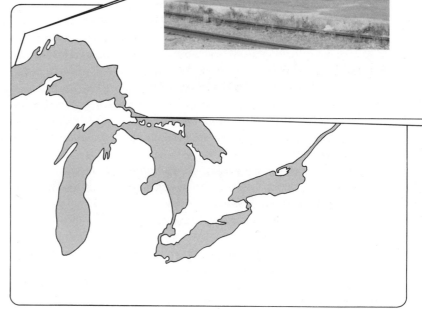

CHAPTER 9
LAKE SUPERIOR

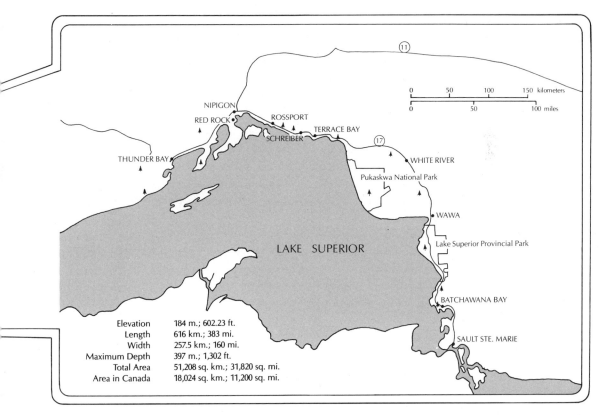

Elevation	184 m.; 602.23 ft.
Length	616 km.; 383 mi.
Width	257.5 km.; 160 mi.
Maximum Depth	397 m.; 1,302 ft.
Total Area	51,208 sq. km.; 31,820 sq. mi.
Area in Canada	18,024 sq. km.; 11,200 sq. mi.

IN THE EARLY 1600s when Samuel de Champlain drew a map of the dim regions beyond Lake Nipissing and Georgian Bay, he called Lake Superior the Great North Sea. Then, following the European habit of giving every piece of geography the name of a king, saint, or top politico, the Great North Sea became Lake Tracey, honoring the lieutenant-governor of New France. Whatever the virtues of Monsieur Tracey, *that* was no name for a giant, the deepest, coldest, largest, and often most ferocious of the Great Lakes. "Superior" it had to be.

The lake fills a hollow, chiseled by glaciers, that plunges to a depth of a quarter of a mile at one point. To geologists this area is part of the Precambrian shield, among the oldest exposed rock formations on the planet.

A tough French scout, Etienne Brulé, is supposed to have been the first white man to paddle across Lake Superior's unpredictable surface where storms of the last two centuries have sunk more than 500 ships and taken thousands of lives.

Beacons guide today's navigators and the flash of headlights can be seen through the trees, yet commerce and a rising population have not changed much of Superior's coast. On the rugged north shore sheer cliffs stand like fortress walls against assaulting waves, exactly as they did in Brule's day. A sparkling network of streams and rivers weaves through the thick forests tumbling toward the lake, and enormous fields of boulders trim the water's edge.

Cutting its twentieth-century swath through this ancient terrain, Hwy. 17—the Voyageur Route—follows the water, pulls far inland, curves, rises, and dips close to a dozen provincial parks, another dozen roadside picnic areas, and a solid line of scenic points. The hospitality business has grown steadily in recent years; food, gas, and lodging wave at you from every junction.

Plumbing, pasta, padding, and brinkmanship with true wilderness. ("Moose crossing" signs indicate deep, unpopulated woods.) The clock spins easily backward as you leave the car and hike down a park trail or sit on a log to stare across the lake with the perfect name. A long freighter may be on the horizon, but if a Voyageur's canoe went past it wouldn't be a surprise.

SAULT STE. MARIE TO THUNDER BAY

Sault Ste. Marie

Although the nickname "twin cities" is quickly tossed at communities sharing lot lines, few are more alike than the Sault Ste. Maries of Michigan and Ontario. These civic siblings grew up with the same name; the same Algonquin Indians fished from their shores; the same Jesuit missionaries, fur traders, and explorers built campfires and altars on both sides of the

river. Destiny put an international boundary line between them, but their roles as gateway to Lake Superior and the need to provide locks for cargo vessels are forever mutual.

On the heels of the earliest trappers and swappers came the North West Fur Trading Company, who built an official post and then went on to build the original Soo canal in 1799. Today there are five locks, four on the American side and the other Canadian, to assist long freighters past a whitewater stretch in the St. Mary's River where the flow from Lake Superior abruptly drops over six m. (twenty-one ft.).

Modern Sault Ste. Marie has nearly 80,000 folks to do the trading, work the giant steel mill, or guide visitors through the locks. On the list of sees and dos:

Built by an early white householder, fur trader, and husband of an Indian • THE ERMATINGER
princess. Ermatinger's first house was destroyed by the Americans in the HOUSE
War of 1812. This stone house replaced it, now stands as oldest Canadian
stone house west of Toronto, home to a lot of information about life in a
rougher time. Open May through October. 831 Queen Street; donation.

Back up among the northside hills are waterfalls, woods, picnic benches, • KINSMEN PARK
and playgrounds. A marvelous place when autumn starts showing its colors.
Bellevue Park on the riverfront a few kilometers east of downtown boasts
a small zoo, marine museum, gardens under glass, gardens along paths, and
fine stretches of lawn to spread a blanket and watch the ships go by. All for
free. Home of an old lighthouse and the Algoma Sailing Club.

The last overnight passenger cruise ship built on the Great Lakes, the • M.S. *NORGOMA*
Norgoma ran from Tobermory to South Baymouth between 1950 and '63. MUSEUM SHIP
Open June 1 to October 1, adults $2.50, children $1.25, seniors $2.00.
Norgoma Dock at Foster Drive.

World's largest forest fire fighting service invites the public to inspect their • FOREST FIRE FIGHTERS
headquarters. East end of the waterfront, July and August. No weekends.
Check by phone for correct times. 705/949-7152 or 942-1800.

Watching a freighter go through a lock is simple, fascinating fun, but going • SOO LOCK TOURS
through yourself is even better. The giant doors close and there you are,
sinking or rising on the water that is merely seeking its own level. The tour
boat (*Chief Shingwauk* or the *Bon Soo*) takes you through both American

and Canadian locks, past the steel mills, vessels from home and abroad, and points of general interest. A two-hour cruise starts from the Norgoma Dock off Foster Drive near the Civic Center, June 1st through the first week in October. Schedule steps up in July and August. 705/253-9850.

Drive into Michigan for a look at the other Soo via the Sault Ste. Marie International Bridge. The S.S. *Valley Camp* (a freighter-turned-museum), the Tower of History, locks viewing stands, and the chance to photograph the passing ships without dazzling backlighting (camera buffs will know what I'm talking about) are reasons to go. You'll find others. See Chapter 10 for Customs and Bridge fare information.

ALGOMA CENTRAL RAILWAY
Budget a day for a train ride into your plans before you leave home, then let NOTHING interfere. The Algoma train winds through rugged, untouched wilderness for 231 km. (144 mi.), giving you a genuine 3-D easy chair adventure. Past waterfalls, rivers, high cliffs . . . over trestles and bridges, around lakes toward Eton in Agawa Canyon for a two-hour pause. That's enough to let you climb to the lookout or maybe catch a fish. Dining service includes breakfast, hot and cold lunches, et. al. Or you can buy snazzy box lunches at the restaurants in the depot mall. You leave at 8:00 A.M. and are back by 5:00 P.M. Free depot parking. Adults $25.50; children

and high schoolers $12.75. Under five, free. Sorry, but you can't bring Fido. Write Passenger Sales Service, Algoma Central Railway, Sault Ste. Marie, Ontario P6A 5P6. 705/254-4331.

Ask them about overnight trips to Hearst and regional fishing or back-packing suggestions.

The top of Sault Ste. Marie's gleaming new civic center is another place to squint into the sun and take pictures. Stop at the front desk for information on special Soo events, etc., such as the **Algoma Fall Festival.**

A six-week spree with heavy emphasis on the arts. Several exhibitions • ALGOMA going on at once, starring big-name collections from private and museum FALL FESTIVAL sources. Professional and amateur shows, craft demonstrations, music from folk to jazz and classics. September through mid-October.

A slick new display case for Canadians and selected others, 10 East Street. • ART GALLERY 705/949-9067. As of this writing a prize heritage building in the downtown OF ALGOMA district is being updated into a new history museum. Call 256-2566 for more information, or wander over to Queen Street. Won't be hard to find.

Bellevue Marine Park, Pine Street South on the St. Mary's River (Hwy. 17 B), has docking space for boats of 240 cm. (8 ft.) draft, gasoline and diesel fuel, launch ramp, and full facilities except rentals and repairs. Box 580, Soo, Ontario P6A 5N1. 705/253-2290.

For more Ontario information write: Sault Ste. Marie, 120 Huron Street, International Bridge, Ontario. For Soo facts, write: 360 Great Northern Road, Sault Ste. Marie, Ontario P6B 4Z7. 705/949-7152.

Almost twenty-six km. (sixteen mi.) west of Ste. Marie on Hwy. 550, a • GROS GAP grand lookout over the St. Mary's River and choice spot for rock hounds.

Once a lumber town, there's a picnic spot on 556 not far from the Hwy. 17 • HEYDEN junction.

One-hundred-year-old hamlet just down the road from Hwy. 17 on 552. • GOULAIS Bishop Baraga, the pioneer "Snowshoe Priest," built a church here; its successor built in 1862 is still used by summer visitors and Indians.

Inlet and town. As the Highway of the Voyageurs skirts around the Bay it • BATCHAWANA BAY passes two picnic sites plus a Provincial Park. Shallow, sheltered B.B. took its name from the Indians, means "narrows and swift waters." The Hudson's

MOOSE TALK

The legendary committee that designed the camel hit its stride putting together the moose. A massive land animal with an unlandish love of grazing under water, a moose looms homely and ponderous compared to its sleek cousins, the deer and elk.

Looks deceive. A bulky 1,800-lb. moose, seven feet high and five or six feet wide at the antlers, can dive to eighteen feet, swim a dozen miles, run at thirty-five mph, and dodge between the trees—antlers and all—with the ease of a rabbit.

Solitary creatures, they prefer to go it alone rather than herd. In the fall, however, the big bulls with full racks will play Prince Charming to a prospective mate and use up a lot of energy fighting off the competition. The antlers drop off in winter when the combat is over and a new set begins to grow.

A vegetarian moose can make a summer-long, one-course-meal out of water lilies; will consume fifty pounds of pond weeds, bushes, the lower branches of balsam fir, or the bark of young hardwoods in one day.

Ironically, however, the dense forest-loving creature thrives where there are clear-cut areas, allowing development of fresh growth.

Coping with his own anatomy is often a moose's number one headache. The long legs that allow him to reach for tree food and swim with ease also force the animal to kneel when grazing on short grasses, and his wide feet and bulk may be just dandy in muddy lakes but often cause him to break through the crusts of deep snow; a floundering moose is a prime target for wolves.

Although moose are present in the forests east of Georgian Bay, you are more likely to glimpse one driving around Lake Superior; chances for encounters go up the farther you get into the back country.

You may hear one long before you see it. A moose does not go gentle into those deep ponds. He ker-plops mightily and the loud snorts as he comes up for breath echo through the hills.

There is a parasite that attacks the animal's spinal cord and causes great disorientation, so that once in a while a moose is seen poking around a town like a lost dog. Whether at lakeside or any other spot, however, never approach a moose, no matter how tranquil they seem. A moose is feisty and bad tempered, especially females with calves to defend. The best place to get a close-up of a moose is in a zoo.

Bay Company had a fur-trading post near the mouth of the Batchawana River, but it's fish for today's bargainer.

BATCHAWANA BAY • A nice sandy beach for swimming, picnic facilities, etc., but no camping—
PROVINCIAL PARK day use only. This is a spot where Superior's water does get a chance to warm up a degree or two. Brrr-rrrrr anyhow. Boat rental nearby.

PANCAKE BAY • An excellent beach, trout fishing, and a special children's fish pond. Hand-
PROVINCIAL PARK icap facilities, 340 campsites, 65 of them with electricity. Best to get a reservation. Stores and boat rentals nearby, self-guided trails and interpretive program. Pancake Bay Provincial Park, Batchawana Bay, Ontario P0S 1A0. 705/882-2209.

Campgrounds, picnicgrounds, exhibit center; facilities are minimal and • LAKE SUPERIOR
nature maximal in this huge 600-square-mile (960 sq.-km.) preserve. PROVINCIAL PARK
Established in 1944 to preserve the untouched shoreline, the countless
lakes and webbing of sparkling streams remain untouched as well. The 316
campsites in three areas have all the very-basics but no electricity. There
are three designated picnic places with no camping, and you're invited to
join the conducted hikes. Canoeing, fishing, Indian pictographs. Don't
wander off by yourself, however; getting lost can be fatal. Reservations
taken for one campground only: L.S.P.P., Agawa Bay, 22 Mission Road,
Wawa, Ontario P0S 1K0. 705/856-2396.

If Wawa seems to be a less-than-dignified name for a town, remember that • WAWA
it is Ojibway for "wild goose," a large, handsome bird that reigns—by the
tens of thousands—as monarch of the sky during spring and fall migrations.
A huge, much-photographed steel sculpture of Canada's symbolic goose is
next to the **Wawa Information Center** where migrating humans can
gather data on a solid little town of 5,000 with an airport, hospital, police
post, good eating, and other reinforcements.

   The Hudson's Bay Company had a small post in Wawa, but it was the
discovery of gold that brought in a population. The area was also rich in
iron, which has sustained the economy even while gold (more than a
million dollars' worth was taken from one mine) petered out. Wawa is the
main supplier of ore for the Algoma Steel Corporation at the Soo.

   "Gold Mine Road" runs (one-way traffic) from Hwy. 17 a few miles south
of town to Hwy. 101, past abandoned digs, mills, and the traces of gold
fever. A gold mine, of sorts, for rockhounds.

   Wawa could easily have been named for the number of delightful waterfalls nearby, such as the Upper Falls of the Magpie River, 22 m. (73 ft.) high
and 45 m. (150 ft.) wide; a short 3.2 km. (2 mi.) off Hwy. 17 south of town.
Silver Falls is further south on the Magpie and another tumbling beauty is
on the Michipicoten River. After aiming your Minolta at Silver Falls, cross
the bridge and turn left just past the Cemetery Trail to see the old burial
ground; plots dating back to the 1830s.

   If staring at a northern Ontario map has kindled a yen for a fly-in experience, an urge to go where no man has gone before, Wawa is famed for
putting people into outpost camps, lodges, and spots where hardly anybody
goes. (Polar Bear Provincial Park on Hudson's Bay gets about fifty visitors a

year.) Some of these remote retreats have more comforts than home, plus fishing that eliminates the need to lie. For more information about this kind of adventure or additional local fun, write to Wawa, Michipicoten Chamber of Commerce, Box 858, Wawa, Ontario P0S 1K0. May 1 to September 30 call 705/856-4538.

MICHIPICOTEN RIVER • Great high bluffs near a sandy bay—the name is an Indian word describing the scene. After 1821 Michipicoten was the chief post of the Hudson's Bay Company on Lake Superior. At that time it took sixteen days to get from here to James Bay—the export route. Today Michipicoten exports ore for Algoma Steel Corporation at Sault Ste. Marie.

OBATANGA • Another super-sized bird, a sandhill crane, greets you at the entrance to a
PROVINCIAL PARK natural environment park. "Unnatural" but necessary are handicap-type comfort stations, an Interpretive Building, and electricity at 23 of the 117 campsites. No reservations taken. Swimming, boating (rentals nearby), and excellent hiking.

PICNICGROUND • About sixteen km. (ten mi.) south of White River.

WHITE RIVER • A junction settlement of 1,000 people who go for cold. They talk about the time in '35 when the temperature dipped to 72° below zero (without adding the wind-chill factor) and an out-sized thermometer proclaims this as the "coldest spot in Canada."

Not to worry: such mercurial violence seldom disturbs the summer and White River is a popular resort area. A center for sportsmen bound for the bush, fishermen and hunters come by train, float plane, bus (Canadian Pacific), and van loads. Going to Hornepayne and a stop for the Canadian National R.R. or on up to the upper loop of Trans-Canada Highway? Turn at 631.

WHITE LAKE • All-services recreational park . . . as long as you don't need to buy bread or
PROVINCIAL PARK plug in your toaster. Has 287 campsites, showers, laundromat, boat rental nearby, hiking trails, interpretive program. Make a reservation: W.L.P.P., White River Office, 200 Winnipeg Street, White River, Ontario P0M 2C0. 705/966-2315. Mobert Indian Reservation is also on White Lake. Campers are invited to visit the Hudson's Bay Post across the lake.

JUNCTION, • The latter follows the R.R. tracks to Manitouwadge, then you have a *long*
HWY. 17 AND 614 meandering gravel stretch until you reach Caramar, Hwy. 625, and the Trans-Canada Highway 11. Watch the gas gauge!

A wilderness area with no facilities. Only a small part of the park is accessi- • PUKASKWA
ble by road; to get far into it you must hike or paddle your canoe . . . if you   NATIONAL PARK
can handle white water. A seventy-five-site semiserviced campground is
located on the northwest corner of the reserve and would-be adventurers
are generally advised to hire a guide. For more information: Pukaskwa Park
Superintendent, P.N.P., P.O. Box 550, Marathon, Ontario P0T 2E0. 807/
825-0801.

Heron Bay

Picnic area near 627, the road to tiny Heron Bay.

Turn at the 626 sign for the short drive to Marathon, a new name on the • MARATHON
map. Two paper mills needed to be where the logs were, hence the town.
Visitors can have the best in accommodations and Lake Superior sunsets as
well. Golf course, shopping, and a "beach" that looks like a field of dinosaur
eggs. On the outskirts is a Scout Forest, where Boy Scouts and Girl Guides
plant over 10,000 seedlings every year. Largest project of its kind in the
world.

Marvelously scenic park, the site of a World War II P.O.W. camp. The • NEYS PROVINCIAL PARK
Ontario Provincial Park guide mentions that "Neys has one of the finest
beaches on Superior's north shore." (True!) "Cool, refreshing swims"!!! Ice
floes can last until June up here, but people *do* go swimming . . . sometimes
up to a whole minute.
   Superb hiking and fishing, and you may even get a glimpse of the woodland caribou in this natural environment area. Of its 146 campsites, only 26
have electricity; showers, laundromat, self-guided trails, and interpretive
center with programs. Reservations taken, write: c/o M.N.R., P.O. Box 280,
Terrace Bay, Ontario P0T 2W0. 807/825-3205.

Company towns are not what they used to be. Planned by the company that • TERRACE BAY
owns the pulp mill, T.B. is built on a series of glacially-formed steps (hence
"Terrace") in a beautiful locale. Take your wide-angle lens to the **Aqua-
sabon** (ah-qwah-*sah*-bun) **Gorge,** where the river of the same name goes
over a 30-m. (100-ft.) cliff into a dramatic chasm. Hospital and airport.

Two thousand people, some very nice motels, and places to eat in a lovely, • SCHREIBER
scenic (there isn't any other word) valley. Fly-in services, great hunting and
fishing.

RAINBOW FALLS • The hiking trails offer views of the Selim River and waterfalls, a chance to
PROVINCIAL PARK   hike close to the north shore. None of the 230 campsites has electricity,
but there are showers, laundromats, swimming, boat launching, and a store
within two miles. Reservations taken, see address under Neys Provincial
Park.

ROSSPORT • Only forty-five sites, no electricity, no showers, nor clothes wash, but there's
PROVINCIAL   swimming and a boat rental nearby. For reservations, see above under Neys
CAMPGROUND   P.P.

ROSSPORT • Photogenic little village on Superior, the favorite spot of lake trout fishing
fans. They fish commercially from Rossport, charter boats, and hold an
annual fishing derby in late summer. Two picnic parks just east of the village,
two more just west of it make Rossport a good place to pause and reflect.

    The official Ontario road map indicates four picnic spots between Ross-
port and Nipigon, so you know that the scenery is what they want to show
off. Of course!

NIPIGON • Color it green, blue, and amethyst. The Nipigon vicinity has produced a
bounty of museum-quality amethyst crystals, the lovely purple gemstones
sometimes used as a symbol of purity. Visit an amethyst mine and hunt for
your own specimens, or simply go into any store. Every shopkeeper in
town has a large counter or small drawer full of rocks to sell.

    Positioned at the upper tip of Lake Superior on the best river passage to
the north, Nipigon has had humankind around for centuries. Long *long* ago
the Ojibways set their tepees beside the Nipigon River, one of the most
populous of all Indian encampments. Today's van drivers can do the same
amid tall pines and superb vistas.

    The **Nipigon Museum** will fill gaps between wigwams and campers;
help you get an understanding of area history, mining, and the pulp-paper
biz. Second at Newton Street, open mid-June to September daily.

    World record brook trout caught in Nipigon River—fourteen lbs., eight oz.

    Fall fishing festival is Labor Day weekend. Write Box 669, Nipigon,
Ontario P0T 2J0.

RED ROCK • Another paper mill town on Nipigon Bay. Public facilities include a swimming pool, tennis court. Want to see how newsprint is made? Tours can be
arranged upon request.

Small village on Black Bay just off the highway. There's a commercial fishing • HURKETT
business and a flying service here. Otherwise, very quiet.

Speckled trout and lake trout fingerlings are on view at the Dorion fish • DORION
hatchery. More and magnificent viewing of a different school if you climb
to the top of the C.N.R.-C.P.R. communications tower hill for a splendid
look at the whole scenic area . . . on a clear day a sixty-four-km. (forty-mi.)
sweep.

Just west of Dorion on Hwy. 17. • PICNIC AREA

A natural reserve, day-use park with no facilities, "only" a breathtaking • OUIMET CANYON
canyon 3 km. (2 mi.) long, 137 m. (450 ft.) deep, and 152 m. (500 ft.)   PROVINCIAL PARK
wide. The gravel road that takes you there from Hwy. 17 seems to go on
and on. Be patient, you'll find it, and then be careful; there are no railings
guarding the abrupt edge. There is a well-worn trail to the canyon floor,
but no elevators back up. Know thy condition before heading down.

A few kilometers off Hwy. 17, the **Ontario Gem Co. Ltd.'s** mine welcomes • AMETHYST MINE
visitors who can pay a low fee and mine their own. Gift shop and information about the legends of amethyst. Between Dorion and Pearl; turn toward
the lake.

South of Hwy. 17-11 on 587, a supply depot for folks going on out to the • PASS LAKE
park.

From Thunder Bay the profile of this exemplary park looks like a dozing • SIBLEY
giant; on the premises it's a rugged scramble of forest, trails (some really   PROVINCIAL PARK
rough ones), a ghost town, and endless panorama. Make a reservation for
the **Lake Mary Louise Campground,** where there's no electricity or hot
water, but swimming, boating, and playgrounds are near. Self-guided trails,
Building and Interpretive programs. Maybe you'll see a moose. Write: Pass
Lake, Ontario P0T 2M0. 807/933-4332.

On maps printed before 1970 the cities of the "Lakehead" are Port Arthur • THUNDER BAY
and Fort William, rivals who joined to assume the booming name of
Thunder Bay. A lively center of 109,000 population, T.B. is clearly in charge
of the western end of Canada's Lake Superior . . . as far inland as Atlantic
freighters bound for an Ontario port can do, and the major exit for grain
from the prairies.

The splendor of the north shore does not taper off as it goes west. From *many* Thunder Bay vantage points you can get a great view of rooftops, steeples, enormous wheat silos beside a gleaming harbor, and the long outline of the "Sleeping Giant," silhouette of the Sibley Peninsula.

In a region peppered with French and Indian names, it's interesting to note the number of Scotsmen in Thunder Bay's history. They came long after Radisson and Grosiellers first explored these far shores, long after missionaries and traders penetrated the area and Daniel Greysolon Sieur du Lhut (founder of Duluth) built the initial trading post in 1678 on the banks of the Kaministiqua River. Prosperity came and ebbed; a new fort, erected in a slightly different spot, was later purchased by a group of savvy Scots with their eyes on the fur trade. They were the gentlemen of the North West Company and they renamed the post Fort William after one of their own brethren. The North West Company and the Hudson's Bay Company were not friendly competitors. Gang warfare, northwoods style, continued until the forces of sanity brought a merger.

In 1857 three families led by pioneer pathfinder Simon Dawson built a settlement (about six km. [four mi.] from Fort William) to act as base camp on the Dawson Trail, first overland route to the West. "The Station," as it was called, grew into "Prince Arthur's Landing," and finally into the sizable town of Port Arthur.

Today's Thunder Bay has a university, one of the highest ski jumps in the world, a population reflecting forty ethnic origins, and enough grain in its elevator units to make two loaves of bread for every person in North America. Gardens, parks, pleasure boat marinas; images of Thunder Bay as an Arctic outpost don't compute. . . not amid the warm smells and sounds of summer. Bring your jackets, however, for those chills in the night.

Thunder Bay itinerary:

Thunder Bay Harbor and Fort Cruises on the *Welcome* gives you a chance to munch a snack lunch while eyeing the long ships, elevators, and harbor bustle at close range, the general scenery at a pleasant distance. The boat also goes fourteen km. (nine mi.) up the Kaministiqua River to the forest locale of **Old Fort William** for an almost three-hour visit. Schedules for short or long trips. Adult fare $7.00, children $3.50, special family rates. Write Welcomeship Ltd., 467 Parkwood Drive, Thunder Bay, Ontario P7A 2J3, or call 807/344-2512.

A time warp behind the log stockade walls might have you trading your • OLD FORT WILLIAM
wristwatch for a candle with notches. Ask a craftsman building a canoe
what year it is and he'll answer in a voice reserved for the tetched, "1816, of
course!" After grumbling about the North West Company being slow in
sending tools from Montreal, he may let you apply some pitch to the seams
and tell how he chooses the right bark. Others are baking bread in small
outdoor ovens, making snowshoes or barrels, farming, or bringing pelts up
to the dock for unloading and inspection. Company officials in high felt
hats do their daily rounds accompanied by a bagpiper to give their pomp
the proper circumstance.

These are all young Canadians who speak—with researched accuracy—
the jargon of 1816 in the present tense. It works. You are in a rarely
portrayed arena of North American history.

The $12 million, meticulously rebuilt Fort has fifty structures on a ten-
acre layout and special events throughout its mid-May to October season.
The highlight is a dilly, an Annual Great Rendezvous Pageant beginning on
the first Sunday in July. No way could they duplicate the boisterous shenan-
igans of the original rendezvous, when Voyageurs, Indians, and buyers met
for a cheat-'em-if-you-can business convention with brawls and wild drinking at fever pitch. The modern version is marvelous family fun, though.

Fees, subject to change, are $2.00 adults, $1.00 students, maximum of
$5.00 per family, children under 6 years free, 6-12 50¢. Get there by car,
city bus, or cruise ship from downtown up the river. Write to Information,
Old Fort Williams, Vickers Heights Post Office, Thunder Bay.

Drive and hike up 305 m. (1,000 ft.) higher than Lake Superior, for an • MOUNT MCKAY
eagle's view of Thunder Bay. Part of the Ojibway reservation, the lookout
station at 182 m. (600 ft.) is reached by their toll road (nominal fee), and
the summit is at the end of a trail from a parking lot. An easy path, yet not
recommended for the infirm. After feasting your eyes on the panorama,
hike a short distance across the mesa to the southwest corner for another
spectacular overlook of forests and rolling hills.

To reach, drive along City Road on the west side of the Kaministiqua
River.

Built in 1967, has flora superabunda and beautifulum. Even nongardeners • CENTENNIAL
will enjoy the large display of plant life. On the corner of Dease Street and   CONSERVATORY
Balmoral, open 1:00-4:00 P.M. every day.

Maybe it's the effect of deep winters, but T.B.'s parks and gardens get special care. **Hillcrest Park** has sunken flower beds plus a photographer's choice view of the city and lakefront. In **Centennial Park** a reconstructed lumber camp with a cookhouse serving meals all summer is fun to wander through. Lumber Camp Museum, logging train rides, more flowers.

KAKABEKA FALLS AND • Not far from the city along Hwy. 17-11, a roaring Niagara of the North. A
PROVINCIAL PARK 39-meter (128-foot) drop of water into a stunning gorge. Although comparing it to Niagara may be a bit much, it *is* a beautiful sight that no visitor to the area should miss . . . from kids to honeymooners. Photographers will be pleased with all the angles offered by guarded walkways on both sides of the river.

Electricity for 50 campers in the 156-site campground, plus hot showers and laundry aids. Make a reservation for top-season times. c/o M.N.R., Ontario Gov. Bldg., P.O. Box 5000, Thunder Bay, Ontario P7C 5G6. 807/475-1531.

Special event is the Canadian Lakehead Exhibition, a ten-day agricultural fair with horse and cattle shows, craft demonstrations, and entertainment. End of June.

For more Thunder Bay Information: Public Affairs, Visitors and Convention Dept., Main Office in Patterson Park, 520 Leith Street, Thunder Bay South, Ontario. 807/623-2711.

MIDDLE FALLS • Delightful spot on the Pigeon River very close to Rt. 61. Cascades and
PROVINCIAL PARK waterfalls, eleven-km. (six-mi.) hiking trail, twenty-five rustic campsites.

PIGEON RIVER • International border, entrance point. (See Chapter 10 for customs regulations, etc.) Information station with all the answers and maps you'll need for the road ahead. The Pigeon leads to Quetico Provincial Park, a wilderness preserve shared with the U.S.'s Boundary Waters Canoe Area.

EAGER FOR BEAVER

Carved into the stonework of a Canadian government building in Toronto, over the doors, over the windows, and who knows where else, are the sturdy shapes of beavers, the eager legendary mascot-symbol of Canada. Why not? The flat-tailed toothy engineering rodent of the north streams has had a profound effect on our environment, development, economy, fashions, et al. and seems to have earned this tribute.

In the 1600s and 1700s he was a new kind of gold: "The people of the Countrie came flocking aboord, and brought us . . . Bevers skinnes, and Otters skinnes, which wee bought for Beades, Knives, Hatchets, (and other) trifles" (Robert Juet, 1609).

"The English have no sense; they give us twenty knives like this for one Beaver skin" (A Montagnais Indian, 1634).

The fur trade—dominated by beaver—brought two worlds, two cultures together and neither was ever the same again. The resourceful Indian was quick to see the value of the Europeans' tools, and competing tribal networks fought bitterly for their trade. The French tried to hold a monopoly but unwisely levied poaching fines on the wrong men and heavy competition soon came from the British. Anything so lucrative could hardly be held in check.

Beavers live in loose colonies, have families of eight to twelve, and mate for life. They don't *always* build lodge dams but sometimes live in burrows under the river banks and use an underwater entrance. Those thoughtfully constructed log dwellings have long been a wonder to human-kind with their subsurface entrances, ventilating chimneys, snug dry interiors, etc. Sometimes, after a young tree is felled and chewed into workable size, even a special canal is dug to float the log to the pond. We are apt to find such expertise in animals a little eerie.

However, the beaver also goofs a lot. Trees fall hit and miss, get caught in the branches of other trees, and rot into uselessness. In densely wooded areas these loggers have been known to waste half the trees. A beaver's teeth are not sharpened by chewing logs; he gets them in shape by gnashing them together, must pause regularly in his tree chomping to do so.

The Indians, after catching and skinning the beaver, wore the hide furry side in, thus wearing off the course outer hairs. When the pelts reached England, the remaining fine hair was shaved off and pressed with hot irons into beaver felt, the material for gentlemen's high hats . . . a fashion that had as much influence on far removed populations as the custom of tea time or smoking tobacco.

The tale of the beaver trade is another book, but suffice it to say that *mammalia rodentia castoridae canadensis* was a hot item and avarice a factor in opening up the Great Lakes.

The Ministry of Natural Resources has an excellent booklet, "The Beaver in Ontario." Fifty cents plus postage. Write M. of N.R., Queen's Park, Toronto, Ontario M7A 2E5.

CHAPTER 10
FOR MORE INFORMATION

MAY I SUGGEST ...

Around the Shores of Lake Superior: A Guide to Historic Sites. M. Bogue and V. Palmer. University of Wisconsin Press.

Canada. Michelin Guide. Michelin Tires Ltd.

Canada: A Candid Guide. G. Hall. Gage, Ltd.

Canadian Facts. Edited by C. J. Harris and R. C. Butchard. CanExpo Publishers.

Dollarwise Guide to Canada. Godwin, Brosnahn, and Wood. Frommer/ Pasmantier.

The Enduring Great Lakes. Edited by J. Rousmaniere. Norton Press.

The Faces of the Great Lakes. J. Ela and B. King. Sierra Club Books.

Fisher's Canada Travel Guide. R. Turnbull. Fisher Travel Guides.

Georgian Bay: The Sixth Great Lake. J. Barry. Clark, Irwin & Co., Ltd.

The Great Lakes Guidebooks. G. Cantor. University of Michigan Press.

The Long Blue Edge of Summer: A Vacation Guide to the Shorelines of Michigan. Doris Scharfenberg. Wm. B. Eerdmans.

Ontario. A. Hocking. McGraw-Hill Ryerson Ltd.

Ontario Country Diary. Perry and McKendy. Centennial College Press, Nelson Ltd.

A Pictorial History of the Great Lakes. H. Hatcher and E. Walter. Bonanza Books.

Trading and Shipping on the Great Lakes. 1899 volume republished by Coles Ltd.

A Well-Favored Passage. Marjorie Brazer. Peach Mountain Press.

Where Two Worlds Meet: The Great Lakes Fur Trade. Fridley and Brookins. Minnesota Historical Society.

ONTARIO PROVINCIAL PARKS RATES

		FULL RATES	REDUCED RATES
CAMPING/NIGHT	Campsite with electricity	$ 8.25	$ 5.00
	Campground with comfort station	6.75	4.00
	Campground without comfort station	6.25	4.00
	Additional vehicle	3.00	2.00
	Interior camping (per boat)	4.00	4.00
	Campsite Reservation Fee	2.00	
GROUP CAMPING	Qualifying youth groups	free	free
	Adult groups—up to 20 persons	30.00	
	—each person in addition to 20	1.00	
DAY-USE	Daily Vehicle Permit	2.50	1.00
	Annual Vehicle Permit	25.00	12.50*
	Bus Permit	10.00	
	Ontario Senior Citizens	free	free

*purchased after Labour Day

Camping for ONTARIO SENIOR CITIZENS is free except on Friday and Saturday night during the peak season (June 17–Labour Day).

For other pertinent information:

Call these Ministry of Tourism and Recreation Toll Free Numbers for up-to-the-minute information on any Ontario Park.

Canada	1–800–268–3735
New York	1–800–462–8404
Continental U.S.A.	1–800–828–8585
Metro Toronto Area	965–4008

CAMPSITE VACANCY REPORTING SERVICE

Provides traveling public with up-to-date information on the availability of campsites in 54 Southern Ontario parks. This service is in operation during the peak season only. (Mid-June to Labour Day).

HOURS OF OPERATION

Information can be obtained from Ontario Travel Toronto (see previous telephone numbers), during their normal hours of operation: Monday through Friday, 8 A.M. to 5 P.M.

In addition, Barrie Travel Centre provides a taped vacancy report 24 hours a day, 7 days a week, along with weather information. (416) 364–4722 (free in Toronto area).

WHERE TO FIND IT . . .

Antique Shops of Country Ontario
Prentice-Hall Canada
1870 Birchmont Rd.
Scarborough, Ontario M1P 2J7
416/293-3621

Art Galleries (Public)
Ontario Assn. of Art Galleries
38 Charles St. E., 2nd floor
Toronto, Ontario M4Y 1T3
416/920-8378

Bicycle Tours
Canadian Cycling Association
333 River Road
Vanier, Ontario K1L 8B9
613/746-5753

Ontario Cycling Association
160 Vanderhoof Ave.
Toronto, Ontario M4G 4B8
416/424-6866

Canals
Rideau Canal Superintendent
Rideau Canal Office
Ministry of Environment
12 Maple Ave. North
Smiths Falls, Ontario K7A 1Z5
613/283-5170

Trent-Severn Waterway Superintendent
Parks Canada
Trent-Severn Waterway
P.O. Box 567
Peterborough, Ontario K9J 6Z6
705/742-9267

Canoe Routes
Ontario Ministry of Natural Resources
District Manager (in appropriate area)
and
Ont. Ministry of Natural Resources
Park Information Section
99 Wellesley Street W., Room 3319
Whitney Block, Queen's Park
Toronto, Ontario M7A 1W3
416/965-3081

Conservation Areas
Ministry of Natural Resources
Conservation Authorities &
Water Management Branch
5th floor, Whitney Block
Toronto, Ontario M7A 1W3
416/965-6287

Customs Regulations
Customs and Excise Branch
Revenue Canada
Connaught Building
Mackenzie Ave.
Ottawa, Ontario K1A 0L5
613/996-9623 (tourist information)

Fall Fairs
Ministry of Agriculture & Food
Legislative Buildings
Queen's Park
Toronto, Ontario M7A 2B2

Farm Vacations
Ontario Vacation Farm Assoc.
c/o R. Clipsham
R.R. #2
Erin, Ontario N0B 1T0
519/833-2814 (residence phone)

Fishing & Hunting Clubs
Ontario Federation of Anglers & Hunters
P.O. Box 28
Peterborough, Ontario K9J 6Y5
705/748-3115

General—Canada
(federal publications—for which there is a charge.
For others, contact the department concerned.)
Supply & Services Canada Publishing Centre
Hull, P.Q.
613/994-3475

Golf
Ontario Golf Association
400 Esna Park Dr., Unit 11
Markham, Ontario L3R 1H5
416/495-5238

Handicapped
(information on establishments, hotels, motels, resorts that can accept wheelchair occupants)
Canadian Paraplegic Association
520 Sutherland Drive
Toronto, Ontario M4G 3V9
416/422-5640

Horseback Riding
(for a listing of establishments)
Min. of Industry & Tourism
Ontario Travel
Hearst Block, 3rd Floor
900 Bay Street
Queen's Park
Toronto, Ontario M7A 2E5
and
(literature for members only; will answer general inquiry)
Mrs. Mavis McCullum
Ontario Trail Riders' Association
Cherry Street, R.R. #3
Stouffville, Ontario L0H 1L0
416/473-3445

Hostel Accommodation
Ontario Hostelling Association
8 York Street, 2nd Floor
Toronto, Ontario M5J 1R2
416/368-1848

Canadian Hostelling Association
333 River Road
Vanier, Ontario K1L 8B9
613/746-0060, ext. 235 or 302

Indians & Eskimos
Canadian Assn. in Support of the Native Peoples
16 Spadina Rd., Suite 201
Toronto, Ontario M5R 2S7
416/964-0169
and
Indian Branch
Dept. of Indian Affairs & Northern Dev.
55 St. Clair Ave. E. 5th Floor
Toronto, Ontario M4T 2P8
416/966-5544

(information on Indians only)
Native Community Branch
Ministry of Culture and Recreation
77 Bloor St. West, 5th Floor
Toronto, Ontario M7A 2R9
416/965-5003

Medical Assistance
International Association for Medical Assistance to Travellers
123 Edward St., Suite 725
Toronto, Ontario M5G 1E2
416/977-6059
(also have office in Guelph)

Mineral & Mine Information
Ministry of Natural Resources
Public Service Centre, Whitney Block
Queen's Park, Toronto, Ontario M7A 1W3
416/965-1348

Mobile Homes
(guidelines, regulation, information for mobile homes)
Canadian Mobile Home Assn.
55 York St., Suite 512
Toronto, Ontario M5J 1S2
416/363-8374

Motorcycling
Canadian Motorcycle Association
500 James St. N., Suite 201
Hamilton, Ontario L8L 1J3
416/522-5705
and
(Regulations "The Law and Your Motorcycle" & "The Driver's Handbook")
Public and Safety Information Branch
Min. of Transportation & Communications
1201 Wilson Avenue, West Tower
Downsview, Ontario M3M 1J8
416/248-3501

Nature
Canadian Nature Federation
75 Albert St., Suite 203
Ottawa, Ontario K1P 6G1
613/238-6154

Northern Ontario Outfitters
(an association of camps, outfitters for fly-ins, etc.)
N. Ont. Tourist Outfitters Assoc. (N.O.T.O.)
P.O. Box 1140
North Bay, Ont. P1B 8K4
705/472-5552

Parks Commission
Niagara Parks Commission
Box 150
Niagara Falls, Ontario L2E 6T2
416/356-2241
St. Clair Parkway Commission
P.O. Box 700
Corunna, Ontario N0N 1G0
519/862-2291
and
St. Lawrence Parks Commission
P.O. Box 740
Morrisburg, Ontario K0C 1X0
613/543-2951

Pilot Licence—Tourist Permits
Dept. of Transport
Personnel Licencing
Air Regulations
4900 Yonge St., Suite 300
Willowdale, Ontario M2N 6A5
416/224-3124
(requests and booklet containing regulations for U.S. visitors)

Provincial Parks Vacancy Report
(July–September)
416/364-4722
416/965-4008

Royal Canadian Mounted Police
Royal Canadian Mounted Police
1200 Alta Vista Drive
Ottawa, Ontario K1A 0R2
613/993-1085 (Public Relations Office)

Roads
Road Information Services
Ministry of Transportation & Communications
1201 Wilson Ave., East Bldg.
Downsview, Ontario M3M 1J8
416/248-3561

St. Lawrence Seaway
St. Lawrence Seaway Authority
Place de Ville
Tower "A," 18th Floor
320 Queen Street
Ottawa, Ontario K1R 5A3
613/992-3949

Sailing
Ontario Sailing Association
160 Vanderhoof Ave.
Toronto, Ontario M4G 4B8
416/424-6700

Student Card
Canadian University Travel Service
(International Student (Scholar) Card)
Association of Student Councils
44 St. George Street
Toronto, Ontario M5S 2E4
416/979-2604

Scuba Diving
Ontario Underwater Council
160 Vanderhoof Ave.
Toronto, Ontario M4G 4B8
416/424-6700

Skiing
(listings of alpine and cross-country areas and winter accommodations)
Ministry of Industry & Tourism
Ontario Travel
Hearst Block, 3rd Floor
Queen's Park
Toronto, Ontario M7A 2E5

Snowmobiling
Ontario Federation of Snowmobile Clubs
Box 318
Port Sydney, Ontario P0B 1L0
705/385-2773

Sports
Ontario Sports Administrative Centre Inc.
160 Vanderhoof Ave.
Toronto, Ontario M4G 4B8
416/424-6700

ONTARIO TRAVEL ASSOCIATIONS

Touring Services
Ontario Motor League
Domestic Travel Dept.
2 Carlton Street
Toronto, Ontario M5B 1K4
416/964-3130 (Domestic Travel)
416/964-3140 (International Travel)
(publications available to CAA members only)

Traffic Regulations—Ontario
(driver's handbook)
Min. of Transportation & Communications
Public and Safety Information Branch
1201 Wilson Avenue, West Tower
Downsview, Ontario M3M 1J8
416/248-3501

Transportation
Bus
(list of bus lines in Ontario)
Ministry of Industry & Tourism
Ontario Travel
900 Bay Street, 3rd Floor
Hearst Block, Queen's Park
Toronto, Ontario M7A 2E5
(NOTE: bus lines must be contacted directly for schedules and fares.)

Railways
Algoma Central Railway
Passenger Sales
129 Bay St., P.O. Box 7000
Sault Ste. Marie, Ontario P6A 5P6
705/254-4331

VIA Rail Canada
20 King St. W., 5th Floor
Toronto, Ontario M5H 1C4
416/366-8411

Ontario Northland Railway
Passenger Service
195 Regina Street
North Bay, Ontario P1B 8L3
705/472-4500
and
805 Bay Street
Toronto, Ontario M5S 1Y9
416/965-4268

U.S. Travel Information
Travel U.S.A.
2 Carlton St., 11th Floor
Toronto, Ontario M5B 1K4
416/964-3094

Water
(testing kit for drinking water)
Ministry of Health
Laboratory Services
81 Resources Road (at Islington Ave.)
Rexdale, Ontario M9W 5K9
416/248-3171

Weather
Atmospheric Environment Services
Environment Canada
4905 Dufferin Street
Downsview, Ontario M3H 5T4
416/676-3066 (current weather)
416/667-4614 (records)
416/667-4551 (general education)
416/667-4551 (department information)

ONTARIO TRAVEL ASSOCIATIONS

Algoma Kinniwabi Travel Association
Suite 203
616 Queen Street East
Sault Ste. Marie P6A 2A4
705/254-4293

Almaguin Nipissing Travel Association
269 Main Street West
Box 351
North Bay P1B 8H5
705/474-6634

Central Ontario Travel Association
165 King Street
P.O. Box 191
Peterborough K9J 6Y8
705/745-3694

Cochrane Timiskaming Travel Association
Box 1162
Timmins P4N 7H9
705/264-9589

Eastern Ontario Travel Association
Lansdowne Travel Centre
Lansdowne K0E 1L0
613/659-2188

Georgian Lakelands Travel Association
Simcoe County Complex
Midhurst L0L 1X0
705/726-9300

Metropolitan Toronto Travel Association
Toronto Eaton Centre
Box 510
220 Yonge Street
Toronto, Ontario M5B 2H1
416/979-3133

Niagara and Mid-Western Ontario Travel
Association
370 Main St. E., Suite 107
Hamilton L8N 1J6
416/522-8351

North of Superior Travel Association
107 Johnson Avenue
Thunder Bay P7B 2V9
807/344-6659

Northwest Ontario Travel Association
102 Main St., Box 647
Kenora P9N 3X6
807/468-5853

Rainbow Country Travel Association
1543 Paris St.
Sudbury P3E 3B7
705/522-0104

Southwestern Ontario Travel Association
Visitors & Convention Services
300 Dufferin Ave., P.O. Box 5035
London N6A 4L9
519/672-1970

MAPS AND WHERE TO OBTAIN THEM . . .

Aerial Photos
Ministry of Natural Resources
Public Service Centre, Room 1640
Whitney Block
Queen's Park
Toronto, Ontario M7A 1W3
416/965-1123 (no phone orders)
or
National Air Photo Library
Department of Energy, Mines and Resources
615 Booth Street, Room 180
Ottawa, Ontario K1A 0E9
613/995-4560

Aeronautical Charts and Topographical Maps
Canada Map Office
615 Booth Street
Ottawa, Ontario K1A 0E9
613/998-9900

City Maps
Tourist Guide Maps and detailed Street Maps are usually available from Chambers of Commerce in various cities or map distributors listed in the "yellow pages." They may also be purchased upon your arrival in a city at a local book, variety, or department store.

County and District Maps; Wall Maps
Ministry of Transportation and Communications
Record Services Office
Map Office
1201 Wilson Ave., East Building
Downsview, Ontario M3M 1J8
416/248-3476 (no phone orders)
See also above address for Ministry of Natural
Resources (over the counter only).
416/965-6511

**Fishing Maps; Geological Maps; Lake Maps;
Topographical Maps; Territorial Maps**
Algonquin Park Canoe Routes
($1.00)
See above address for Ministry of Natural
Resources.
416/965-6511

Marine Navigational Charts
Canadian Hydrographic Services
Hydrographic Chart Distribution
Dept. of Fisheries and Oceans
1675 Russell Road, P.O. Box 8080
Ottawa, Ontario K1G 3H6
613/998-4931 (no phone orders)

Marine Charts also available from chart distributors listed in the "yellow pages."

Provincial Maps
Canada Government Office of Tourism
235 Queen Street
Ottawa, Ontario K1A 0H6
613/996-4610
Provincial Maps are also available from the Tourist
Information Department, Parliament Buildings, of
the capital city of the province in which you are
interested.

Provincial Park Maps
Ministry of Natural Resources
Parks Branch
Whitney Block, 3rd Floor
Queen's Park
Toronto, Ontario M7A 1W3
416/965-3081

Rideau Canal System Charts
Superintendent
Rideau Canal Office
12 Maple Avenue North
Smiths Falls, Ontario K7A 1Z5
613/283-5170

Trent Canal System Charts
Superintendent
Parks Canada
Trent-Severn Waterway Office
P.O. Box 567
Peterborough, Ontario K9J 6Z6
705/742-9267

A NOT-SO-TAXING SITUATION

Tourists do not have to pay the seven percent provincial sales tax if goods are to be used outside the province.

Goods purchased in Ontario may be sent out of the province tax-free. The purchaser will not be charged at the time of the sale. The vendor will arrange to have the goods delivered to purchaser's home and keep documentary evidence of the sale.

If visitors purchase goods but decide to take them home themselves, the sales tax must be paid at the time of purchase, but a refund of the tax will be made if the goods are taken out of Ontario within thirty days.

To receive a refund, a form from the ministry of revenue must be completed. Such forms are available at tourism offices and chambers of commerce.